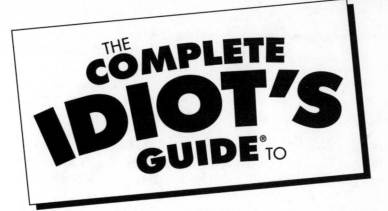

THE COMPLETE IDIOT'S GUIDE® TO

Windows® XP

Second Edition

by Paul McFedries

ALPHA

A member of Penguin Group (USA) Inc.

To Karen and Gypsy, who are always happy to see me.

ALPHA BOOKS

Published by the Penguin Group

Penguin Group (USA) Inc., 375 Hudson Street, New York, New York 10014, U.S.A.

Penguin Group (Canada), 10 Alcorn Avenue, Toronto, Ontario, Canada M4V 3B2 (a division of Pearson Penguin Canada Inc.)

Penguin Books Ltd, 80 Strand, London WC2R 0RL, England

Penguin Ireland, 25 St Stephen's Green, Dublin 2, Ireland (a division of Penguin Books Ltd)

Penguin Group (Australia), 250 Camberwell Road, Camberwell, Victoria 3124, Australia (a division of Pearson Australia Group Pty Ltd)

Penguin Books India Pvt Ltd, 11 Community Centre, Panchsheel Park, New Delhi—110 017, India

Penguin Group (NZ), cnr Airborne and Rosedale Roads, Albany, Auckland 1310, New Zealand (a division of Pearson New Zealand Ltd)

Penguin Books (South Africa) (Pty) Ltd, 24 Sturdee Avenue, Rosebank, Johannesburg 2196, South Africa

Penguin Books Ltd, Registered Offices: 80 Strand, London WC2R 0RL, England

International Standard Book Number: 1-59257-084-4
Library of Congress Catalog Card Number: 021898570840

06 05 04   8 7 6 5 4 3 2 1

Interpretation of the printing code: The rightmost number of the first series of numbers is the year of the book's printing; the rightmost number of the second series of numbers is the number of the book's printing. For example, a printing code of 04-1 shows that the first printing occurred in 2004.

Printed in the United States of America

Note: This publication contains the opinions and ideas of its author. It is intended to provide helpful and informative material on the subject matter covered. It is sold with the understanding that the author and publisher are not engaged in rendering professional services in the book. If the reader requires personal assistance or advice, a competent professional should be consulted.

The author and publisher specifically disclaim any responsibility for any liability, loss, or risk, personal or otherwise, which is incurred as a consequence, directly or indirectly, of the use and application of any of the contents of this book.

Most Alpha books are available at special quantity discounts for bulk purchases for sales promotions, premiums, fund-raising, or educational use. Special books, or book excerpts, can also be created to fit specific needs.

For details, write: Special Markets, Alpha Books, 375 Hudson Street, New York, NY 10014.

Publisher: *Marie Butler-Knight*
Product Manager: *Phil Kitchel*
Senior Managing Editor: *Jennifer Chisholm*
Acquisitions Editors: *Mikal E. Belicove, Tom Stevens*
Development Editor: *Ginny Bess Munroe*
Production Editor: *Janette Lynn*

Copy Editor: *Amy Borrelli*
Illustrator: *Richard King*
Cover/Book Designer: *Trina Wurst*
Indexer: *Angie Bess*
Layout: *Becky Harmon*
Proofreading: *Donna Martin*

Contents at a Glance

Contents

Foreword

In an ideal world, there would be no need for *The Complete Idiot's Guide to Windows XP, Second Edition*, because the operating system would be easy to learn yet powerful, simple yet versatile, and you'd never, ever see the dreaded "blue screen of death."

Unfortunately, we don't live in an ideal world. Rather, we live in a world where driver conflicts can derail your printer, corrupted files can cause you to lose important Word documents, and surfing the Internet without an antivirus program can lead to disaster. And that's just the tip of the iceberg. Whether you're new to Windows XP or a grizzled veteran with years of experience under your belt, and whether you use the Home or Professional edition, chances are you've managed to run across something in the OS that has at best baffled you and at worst stopped your PC dead in its tracks. No, you're not an idiot, but computer problems sure have a way of making you feel like one. It's almost enough to make you trade in your PC for an abacus. But now, thanks to Paul McFedries, you won't have to.

I've been writing about Windows since before Windows 95, and have always done my best to explain and deal with even the most complicated of issues. Because of my own experience, I've always had a lot of respect for anyone who can take an issue and break it down for the readers, leaving them with more than just the solution to a particular problem in the process. McFedries easily accomplishes this goal, while writing in an easy-to-read and enjoyable style. He actually helps us to *understand* Windows without talking down to the reader, which is exactly what "idiots" like us need.

This book makes even the most frustrating and complex problems easy to work through and understand. Difficult concepts are often accompanied by illustrations, and the book is filled with funny cartoons. And because this is the second edition, a lot of new and timely information has been added, including coverage of the latest and greatest Windows XP additions and service packs. In fact, this guide contains everything you need to use Windows XP efficiently, skillfully, and to its fullest potential.

So the next time you receive the dreaded "blue screen of death," don't waste time searching the Web for information or calling Microsoft support; just read this book. Chances are, you'll not only find the solution to your troubleshooting woes but also learn how to make Windows work *for* you instead of *against* you. And, really, who has time for anything less than that?

—Joe DeRouen

Joe DeRouen is a contributing editor for *Computer User* magazine (www.computeruser. com) and authors the monthly "Windows Advisor" column. He lives in Arkansas and has just finished *Small Things*, his first novel.

Introduction

Never let a computer know you're in a hurry.

—Anonymous

The world's gardeners have told us for years that if you want to keep your plants healthy and happy, then you should talk to them in a kindly, soothing voice. The world's gardeners are, I suspect, an eccentric bunch, but who can argue with their success?

Certainly not me, so perhaps that's why I've taken to talking to my computer using the same gentle, comforting tones. "Now, my good fellow, I have a *very* important deadline tomorrow, oh yes, and I just need you to be a good boy and not crash between now and then. Okey-dokey?" (This is made *much* easier by the fact that I work at home.)

I think that, subconsciously, I view my computer as though it's the electronic equivalent of some deranged lunatic who'll snap at the least provocation. Or perhaps I see it as more of a fragile, high-strung, Southern belle type, a digital Blanche DuBois who is depending on the kindness of a stranger (that is to say, me) to keep it together.

Of course, what's really happening here is that years of using various incarnations of Windows have made me certifiably paranoid. I've simply come to expect that Windows will do something weird or toss me some semicomprehensible message that will have me scratching my head for hours. So even though it has been over 14 years since Windows 3.0 was foisted upon an unsuspecting world, Windows remains both devilishly difficult and fiendishly fickle. Windows can, in other words, make any of us feel, temporarily, like a complete idiot.

That, in the end, is why I wrote *The Complete Idiot's Guide to Windows XP, Second Edition.* My goal here is to help you and Windows XP get along. If you aren't a computer wizard (and don't even want to be one), this book is for you; if you have a job to do—a job that includes working with Windows XP—and you just want to get it done as quickly and painlessly as possible, this book is for you; if you don't want to learn about Windows XP using absurdly serious, put-a-crease-in-your-brow-and-we'll-begin tutorials, this book is for you.

No experience with Windows XP? No problem. In fact, this book doesn't assume you have *any* previous experience with *any* version of Windows. I begin each topic at the beginning and build your knowledge from there. So even if you've never used a computer before, this book will get you through those crucial (and scary) early stages.

No time? No problem. With *The Complete Idiot's Guide to Windows XP, Second Edition*, you get just the facts you need—not everything there is to know. This means I avoid long-winded discussions of boring, technical details. Instead, you get all the information in short, easy-to-digest chunks that you can quickly skim through to find just the tidbits you need.

How This Book Is Organized

With Windows, *anything* can happen (and often does). So my best advice as you cross over into Windows XP territory is to expect (you guessed it) the unexpected. However, the last thing you need is to be thrown a few curve balls by the book that's supposed to be your trusted guide in this newfound land. So, to get you better prepared for the journey to come, let's bone up on some of the flora and fauna you'll be seeing along the way.

First, the itinerary. *The Complete Idiot's Guide to Windows XP, Second Edition*, is organized into five reasonably sensible parts. To help you locate what you need fast, here's a summary of what you'll find in each part.

Part 1: "Windows XP Everywhere: A Few Things You Need to Know." The lucky six chapters that open the book are designed to help you get your Windows XP travels off on the right foot. New Windows users will want to start with Chapter 1, which gives you a tour of the Windows XP screen and offers some mouse and keyboard basics. From there, you learn about controlling programs (Chapter 2), working with windows (Chapter 3), dealing with documents (Chapter 4), working with files and folders (Chapter 5), and installing and uninstalling programs and devices (Chapter 6).

Part 2: "Windows XP at Home." Using a computer at home, we tend more toward the fun end of the computer spectrum. (Yes, there *is* a fun end.) With that in mind, I structured Part 2 to cover some of the more fun features that can be found in Windows XP. This includes working with pictures (Chapter 7); using scanners and digital cameras (Chapter 8); and working with music, videos, and other multimedia (Chapter 9). For good measure, I also show you an easy way to share your computer with other family members (Chapter 10).

Part 3: "Windows XP at Work." This part is short but sweet (assuming that using Windows at work could be described as "sweet," that is). The three chapters in Part 3 cover workaday tasks such as using Windows XP's writing programs (Chapter 11), sending and receiving faxes (Chapter 12), and using Windows XP's notebook computer features (Chapter 13).

Part 4: "Windows XP on the Internet." There are plenty of days when it seems that our computers are just one giant communications terminal. Electronic communication in all its forms is a huge part of our daily lives, and Part 4 devotes no less than six chapters to Windows XP Internet and communications goodies. You'll learn step-by-step how to get connected to the Internet (Chapter 14), how to surf the World Wide Web with Internet Explorer (Chapters 15 and 16), how to exchange Internet e-mail with Outlook Express (Chapters 17 and 18), and how to keep you and your computer safe while online (Chapter 19).

Part 5: "Windows XP at the Shop: Customizing, Maintaining, and Trouble-shooting." Like people living in row houses who paint their doors and windowpanes to stand out from the crowd, most Windows users like to personalize their computing experience by adjusting the screen colors, changing the background, and performing other individualistic tweaks. The first two chapters in Part 5 show you how to perform these customizations in Windows XP. You'll learn how to customize the desktop (Chapter 20) and the Start menu and taskbar (Chapter 21).

Thanks to higher-quality parts and improved manufacturing, modern computers are fairly reliable and will often run for years without so much as an electronic hiccup. However, that doesn't mean some disaster—be it a nasty computer virus, an ill-timed power failure, or some other spawn of Murphy's Law—can't strike at any time. The other two chapters in Part 5 can help you to prepare for problems. You'll get a step-by-step plan for maintaining your system (Chapter 22) and basic strategies for solving problems (Chapter 23).

Some Things to Help Out Along the Way

In a book such as this, I believe that it's not only important *what* you say, but also *how* you say it. So I've gone to great lengths to present the info in easy-to-digest tidbits that can be absorbed quickly. I've also liberally sprinkled the book with features that I hope will make it easier for you to understand what's going in. Here's a rundown:

◆ Stuff that you have to type will appear in a `monospaced font`, like that.

◆ Menus, commands, and dialog box controls that you have to select, as well as keys you have to press, appear in a **bold font.**

◆ Whenever I tell you to select a menu command, I separate the various menu and command names with commas. For example, instead of saying "click the **Start** button, then click **All Programs,** and then click **Internet Explorer,**" I just say this: "select **Start, All Programs, Internet Explorer.**"

◆ Many Windows XP commands have equivalent keyboard shortcuts, and most of them involve holding down one key while you press another key. For example, in most Windows programs, you save your work by holding down the **Ctrl** key, pressing the **S** key, and then releasing **Ctrl**. I'm *way* too lazy to write all that out each time, so I'll just plop a plus sign (+) in between the two keys, like so: **Ctrl+S.**

I've also populated each chapter with several different kinds of sidebars (some appear in the middle of the page and others appear in the margin):

Windows Wisdom

These asides give you extra information about the topic at hand, provide you with tips for making things work easier, and generally just make you a more well-rounded Windows XP user.

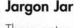

Jargon Jar

These notes give you definitions of Windows words suitable for use at cocktail parties and other social gatherings where a well-timed bon mot can make you a crowd favorite.

Look Out!

These notes warn you about possible Windows XP pitfalls and tell you how to avoid them.

Cross-Reference

Each of these elements points you to another section of the book that contains related material.

Hacking Windows

These juicier tidbits take you deeper into Windows XP and show you useful tweaks that enable you to supercharge your system and take control of various aspects of Windows XP.

Acknowledgments

Substitute damn every time you're inclined to write very; your editor will delete it and the writing will be just as it should be.

—*Mark Twain*

I didn't follow Mark Twain's advice in this book (the word *very* appears throughout), but if my writing still appears "just as it should be," then it's because of the keen minds and sharp linguistic eyes of the editors at Alpha Books. Near the front of the book you'll find a long list of the hard-working professionals whose fingers made it into this particular paper pie. However, there are a few folks whom I worked with directly, so I'd like to single them out for extra credit. A big, heaping helping of thanks goes out to acquisitions editor Mikal Belicove, development editor Ginny Munroe, production editor Jan Lynn, copy editor Amy Borrelli, and technical editor Bill Bruns.

Special Thanks to the Tech Reviewer

The Complete Idiot's Guide to Windows XP, Second Edition was reviewed by an expert who double-checked the accuracy of what you'll learn here. Thanks are extended to Bill Bruns.

Bill Bruns is a veteran of finance and data retrieval in the information age. Bill is the chief financial officer for Jacob Marlie Financial, Inc. (www.jacobmarlie.com), a web-based invoicing and collections agency for fraternal organizations. Currently, he is the assistant director for Business Systems at the University of Illinois College of Medicine. Billy has been a technical editor, working on at least 125 books relating to the Internet, web servers, HTML, operating systems, and Office applications. You can reach him at bill@jacobmarlie.com.

Trademarks

All terms mentioned in this book that are known to be or are suspected of being trademarks or service marks have been appropriately capitalized. Alpha Books and Penguin Group (USA) Inc. cannot attest to the accuracy of this information. Use of a term in this book should not be regarded as affecting the validity of any trademark or service mark.

Part 1

Windows XP Everywhere: A Few Things You Need to Know

One of the great things about Windows XP is what technoid types refer to as its "consistent interface." In plain English, this just means that a lot of the techniques you learn in one Windows program today can also be used in another Windows program tomorrow. These techniques are things you'll be using day in and day out: starting programs, using menus and toolbars, manipulating windows, opening and printing documents, and installing programs and devices. The six chapters that populate Part 1 take you through all of these techniques and quite a few more.

A Field Guide to Windows XP

In This Chapter

- ◆ Checking out the Windows XP screen
- ◆ Handy mouse and keyboard techniques
- ◆ A cautionary tale about shutting Windows down

Thrill-seeking types enjoy diving into the deep end of any new pool they come across. The rest of us, however, prefer to check things out first by dipping a toe or two into the waters and then slipping ever so gently into the shallow end. The latter is the most sensible approach when it comes to Windows waters, which can be cold and murky to the uninitiated. You need to ease into the pool by learning a few basics about the layout of the screen and a few useful mouse and keyboard techniques. That's exactly what you'll do in this chapter.

Note, however, that this chapter assumes your Windows XP pool has already been built and filled with water. That is, I assume that either your computer came with Windows XP already installed or else you have (or a nearby computer guru has) upgraded your computer to Windows XP.

Starting Windows XP

After you poke your computer's power switch, Windows XP begins pulling itself up by its own bootstraps. This *booting* process takes a few minutes on most machines, so this is an excellent time to grab a cup of coffee or tea and review your copy of *Feel the Fear and Do It Anyway*.

After your machine has churned through a few behind-the-scenes (and happily ignorable) chores, Windows XP's next move depends on which version you're using and on how it has been set up.

> **Jargon Jar**
>
> The idea of Windows pulling itself up by its own bootstraps is actually a pretty good way to describe the whole process of Windows starting itself up from scratch. In fact, it's the source of the verb **boot**, which means "to start a computer."

If you have Windows XP Home Edition, one of two things will happen:

♦ You end up at the Windows XP "desktop," which is the screen shown in Figure 1.3. If that's the case, you get a free pass to the "What's What in the Windows Screen" section in this chapter.

♦ You're left staring at the "Welcome" screen, which will be similar to the one shown in Figure 1.1. In this case, just press the **Enter** key on your keyboard. I'll talk more about the Welcome screen later in Chapter 13.

Figure 1.1

This box might appear while Windows XP Home Edition loads.

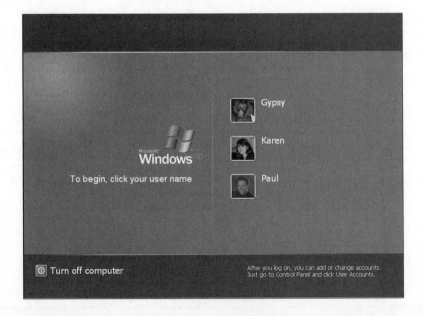

If you're running Windows XP Professional instead, then you'll see a box titled Welcome to Windows. Here's what you do:

1. The box asks you to **Press Ctrl+Alt+Delete to begin.** This arcane instruction means that you press and hold down both the **Ctrl** key and the **Alt** key on your keyboard, and then tap the **Delete** key. This gets you to another box that's titled Log On to Windows, as shown in Figure 1.2. (At this point, you can release the **Ctrl** and **Alt** keys if you've still got them held down for dear life.)

2. What's happening here is that Windows XP wants you to supply the appropriate password before going any further. (The person who set up your system, or the person at work who administers your computer system, should have told you what your password is.) Go ahead and type your password in the **Password** box. (The letters you type will appear as dots, but that's okay. It's a security feature that prevents a snoop from eyeballing your password.) Then press **Enter** to continue loading Windows XP.

Figure 1.2

This box might appear while Windows XP Professional loads.

A few seconds later, the dust clears and—voilà!—Windows XP is ready to roll.

What's What in the Windows Screen

The screen shown in Figure 1.3 is typical of the face that Windows XP Home Edition presents to the world. (The screen for XP Pro looks a bit different. Note, too, that your screen might have a different look, depending on how your computer manufacturer chose to set up your machine.) If you're new to Windows XP, you need to get comfortable with the lay of the Windows land. To that end, let's examine the vista you now see before you, which I divide into two sections: the desktop and the taskbar.

Figure 1.3

The Windows XP Home Edition landscape.

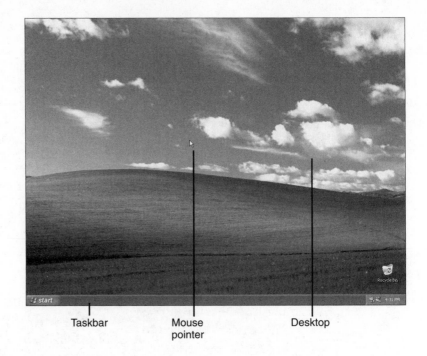

Taskbar   Mouse pointer   Desktop

The Desktop

Ivory-tower computer types enjoy inventing metaphors for the way the rest of us use a computer. The idea is that more people will put up with a computer's shenanigans if using the computer reflects the way we do things in real life.

For Windows, the metaphor of choice is the humble desktop. That is, you're supposed to think of the Windows screen as being comparable to the top of a real desk in a real office or den. Starting a program is like taking a folder full of papers out of storage and placing it on the desk. To do some work, of course, you need to pull papers out of a folder and place them on the desk. This is just like opening a file within the program (it could be a letter, a drawing, an e-mail message, or whatever). To extend the metaphor a little, most programs also come with tools, such as a ruler, a calculator, and a calendar, that are the electronic equivalents of the tools you use at your desk.

So, officially, the vast expanse that takes up the bulk of the screen real estate is the Windows XP desktop, and it's where you'll do your work. (If looking at the same old screen all day long makes you feel a bit batty, changing to a different image, color, or psychedelic pattern is no sweat. I'll tell you how in Chapter 20.)

The Taskbar

The multicolored strip along the bottom of the Windows XP screen is called the *taskbar*. The taskbar sports three distinct features (pointed out in Figure 1.4).

Start button   Notification   Clock
                                                      area

Figure 1.4

The features of the Windows XP Home Edition taskbar.

◆ **Start button**   Believe it or not, this tiny chunk of screen real estate is one of the most important features in all of Windows XP. As its name implies, the Start button is your starting point for most of the Windows XP features and goodies. I discuss the Start button in depth in Chapter 2.

◆ **Notification area**   Windows XP populates this area with even more icons. In this case, these icons tell you a bit about what's happening with your machine. For example, an icon appears here when you add new hardware to your machine and another icon shows up while you're connected to the Internet.

Windows Wisdom

The taskbar's clock can also show you the date. To try it, move your mouse pointer until it sits over the time. After a second or two, the date pops up, just like that. If you ever need to change the time or date, double-click the clock.

◆ **Clock**   The clock's purpose is obvious enough: It simply tells you the current time.

The rest of the taskbar is empty right now, but that will change soon enough. As you'll see in the next chapter when I show you how to start programs, Windows XP uses the taskbar to keep track of all your running programs. You can use the taskbar to switch between the programs, shut them down, and do other handy things.

As a final note on the taskbar, Windows XP comes with a useful feature for the notification area. This feature automatically hides those notification icons that you haven't used in a while. (I explain how you "use" a notification icon in various places throughout this book.) One fine day you'll start your computer and see a notice that tells you your unused icons have been hidden from view. If you want to see those icons, click the left-pointing arrow, as shown in Figure 1.5.

Figure 1.5

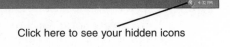

*Windows XP eventually hides
your unused notification icons.*

Click here to see your hidden icons

Some Mouse and Keyboard Fundamentals

Windows XP is supposed to have all kinds of fancy-schmancy features. How do I get at 'em?

Ah, that's where your mouse and keyboard come in. You use them as "input devices" to give Windows XP its marching orders. The next few sections show you the basic mouse and keyboard techniques you need to do just that.

Basic Mouse Maneuvers

If you're unfamiliar with Windows, there's a good chance that you're also unfamiliar with the mouse, the electromechanical (and, thankfully, toothless) mammal attached to your machine. If so, this section presents a quick look at a few mouse moves, which is important because much of what you do in Windows will involve the mouse in some way.

For starters, be sure the mouse is sitting on its pad or on your desk with the cord facing away from you. (If you have one of those newfangled cordless mice, move the mouse so that the buttons are facing away from you.) Rest your hand lightly on the mouse with your index finger on (but not pressing down) the left button and your middle finger on the right button (or the rightmost button). Southpaws need to reverse the fingering.

Figure 1.3, displayed earlier, showed you the *mouse pointer*. Find the pointer on your screen and then slowly move the mouse on its pad. As you do this, notice that the pointer moves in the same direction (although it will stop dead in its tracks when it hits the edge of the screen). Take a few minutes to practice moving the pointer to and fro using slow, easy movements.

To new users, the mouse seems an unnatural device that confounds common sense and often reduces the strongest among us to tears of frustration. The secret to mastering the mouse is twofold. First, use the same advice as was given to the person who wanted to get to Carnegie Hall: practice, practice, practice. Fortunately, with Windows XP being so mouse-dependent, you'll get plenty of chances to perfect your skills.

Second, understand all the basic mouse moves that are required of the modern-day mouse user. There are a half-dozen in all:

♦ **Point** This means that you move the mouse pointer so that it's positioned over some specified part of the screen. For example, "point at the **Start** button" means that you move the mouse pointer over the taskbar's **Start** button.

♦ **Click**   This means that you press and immediately release the left mouse button to initiate some kind of action. Need a "fer instance"? Okay, point at the **Start** button and then click it. Instantly, a menu sprouts up in response to the click. (This is Windows XP's Start menu. I'll discuss it in detail in the next chapter. For now, you can get rid of the menu by clicking an empty section of the desktop.)

♦ **Double-click**   This means that you press and release the left mouse button *twice*, one press right after the other (there should be little or no delay between each press). To give it a whirl, point at the clock in the taskbar's notification area and then double-click. If all goes well, Windows XP will toss a box titled Date and Time Properties onto the desktop. You use this box to change the current date and time. To return this box from whence it came, click the button labeled **Cancel.** If nothing happens when you double-click, try to click as quickly as you can, and try not to move the mouse while you're clicking.

Windows Wisdom

Okay, so clicking initiates some kind of action, but so does double-clicking. What's the diff? The whole single-click versus double-click conundrum is one of the most confusing and criticized traits in Windows, and I'm afraid there's no easy answer. Some things require just a click to get going, whereas other things require a double-click. With experience, you'll eventually come to know which clicking technique is needed. Note, too, that if Windows seems to be missing some of your double-clicks, it's possible to change some settings to fix this.

♦ **Right-click**   This means that you press and immediately release the *right* mouse button. In Windows XP, the right-click is used almost exclusively to display a creature called the *shortcut menu*. To see one, right-click an empty part of the desktop. Windows XP displays a menu with a few common commands related to the desktop. To remove this menu, *left*-click the desktop.

♦ **Click and drag**   This means that you point at some object, press and *hold down* the left mouse button, move the mouse, and then release the button. You almost always use this technique to move an object from one place to another. For example, try dragging any of the desktop icons. (To restore apple-pie order to the desktop, right-click the desktop, click **Arrange Icons** in the shortcut menu, and then click **By Name.**)

♦ **Scroll**   This means that you turn the little wheel that's nestled in between the left and right mouse buttons. In programs that support scrolling, you use this technique to move up and down within a document. The wheel is a relatively new innovation, so your mouse might not have one. If not, never fear, as Windows provides other ways to navigate a document. I tell you about those other ways to navigate a document in Chapter 3.

Common Keyboard Conveniences

I mentioned earlier that getting comfy with your mouse is crucial if you want to make your Windows XP life as easy as possible. That's not to say, however, that the keyboard never comes in handy as a timesaver. On the contrary, Windows XP is chock-full of keyboard shortcuts that are sometimes quicker than the standard mouse techniques. I'll tell you about these shortcuts as we go along. For now, let's run through some of the standard keyboard parts and see how they fit into the Windows way of doing things.

◆ **The Ctrl and Alt keys** If you press **Ctrl** (it's pronounced "control") or **Alt** (it's pronounced "alt" as in *alt*ernate), nothing much happens, but that's okay because nothing much is supposed to happen. You don't use these keys by themselves, but as part of *key combinations*. (The **Shift** key often gets into the act as well.) For example, hold down the **Ctrl** key with one hand, use your other hand to tap the **Esc** key, and then release **Ctrl.** Like magic, you see a menu of options sprout from the Start button. (To hide this menu again, press **Esc** by itself.)

Jargon Jar

A **key combination** is a keyboard technique where you hold down one key and then press another key (or possibly two other keys).

Windows Wisdom

Windows XP has all kinds of keyboard combo shortcuts, so they pop up regularly throughout the book. Because I'm *way* too lazy to write out something like "Hold down the **Ctrl** key with one hand, use your other hand to tap the **Esc** key, and then release **Ctrl**" each time, however, I use the following shorthand notation instead: "Press **Hold+Tap,**" where **Hold** is the key you hold down and **Tap** is the key you tap. In other words, instead of the previous long-winded sentence, I say this: "Press **Ctrl+Esc.**" (On rare occasions, a third key joins the parade, so you might see something like "Press **Ctrl+Alt+Delete.**" In this case, you hold down the first two keys and then tap the third key.)

◆ **The Esc key** Your keyboard's Esc (or Escape) key is your all-purpose get-me-the-heck-out-of-here key. For example, you just saw that you can get rid of the Start menu by pressing **Esc.** In many cases, if you do something in Windows XP that you didn't want to do, you can reverse your tracks with a quick tap (or maybe two or three) on **Esc.**

◆ **The numeric keypad**   On a standard keyboard layout, the numeric keypad is the separate collection of numbered keys on the right. The numeric keypad usually serves two functions, and you toggle between these functions by pressing the **Num Lock** key. (Most keyboards have a Num Lock indicator light that tells you when Num Lock is on.) When Num Lock is on, you can use the numeric keypad to type numbers. When Num Lock is off, the other symbols on the keys become active. For example, the 8 key's upward-pointing arrow becomes active, which means you can use it to move up within a program. Some keyboards (called *extended keyboards*) have a separate keypad for the insertion point movement keys, and you can keep Num Lock on all the time.

Making It Legit: Activating Your Copy of Windows XP

After you've had Windows XP (or a new computer that came with Windows XP) for a short time (a day or two), one of two things will happen:

◆ When you start Windows XP, a message will appear on your screen telling you that **Your Windows product must be activated within X day(s)** (where X is some number between 1 and 15).

◆ When Windows XP is running, a message will pop up from the taskbar's notification area telling you that you have **X days until activation.**

What your computer is trying to tell you is that you have to "activate" Windows XP with Microsoft or else Windows will simply stop working. This is Microsoft's way of checking for illegal copies of Windows. What happens is that Windows checks the hardware configuration of your computer and ties it to the product ID of your copy of Windows XP. Don't worry: No personal information is ever sent to Microsoft and there are no fees or other hidden goings-on. Here's what you have to do:

1. If you see the dialog box at startup, click **Yes;** if, instead, you see the taskbar message, click the message.

2. In the window that appears, click **Next.** If your computer is set up to access the Internet, the activation process will happen automatically, so skip to step 4. Otherwise, another window will show up to let you know that Windows XP will dial a telephone number to process the activation.

3. Click **Next.** The activation program elbows your computer's modem and asks it to dial a number. When the call goes through, try to ignore the very strange noises that your modem makes while it contacts the "activation server."

4. When the activation is done, you'll see a message telling you the good news. Click **Finish.**

Quittin' Time: Shutting Down Windows

When you've stood just about all you can stand of your computer for one day, it's time to close up shop. Please tape the following to your cat's forehead so that you never forget it: *Never, I repeat, never, turn off your computer's power while Windows XP is still running*. Doing so can lead to data loss, a trashed configuration, and accelerated hair loss that those new pills don't help.

Now that I've scared the daylights out of you, let's see the proper procedure for shutting down your computer. To begin, click the **Start** button to pop up the Windows XP Start menu. The route you take from here depends on a couple of different factors:

♦ If you have Windows XP Home, or if you have Windows XP Professional that isn't running on a corporate network, then click the **Turn Off Computer** option. Windows XP displays the little box shown in Figure 1.6. Use your mouse to click the option you want (I explain them in a sec).

Figure 1.6

*In Windows XP Home Edition, when you click the Start menu's **Turn off** computer option, you see this dialog box.*

♦ If you're running Windows XP Professional on a corporate network, click **Shut Down** to see the box shown in Figure 1.7. Use the **What do you want the computer to do?** list to choose the action you want (they're explained below) and then click **OK**. If you're not sure how to work the list, see the "Dealing with Dialog Boxes" section in Chapter 2.

Figure 1.7

*In Windows XP Professional, when you click the Start menu's **Shut Down** option, you see this dialog box.*

Now click one of the following choices:

- **Stand By**   Choose this option (which is only available on some computers) to put your machine in *standby mode*, which powers down just the monitor and hard disk.

- **Turn Off Computer** (XP Home) or **Shut Down** (XP Pro)   Choose this option if you're wanting to turn off the computer's power.

- **Restart**   Choose this option if you want to start Windows XP all over again. For example, if you find that Windows is acting strangely, restarting can often put things right.

- **Log Off** *User* (XP Pro only)   Choose this option to log off your network (where *User* is your network user name).

- **Hibernate** (in Windows XP Home, hold down the **Shift** key to see this option)   Choose this option (which, again, is only available on newer computers) if you're going to shut down your computer, but you also want Windows XP to remember all your open windows and documents and to restore them the next time you crank things up. If you go this route, it takes a bit longer for Windows XP to prepare itself for bed, but your machine will rouse from its slumbers much faster the next time you start it.

The Least You Need to Know

- The Windows XP screen is carved into two main areas: the *desktop*—the large area that covers most of your monitor—and the *taskbar*—the thin strip along the bottom of the screen.

- The taskbar consists of the Start button, a space for running program icons, the notification area, and the clock.

- The three most-used mouse movements are the *click* (quickly pressing and releasing the left mouse button), the *double-click* (two quick clicks), and the *drag* (holding down the left button and moving the mouse).

- A *key combination* involves holding down one key, pressing a second key, and then releasing the first key. I signify such a combo with the notation **Hold+Tap** (where **Hold** is the key you hold down and **Tap** is the key you tap); for example, **Ctrl+Esc.**

- To shut down Windows, click **Start,** click **Turn Off Computer,** and then click **Turn Off.**

2

Making Your Programs Do What You Want Them to Do

In This Chapter

- ◆ A couple of ways to get a program off the ground
- ◆ Learning about pull-down menus, toolbars, and dialog boxes
- ◆ Getting the hang of the taskbar
- ◆ Techniques for switching between programs
- ◆ Shutting down a program

If you want to get your computer to do anything even remotely nonpaperweight-like, you need to launch and work with a program or three. For example, if you want to write a memo or a letter, you need to fire up a word processing program; if you want to draw pictures, you need to crank up a graphics program. If you want to use the Windows spreadsheet program, well … there isn't one. Windows XP comes with a passel of programs, but a spreadsheet isn't among them. If you want to crunch numbers, you need to get a third-party spreadsheet program, such as Microsoft Excel or Lotus 1-2-3.

On the other hand, Windows XP *does* come with a decent collection of programs that enable you to perform most run-of-the-mill computing tasks. This chapter shows you how to get at those programs as well as how to mess with them after they're up and running.

How to Start a Program

If you're interested in starting a program, then you might think that the Start button in the lower-left corner of the screen would be a promising place to begin. If so, give yourself a pat on the back (or have a nearby loved one do it) because that's exactly right. Go ahead and use your mouse to point at the Start button and then click. As you can see in Figure 2.1, Windows XP responds by tossing a rather large box onto the screen. This is called the *Start menu*, and you'll be visiting this particular place a lot in your Windows XP travels.

Figure 2.1

The Start menu: your Windows XP launch pad.

The current user

Icons for folders

Icons for programs

Icons for Windows XP features

Click the Start button to unfurl the Start menu

Icons for exiting Windows XP

A Start Menu Summary

The Start menu is populated with all kinds of interesting-looking pictures and text. Each little picture and the text beside it is called an *icon* in the Windows world. An icon is a representation of something that exists on your computer. To see what I mean, let's run through the various icons that exist on the Start menu. (Again, however,

I need to point out that computer manufacturers can and will customize the Start menu, so yours may be populated with a different set of icons.) As pointed out in Figure 2.1, I divide the icons into four general categories: programs, folders, features, and exiting.

For the programs, the initial Start menu has eight icons:

♦ **Internet**   This icon represents the Internet Explorer program, which you use to make your way around the World Wide Web. I talk about this program in Chapter 15.

Windows Wisdom

Clicking the Start button is probably the most common way to get at the Start menu, but Windows XP also offers a couple of keyboard methods that you should have in your arsenal. No matter what kind of keyboard you have, you can press **Ctrl+Esc**. But, if you have the Microsoft Natural Keyboard—the one with the alphanumeric keys split down the middle and the curvaceous look—press the key with the Windows logo on it (▓). Most recent keyboards sport the Windows logo key. In almost all cases, the key is located between the Ctrl and Alt keys.

♦ **E-mail**   This icon represents the Outlook Express program, which you use to send and read e-mail messages. You can get the scoop on this program in Chapter 17.

♦ **Windows Media Player**   This icon represents the Windows Media Player program, which you use to play music, watch DVD movies, create audio CDs, and perform other multimedia tricks. (See Chapter 9 for details.)

♦ **MSN Explorer**   This is yet another web browser. I don't talk about this program in this book.

♦ **Windows Movie Maker**   This icon represents the Windows Movie Maker program, which enables you to capture and edit digital video footage.

♦ **Tour Windows XP**   This icon represents a multimedia tour of what Windows XP has to offer.

♦ **Files and Settings Transfer Wizard**   This icon represents a program that makes it easy for you to transfer your documents and settings from an old computer to Windows XP.

♦ **All Programs**   This icon represents another menu that lists all the other programs installed on your computer. (See the next section, "Maneuvering Around the Start Menu," to learn more about this icon.)

You should know, as well, that the space below and including the Windows Media Player icon will soon be filled with more icons that represent the last six *programs* you've worked with most often.

The Start menu is loaded with five icons:

◆ **My Documents**   This icon represents the *folder* where you'll store most of the *documents* that you create. (You'll learn what it's all about in Chapter 4.)

◆ **My Pictures**   This icon represents the folder where you'll store your picture files (which are also known as graphics files and image files; see Chapter 7 for more info).

◆ **My Music**   This icon represents the folder where you'll store your music files, as described in Chapter 9.

◆ **My Computer**   This icon represents the folder that contains everything on your computer, including your hard disk, CD-ROM or DVD-ROM drive, floppy disk drive, and so on. (To get the details, head for Chapter 5.)

◆ **My Network Places**   This icon represents your local area network, if your computer is attached to one.

> **Jargon Jar**
>
> A **folder** is a storage location on your computer's hard disk. What do you store in a folder? You store files, which generally come in two flavors: **documents** that you create yourself and **program files** that run the programs installed on your computer.

For the Windows XP features, the Start menu is home to four icons:

◆ **Control Panel**   This icon represents the Windows XP Control Panel feature, which you use to customize Windows XP. I talk about the Control Panel throughout this book.

◆ **Help and Support**   This icon represents the Windows XP Help feature, which offers guidance and instruction on the various Windows XP bits and pieces.

◆ **Search**   This icon represents the Search feature, which you use to search for files on your hard disk, people in your Windows address book, information on the Internet, and more. I discuss file-searching in Chapter 5 and Internet-searching in Chapter 16.

◆ **Run**   This icon represents the Run feature, which you use to start programs that aren't accessible via the Start menu, and sometimes to install programs. Chapter 5 is the place to go to find out how this works.

Last and quite possibly least, for exiting Windows XP, the Start menu lines up two icons:

- ◆ **Log Off**   This icon represents the logging off process, which enables another person to use Windows XP with their own settings and program. I talk about setting up Windows XP for different users in Chapter 10.

- ◆ **Turn Off Computer** (Windows XP Home) or **Shut Down** (Windows XP Professional)   This icon represents the shutdown process, which you can use to either turn off or restart your computer. (See Chapter 1 for the specifics.)

Maneuvering Around the Start Menu

Now that you've met the denizens of the Start menu, you need to know how to make them do something useful. To launch an icon, you have two possibilities:

- ◆ For every icon except All Programs, you need only click the icon, and Windows XP launches the program, folder, or feature without further ado.

- ◆ Clicking the **All Programs** icon brings up another menu, as shown in Figure 2.2. As you can see, this new menu is filled with even more icons, some of which are duplicates of icons on the Start menu (Internet Explorer, Outlook Express, and Windows Media Player). To launch one of these icons, click it with your mouse.

Figure 2.2

Clicking the All Programs icon displays a menu of programs.

… to see
this menu

Click All
Progams…

Notice, however, that two of the icons (Accessories and Startup) have a little arrow on the right. When you click either one of these icons, a new menu (called a *submenu*) slides out to the right of the icon. For example, clicking the Accessories icon displays the submenu shown in Figure 2.3.

Figure 2.3

Some icons exist only to display a submenu that contains even more icons.

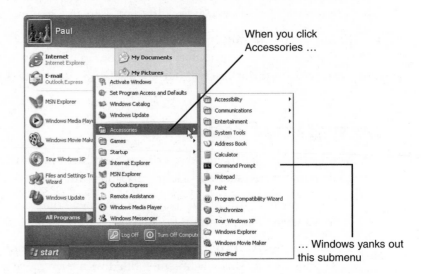

Don't be surprised if you find yourself wading through two or three of these submenus to get the program you want. For example, here are the steps you'd follow to fire up Solitaire, one of Windows XP's addictive card games:

> **Windows Wisdom**
>
> Here's a bonus: To display a submenu, you don't even need to click the icon. Instead, just point at the icon with your mouse and in a second or two the submenu will drift out automatically.

1. Click the **Start** button to display the Start menu.

2. Click **All Programs** to open the menu.

3. Click **Accessories** to open the submenu.

4. Click **Games** to open yet another submenu.

5. Click **Solitaire.** Windows XP launches the Solitaire program.

In the future, I abbreviate these long-winded Start menu procedures by using a comma (,) to separate each item you click, like so: "Select **Start, All Programs, Accessories, Games, Solitaire.**"

Now What? Getting a Program to Do Something Useful

Okay, so I know how to get a program running. What's next?

Ah, now you get to go on a little personal power trip because this section shows you how to boss around your programs. Specifically, you learn how to work with pull-down menus, toolbars, and dialog boxes.

Making It Go: Selecting Commands from Pull-Down Menus

Each program you work with has a set of commands and features that define the majority of what you can do with the program. Most of these commands and features are available via the program's *pull-down menus*. Oh sure, there are easier ways to tell a program what to do (I talk about some of them later in this chapter), but pull-down menus are special because they offer a complete road map for any program. This section gets you up to speed on this crucial Windows topic.

I'm going to use the My Computer program as an example for the next page or two. If you feel like following along, go ahead and launch the program by selecting **Start, My Computer.**

The first thing you need to know is that a program's pull-down menus are housed in the *menu bar*, the horizontal strip that runs just beneath the blue title bar. Each word in the menu bar represents a pull-down menu. Figure 2.4 points out the menu bar in My Computer.

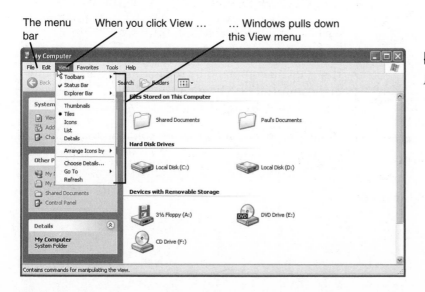

The menu bar   When you click View …   … Windows pulls down this View menu

Figure 2.4

My Computer's View menu.

The various items that run across the menu bar (such as File, Edit, and View in My Computer) are the names of the menus. To see (that is, *pull down*) one of these menus, use either of the following techniques:

◆ Use your mouse to click the menu name. For example, click **View** to pull down the View menu.

◆ Hold down the **Alt** key and examine the menu bar once again. See how each menu name sprouts an underline under one letter. That underline tells you that you can pull down the menu by holding down **Alt** and pressing the underlined letter on your keyboard. For example, the "V" in View gets underlined when you hold down Alt, so you can pull down this menu by pressing **Alt+V.**

Jargon Jar

A **command** is a menu item that initiates some kind of action.

Windows Wisdom

What if you don't want to select the commands from a menu you already opened? You can get rid of the menu by clicking any empty part of the program's window, or by pressing **Alt** by itself. Alternatively, you can choose a command from a different menu by clicking the menu's name in the menu bar, or by pressing **Alt** plus the underlined letter of the new menu.

The various items you see in the menu are called *commands*. From here, you use any of the following techniques to select a command:

◆ Use your mouse to click the command you want.

◆ From your keyboard, use the down arrow key (↓) or the up arrow key (↑) to highlight the command, and then press **Enter.**

◆ Press the underlined letter in the command. For example, the "R" in the View menu's Refresh command is underlined, so you can select this command by pressing **R.** (Go ahead and try this example; you won't hurt anything.)

Throughout this book, I tell you to select a pull-down menu command by separating the menu name and command name with a comma (,), like this: "Select the **View, Refresh** command."

Note, too, that many program commands are also available via *shortcut menus*, which you open by right-clicking something within the program window.

Jargon Jar _____

Many Windows programs (and Windows XP itself) use **shortcut menus** to give you quick access to oft-used commands. The idea is that you right-click something and the program pops up a small menu of commands, each of which is somehow related to whatever it is you right-clicked. If you see the command you want, great: Just click it (using the left button this time). If you don't want to select a command from the menu, either left-click an empty part of the window or press **Esc.**

What happens next depends on which command you picked. Here's a summary of the various possibilities:

◆ **The command runs without further fuss**   This is the simplest scenario, and it just means that the program carries out the command, no questions asked. For example, clicking the Refresh command updates My Computer's display automatically.

◆ **Another menu appears**   As shown in Figure 2.5, when you click the **View** menu's **Arrange Icons** command, a submenu appears on the right (similar to what you saw earlier with the Start menu). You then click the command you want to execute from the new menu.

◆ **The command is toggled on or off**   Some commands operate like light switches: They toggle certain features of a program on and off. When the feature is on, a small check mark appears to the left of the command to let you know. Selecting the command turns off the feature and removes the check mark. If you select the command again, the feature turns back on and the check mark reappears. For example, click the **View** menu's **Status Bar** command, which activates the status bar at the bottom of the My Computer window (see Figure 2.5).

◆ **An option is activated**   Besides having features that you can toggle on and off, some programs have flexible features that can assume three or more different states. My Computer, for example, gives you five ways to display the contents of your computer, according to your choice of one of the following **View** menu commands: **Thumbnails, Tiles, Icons, List,** and **Details** (see Chapter 5 for details). Because these states are mutually exclusive (you can select only one at a time), you need some way of knowing which of the four commands is currently active. That's the job of the *option mark:* a small dot that appears to the left of the active command (see the **Tiles** command in Figure 2.5).

Figure 2.5

A few pull-down menu features.

The check mark indicates an activated feature

Select a command that has an arrow ...

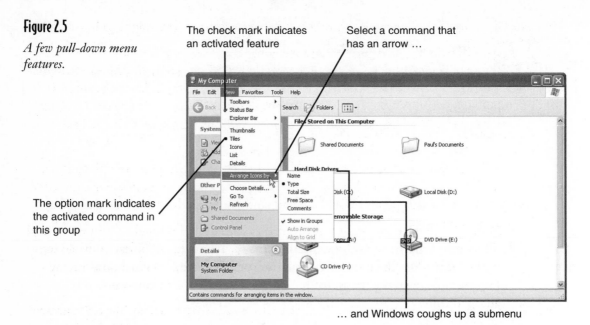

The option mark indicates the activated command in this group

... and Windows coughs up a submenu

◆ **A dialog box appears** Dialog boxes are pesky little windows that show up whenever the program needs to ask you for more information. You learn more about them in the "Dealing with Dialog Boxes" section, later in this chapter.

Your Click Is My Command: Toolbar Basics

The computer wizards who build our programs have come up with some amazing things over the years, but one of their most useful inventions has to be the *toolbar*. This is a collection of easily accessible icons designed to give you push-button access to common commands and features. No unsightly key combinations to remember; no pull-down menu forests to get lost in.

Toolbars play a big role in Windows XP, and you can reap some big dividends if you get to know how they work. Although most Windows XP components have a toolbar or two as standard equipment, let's stick with My Computer. As you can see in Figure 2.6, the toolbar is the horizontal strip located just south of the menu bar.

Most toolbar icons are buttons that represent commands you'd normally access by using the pull-down menus. All you have to do is click a button, and the program runs the command, no questions asked.

Here's a summary of a few other toolbar-related techniques you ought to know:

- ◆ **Toolbar text**   Most toolbar buttons advertise what they do using nothing more than an icon. Rather than trying to decipher the icon, some toolbars let you display text that at least gives you the name of each button. In My Computer, for example, select **View, Toolbars, Customize** to display the Customize Toolbar dialog box. Now use the **Text options** list to select **Show text labels,** and then click **Close.**

- ◆ **Button banners**   If the toolbar doesn't offer text labels, you can still find out the name of a particular button by pointing at it with your mouse. After a second or two, a banner—sometimes called a *tooltip*—with the button name pops up.

- ◆ **Hiding and showing toolbars**   In most programs, you toggle a toolbar on and off by selecting the **View, Toolbar** command. If a program offers multiple toolbars (as does My Computer), select the **View, Toolbars** command to display a submenu of the available toolbars, and then select the one you want.

- ◆ **Drop-down buttons**   You'll occasionally come across toolbar buttons that are really drop-down menu wanna-bes. In My Computer, the View "button" is an example of the species. As shown in Figure 2.6, you click the downward-pointing arrow to see a list of commands.

Here's the toolbar   Click the arrow to display the menu

Figure 2.6

Like most Windows XP components, My Computer comes with a toolbar.

Dealing with Dialog Boxes

I mentioned earlier that after you select some menu commands, the program might require more info from you. For example, if you run a Print command, the program might want to know how many copies of the document you want to print.

In these situations, the program sends an emissary to parley with you. These emissaries, called *dialog boxes*, are one of the most ubiquitous features in the Windows world. This section preps you for your dialog box conversations by showing you how to work with every type of dialog box control you're likely to encounter. (They're called *controls* because you use them to manipulate the different dialog box settings.) Before starting, it's important to keep in mind that most dialog boxes like to monopolize your attention. When one is on the screen, you usually can't do anything else in the program (such as select a pull-down menu). Deal with the dialog box first, and then you can move on to other things.

Jargon Jar

A **dialog box** is a small window that a program uses to prompt you for information or to display a message. You interact with each dialog box by using one or more **controls** to input data or initiate actions.

Conveniently, the WordPad program offers a wide variety of dialog boxes, so I use it for most of the examples in this section. If you're following along, launch the program by selecting **Start, All Programs, Accessories, WordPad.** Begin by selecting WordPad's **View, Options** command to have the Options dialog box report for duty, as shown in Figure 2.7.

Figure 2.7

WordPad's Options dialog box demonstrates quite a few dialog box features.

Okay, let's get started:

- **Command buttons**   Clicking one of these buttons executes whatever command is written on the button. The two examples shown in the Options dialog box are the most common. You click **OK** to close the dialog box and put the settings into effect, and you click **Cancel** to close the dialog box without doing anything.

◆ **Check boxes**   Windows uses a check box to toggle program features on and off. Clicking the check box either adds a check mark (meaning the feature will get turned on when you click **OK**) or removes the check mark (meaning the feature will get turned off when you click **OK**).

◆ **Option buttons**   If a program feature offers three or more possibilities, the dialog box will offer an option button for each state, and only one button can be activated (that is, have a black dot inside its circle) at a time. You activate an option button by clicking it.

◆ **Tabs**   Click any of the tabs displayed across the top of some dialog boxes and you see a new set of controls. (At this point, you no longer need the Options dialog box, so click **Cancel** to shut it down.)

◆ **Text boxes**   You use these controls to type text data. To see some examples, select WordPad's **Format, Paragraph** command to get to the Paragraph dialog box, shown in Figure 2.8. The **Left, Right,** and **First line** controls are all text boxes. (The Paragraph dialog box has served its purpose, so click **Cancel.**)

Highlighted text tells you this text box is currently the active control

These are the text boxes

Figure 2.8

Some sample text boxes.

◆ **List boxes**   These controls display a list of items and you select an item by clicking it. An example can be seen if you select WordPad's **Insert, Date and Time** command, shown in Figure 2.9. (After you've played around a bit, click **Cancel** to close this dialog box.)

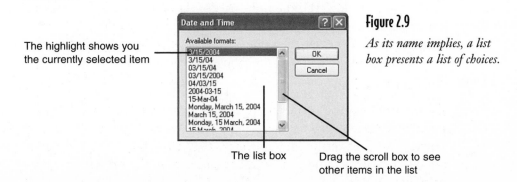

The highlight shows you the currently selected item

The list box

Drag the scroll box to see other items in the list

Figure 2.9

As its name implies, a list box presents a list of choices.

◆ **Combo boxes**   These hybrid controls combine a list box and a text box. You can either select the item you want from the list or type it in the text box. In Figure 2.10, WordPad's Font dialog box shows several examples (select **Format, Font** to get there).

Figure 2.10

WordPad's Font dialog box offers several examples of both combo boxes and drop-down list boxes.

Some combo boxes

Some drop-down list boxes

◆ **Drop-down list boxes**   These controls represent yet another example of the list box genre. In this case, at first you see only one item. However, if you click the downward-pointing arrow on the right, the full list appears and it becomes much like a regular list box. (That's enough of the Font dialog box, so click **Cancel**.)

◆ **Spin boxes**   These controls enable you to cycle up or down through a series of numbers. To see an example, select WordPad's **File, Print** command to wake up the Print dialog box, shown in Figure 2.11. The spin box is named **Number of copies.** The left part of the spin box is a simple text box into which you can type a number; however, the right part of the spin box has tiny up and down arrow buttons. You click the up arrow to increase the value, and you click the down arrow to decrease the value. (When you're finished, click **Cancel** to return the Print dialog box from whence it came.)

Figure 2.11

Click the spin box arrows to cycle up or down through a range of values.

A spin box

Switching from One Program to Another

When you fire up a program, Windows XP marks the occasion by adding a button to the taskbar. If you then coax another program or two onto the screen (remember, Windows XP is capable of *multitasking*—running multiple programs simultaneously), each one gets its own taskbar button.

For example, Figure 2.12 shows Windows XP with two programs up and running: WordPad and Paint. (To run the latter, select **Start, All Programs, Accessories, Paint.**) It looks as though Paint has lopped off a good portion of the WordPad window, but in reality Windows XP is just displaying Paint "on top" of WordPad. In addition, the taskbar has changed in two ways:

◆ There are now buttons for both WordPad and Paint in the taskbar.

◆ In the taskbar, the *active* program's button (the Paint button in this figure) looks as though it's been pressed. (The active program is the one you're currently slaving away in.)

Look Out!

Although it's true that Windows XP is happy to deal with multiple running programs—think of it as the electronic equivalent of walking and chewing gum at the same time—that doesn't mean you can just start every program you have and leave them running all day. The problem is that because each open program usurps a chunk of the Windows resources, the more programs you run, the slower each program performs, including Windows itself. The number of applications you can fire up at any one time depends on how much horsepower your computer has. You probably need to play around a bit to see just how many applications you can launch before things get too slow.

Figure 2.12

Windows XP with two programs on the go.

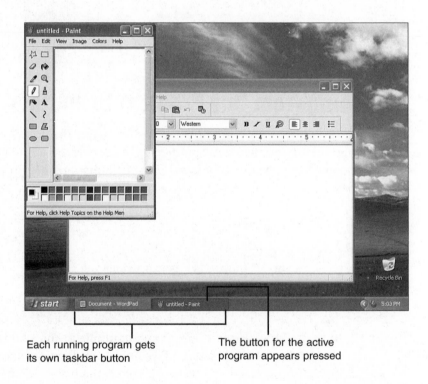

Each running program gets its own taskbar button

The button for the active program appears pressed

The taskbar has another trick up its digital sleeve: You can switch from one running program to another by clicking the latter's taskbar button. For example, when I click the WordPad button, the WordPad window comes to the fore, as shown in Figure 2.13.

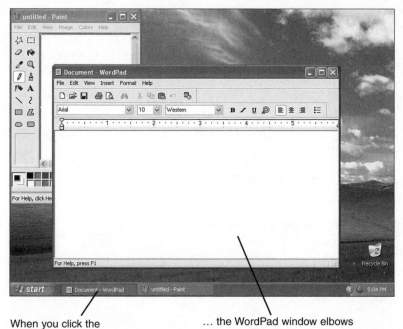

When you click the
WordPad taskbar button …

… the WordPad window elbows
its way to the front

Besides clicking the taskbar buttons, Windows XP gives you three other ways to leap from one running program to another:

♦ **Click the program's window**   This is perhaps the simplest and most obvious method. All you do is point the mouse inside the program's window and then click. This method is most useful if your hand is already on the mouse and you can see at least part of the window you want to activate.

♦ **Hold down Alt and tap Tab**   When you do this, Windows XP displays a box that boasts an icon for each running program. Each time you press **Tab,** the next icon gets highlighted. After you highlight the icon for the program you want, release the **Alt** key, and Windows XP then switches to the program. This technique is useful if your hands are on the keyboard and you have only a few programs running.

♦ **Hold down Alt and tap Esc**   This method is similar to the **Alt+Tab** method in that Windows XP cycles through the open programs. The difference is that with each tap of the **Esc** key, Windows XP brings each program window to the fore. Use this method when you want to check out the contents of each window before you decide which program you want to work with.

When Enough's Enough: Quitting a Program

When you're finished with a particular program, you should close it to keep your screen uncluttered and to reduce the load on Windows' resources. The easiest way to do this is to click the **Close** button—the "X" in the upper-right corner of the program's window.

You can also use a few other methods, which you may find faster under certain circumstances:

> #### Cross-Reference
>
> I tell you how to handle saving documents in Chapter 4. See the section titled "The All-Important Save Command."

♦ Press **Alt+F4.**

♦ Pull down the program's **File** menu and select the **Exit** command (or, more rarely, the **Close** command).

♦ Right-click the program's taskbar button and then click **Close** in the little menu that appears.

Depending on the program you're closing and the work you were doing with it, you might be asked whether you want to "save" some files.

The Least You Need to Know

♦ To start a program, click the **Start** button to display the Start menu, and then click the command or submenus required to launch the program.

♦ To select a pull-down menu command, first display the menu by clicking its name in the menu bar, and then click the command.

♦ In a dialog box, click **OK** to put dialog box settings into effect; click **Cancel** to bail out of a dialog box without doing anything; click **Help** to view the program's Help system.

♦ To switch between running programs, click the taskbar buttons. Alternatively, click the program window if you can see a chunk of it, or else press **Alt+Tab.**

♦ To quit a program, click the **Close** X button. You can also usually get away with selecting the program's **File, Exit** command or pressing **Alt + F4.**

Your Twenty-Minute Windows Workout

In This Chapter

◆ Window gadgets and gewgaws

◆ Minimizing and maximizing windows

◆ Moving and sizing windows

◆ How to wield window scrollbars

Windows gets its name because, as you saw in the previous chapter, each program that you launch shows up on the screen in a box, and that box is called a *window*. Why they named them "windows" instead of, say, "boxes" or "frames," I can't imagine. After all, have *you* ever seen a window on the top of a desk? I thought not.

Nincompoop nomenclature concerns aside, you're going to have to build up some window stamina because they'll come at you from the four corners of the screen. Fortunately, such stamina can be had without resorting to smelly workout clothes or Stairmasters. As you see in this chapter, all that's required is practicing a few handy mouse techniques.

Warming Up: A Window Walkabout

Your average window is a kind of mini Nautilus machine brimming with various gadgets that you push and pull. The secret to a successful window workout is to get to know where these gadgets are and what you use them for. To that end, let's take a tour of a typical window, as shown in Figure 3.1. This is a Notepad window. To get it onscreen, select **Start, All Programs, Accessories, Notepad.** (There's more on the Notepad program in Chapter 11.)

Here's a rundown of the various trinkets pointed out in Figure 3.1:

Figure 3.1

The Notepad window will be your "gym" for this chapter's exercise regimen.

Windows Wisdom

With all those buttons crowded into the upper-right corner of a window, it's tough keeping them straight. To help us out, Windows XP has a feature that tells you the name of each button. To check it out, move your mouse pointer over a button. A second or two later a little "tooltip" shows up with the button's name (as shown in Figure 3.1 by the word "Minimize").

◆ **Title bar**   This is the band (it's usually blue) that forms the top portion of the window. As its name implies, the title bar's job is to tell you the name of the currently open document. (In Figure 3.1, the document is new, so it has the temporary—and decidedly uninspiring—name "Untitled." See Figure 3.7 for a better example.) The title bar also usually shows the name of the program (with a dash in between the two names).

◆ **Buttons galore**   The right side of the title bar is populated with three buttons: The two blue buttons are named **Minimize** and **Maximize,** and the red button is named **Close.** I fill you in on what they do a bit later (see the section "Breaking a Sweat: Window Exercises").

- **Borders**   Most windows are surrounded by four borders that you can manipulate, with your mouse, to change the size of the window (I show you how to do this later in this chapter; see "Breaking a Sweat: Window Exercises").

- **System menu icon**   The system menu sports several commands that enable keyboard users to perform routine window maintenance. If you're dealing with a program window, you drop down the system menu by pressing **Alt+spacebar;** for a document window, the system menu sprouts in response to **Alt+-** (**hyphen**).

Now just hold on a cotton-picking second. What's the difference between a "program window" and a "document window"?

Gee, you *are* paying attention, aren't you? Here you go:

- **Program window**   This is the window in which the program as a whole appears.

- **Document window**   This is a window that appears inside the program window and it contains a single, open document. This isn't something you have to worry about if you run only the programs that come with Windows XP because they're only capable of opening one document at a time. However, lots of other programs—such as those that come with Microsoft Office—are capable of working with two or more documents at once. In this case, each document appears inside its own window.

Breaking a Sweat: Window Exercises

Before getting to the specifics of the four main window techniques—minimizing, maximizing, moving, and sizing—let's see how they can solve some niggling Windows problems and help you work better:

Problem #1: You have an open program that you know you won't need for a while. It's taking up desktop space, but you don't want to close it. The solution is to *minimize* the program's window, which means that it's cleared off the desktop, but it remains open and appears only as a taskbar button.

Problem #2: You want the largest possible work area for a program. The solution here is to *maximize* the program's window. This enlarges the window so that it fills the entire desktop area.

Problem #3: You have multiple programs on the go and their windows overlap each other so some data gets covered up. The way to fix this is to *move* one or more of the windows so that they don't overlap (or so that they overlap less).

CAUTION

Look Out!

You can't move or size a window if it's either maximized or minimized.

Problem #4: No matter how much you move your windows, they still overlap. In this case, you need to resort to more drastic measures: *sizing* the windows. For example, you can reduce the size of less important windows and increase the size of windows in which you do the most work.

The next few sections discuss these techniques and a few more, for good measure.

Minimizing a Window

When you click a window's **Minimize** button, the window disappears from view. The window isn't closed, however, because its taskbar button remains in place, as you can see in Figure 3.2.

Figure 3.2

When you minimize a program's window, the program remains running, but all you see is its taskbar button.

Just the window's taskbar
button is visible

Maximizing a Window

Clicking a window's **Maximize** button is a whole different kettle of window fish. In this case, the window grows until it fills the entire desktop, as you can see in Figure 3.3. Note that the **Maximize** button has, without warning, morphed into a new entity: the **Restore** button. I talk about this new creature in the next section.

Windows Wisdom _____

With Windows XP, Microsoft has made the **Minimize, Maximize, Restore,** and **Close** buttons a bit bigger, but they're still smallish targets. Here are some techniques that can help: minimize the current window by clicking its taskbar button; maximize a window by double-clicking its title bar; restore a maximized window by double-clicking its title bar; close a window by double-clicking its system menu icon.

The Restore button

Figure 3.3

When you maximize a window, it takes over the entire desktop.

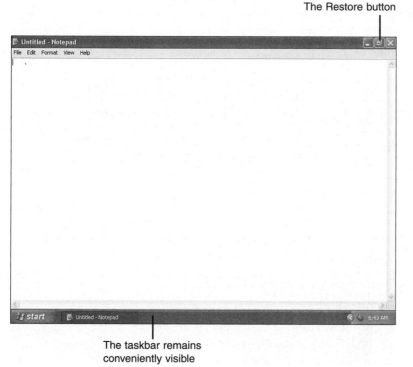

The taskbar remains
conveniently visible

Restoring a Window

In Windows parlance, *restoring* a window means that you put the window back exactly the way it was before minimizing it or maximizing it. How you do this depends on what action you inflicted on the window:

◆ If you minimized the window, click its **taskbar** button.

◆ If you maximized the window, click the **Restore** button (pointed out in Figure 3.3).

Moving a Window

Moving a window from one part of the desktop to another takes a simple mouse maneuver. Here are the steps to follow:

Windows Wisdom

If you want to change both the height and width of a window, you can save yourself a bit of effort by sizing two sides in one fell swoop. To do this, move the mouse pointer over a window corner. (The pointer will change to a diagonal two-sided arrow.) When you drag the mouse, Windows XP sizes the two sides that create the corner.

1. Make sure the window isn't maximized (or that it's not, duh, minimized).

2. Position the mouse pointer inside the window's title bar (but not over the system menu icon or any of the buttons on the right).

3. Click and drag the title bar. (That is, press and hold down the left mouse button and then move the mouse.) As you drag, the window moves along with your mouse. (Although it may lag behind slightly if you have a slower system.)

4. When the window is in the position you want, release the mouse button.

Sizing a Window

If you want to change the size of a window, instead, you need to plow through these steps:

1. Make sure the window isn't maximized or minimized.

2. Point the mouse at the window border you want to adjust. For example, if you want to expand the window toward the bottom of the screen, point the mouse at the bottom border. When you've positioned the pointer correctly, it becomes a two-headed arrow, as shown in Figure 3.4.

3. Click and drag the border to the position you want.

4. Release the mouse button to set the new border position.

5. Repeat steps 2 through 4 for any other borders you want to size.

Figure 3.4

You resize a window by dragging the window borders hither and yon.

At a window border, the mouse pointer changes to a two-headed arrow

Cascading and Tiling Windows

If you're pressed for time, you can take advantage of some Windows XP features that can save you a few steps. To get at these features, right-click an empty section of the taskbar. The shortcut menu that slides into view contains (among others) the following commands:

◆ **Cascade Windows** This command automatically arranges all your nonminimized windows in a diagonal pattern that lets you see the title bar of each window. Figure 3.5 shows three cascaded windows.

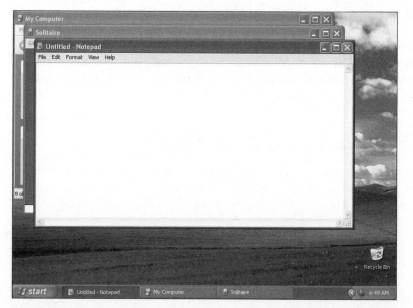

Figure 3.5

The **Cascade Windows** *command arranges your windows neatly in a diagonal pattern.*

◆ **Tile Windows Horizontally** This feature automatically arranges all your nonminimized windows into horizontal strips so that each of them gets an equal amount of desktop real estate without overlapping each other. Figure 3.6 shows the same three windows arranged horizontally.

Figure 3.6

The **Tile Windows Horizontally** *command carves out equal-size horizontal desktop chunks for your windows.*

◆ **Tile Windows Vertically** This command is similar to the **Tile Windows Horizontally** command, except that it arranges the windows into vertical strips.

◆ **Show the Desktop** This command hides all the nonminimized windows so that you can see the full desktop. After you run this command, it changes to **Show Open Windows** which restores all your windows.

Window Weight Lifting: Using Scrollbars

Depending on the program you're using, you often find that the document you're dealing with won't fit entirely inside the window's boundaries, even when you maximize the window. When this happens, you need some way to move to the parts of the document you can't see.

From the keyboard, you can use the basic navigation keys (the **arrow keys, Page Up,** and **Page Down**). Mouse users, as usual, have all the fun. To navigate through a document, they get to learn a new skill: how to use *scrollbars*. Using the Notepad window shown in Figure 3.7, I've pointed out the major features of the average scrollbar. Here's how to use these features to get around inside a document:

Jargon Jar

The **scrollbar** is the narrow strip that runs along the right side of most windows. You sometimes see scrollbars along the bottom of a window, too.

◆ The position of the scroll box gives you an idea of where you are in the document. For example, if the scroll box is about halfway down, you know you're somewhere near the middle of the document. Similarly, if the scroll box is near the bottom of the scrollbar, then you know you're near the end of the document.

◆ To scroll down through the document one line at a time, click the **down scroll arrow.** To scroll continuously, press and hold down the left mouse button on the down scroll arrow.

◆ To scroll up through the document one line at a time, click the **up scroll arrow.** To scroll continuously, press and hold down the left mouse button on the **up scroll arrow.**

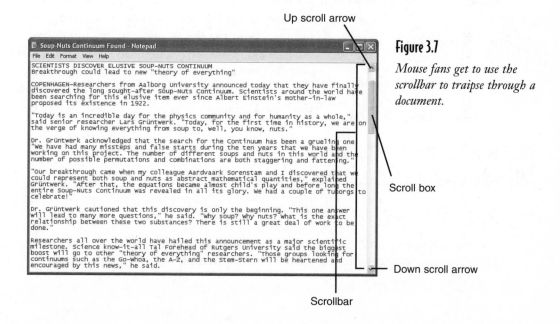

Figure 3.7

Mouse fans get to use the scrollbar to traipse through a document.

◆ To leap through the document one screen at a time, click inside the scrollbar between the scroll box and the scroll arrows. For example, to move down one screen, click inside the scrollbar between the scroll box and the down scroll arrow.

◆ To move to a specific part of the document, click and drag the scroll box up or down.

Note, as well, that many of the windows you work in will also sport a second scrollbar that runs horizontally along the bottom of the window. Horizontal scrollbars work the same as their vertical cousins, except that they let you move left and right in wide documents.

Scrolling with a "Wheel" Mouse

In early 1997, Microsoft introduced a radical new mouse design that incorporates a little wheel between the two buttons. If you have one of these rotary rodents (or one of the knockoffs that many other mouse makers have put out), you can scroll up and down through a document by rotating the wheel forward or backward.

Some applications (such as Microsoft's Internet Explorer and the Microsoft Office 97 and later programs) also support a feature called *panning* that lets you scroll automatically through a document and control the speed. To enable panning, click the wheel button. The application will then display an *origin mark* (the position of this mark varies from application to application). Drag the pointer above the origin mark to scroll up; drag the pointer below the origin mark to scroll down. Note also that the farther the pointer is from the origin mark, the faster you scroll. To turn off panning, click the wheel again.

Jargon Jar

To **pan** means to use the mouse wheel to scroll automatically through a document.

The Least You Need to Know

◆ Minimizing a window means that the window disappears from the desktop, although the program continues to run. You minimize a window by clicking the **Minimize** button in the upper-right corner.

◆ Maximizing a window means that the window expands to fill the entire desktop. You maximize a window by clicking the **Maximize** button in the upper-right corner.

◆ To move a window, use your mouse to drag the title bar to and fro.

◆ To size a window, use your mouse to drag any of the window's borders.

◆ To let Windows do most of the work, right-click an empty part of the taskbar to eyeball several commands for cascading, tiling, and minimizing all windows.

Chapter 4

Saving, Opening, Printing, and Other Document Lore

In This Chapter

♦ Forging a fresh document

♦ Saving a document for posterity

♦ Closing a document and opening it back up again

♦ Handy document editing techniques

♦ Printing a document

The purpose of the chapters in Part 1 is to help you get comfortable with Windows XP, and if you've been following along and practicing what you've learned, you and Windows should be getting along famously by now. However, there's another concept you need to familiarize yourself with before you're ready to fully explore the Windows universe: documents.

This chapter plugs that gap in your Windows education by teaching you all the basic techniques for manipulating documents. This will include creating, saving, closing, opening, editing, and printing documents, plus much more.

"What's Up, Doc(ument)?"

Most folks think a document is a word processing file. That's certainly true, as far as it goes, but I'm talking about a bigger picture in this chapter. Specifically, when I say "document," what I really mean is *any* file that you create by cajoling a program into doing something useful.

So, yes, a file created within the confines of a word processing program (such as WordPad) is a document. However, these are also documents: text notes you type into a text editor; images you draw in a graphics program; e-mail missives you compose in an e-mail program; spreadsheets you construct with a spreadsheet program; and presentations you cobble together with a presentation graphics program. In other words, if you can create it or edit it yourself, it's a document.

Manufacturing a New Document

Lots of Windows programs—including WordPad, Notepad, and Paint—are courteous enough to offer up a new, ready-to-roll, document when you start the program. This means you can just dive right in to your typing or drawing or whatever. Later on, however, you may need to start another new document. To do so, use one of the following techniques:

- ◆ Select the **File, New** command.

- ◆ Click the **New** button in the program's toolbar, pointed out in Figure 4.1. (This is the WordPad program. If you want to follow along, open WordPad by selecting **Start, All Programs, Accessories, WordPad.**)

Figure 4.1

Most Windows programs offer toolbar buttons for easy access to document commands.

- ◆ In many Windows programs, you can spit out a new document by pressing **Ctrl+N.**

In most cases, the program will then toss a fresh document on-screen. Some programs (WordPad is one) display a dialog box that asks you what kind of new document you want.

The All-Important Save Command

"Save your work as soon as you can and as often as you can."

Without even a jot of hyperbole, I'm telling you right here and now that this deceptively simple slogan is probably the single most important piece of advice that you'll stumble upon in this book.

Look Out! _____

If your computer's memory doesn't go into clean slate mode until you shut down Windows, you may be wondering why you can't just wait to save until you're ready to close up shop for the night. If a power failure shuts off your system, or if Windows crashes, all your unsaved work is toast. By saving constantly, you greatly lessen the chance of that happening.

Why all the fuss? Because when you work with a new document (or with an existing document), all the changes you make are stored temporarily in your computer's memory. The bad news is that memory is a fickle and transient medium that, despite its name, forgets all of its contents when you shut down Windows. If you haven't saved your document to your hard disk (which maintains its contents even when Windows isn't running and even if your computer is turned off), you lose all the changes you've made and it's impossible to get them back. Scary!

To guard against such a disaster, remember my "saving slogan" from before and keep the following in mind:

◆ When you create a new document, save it as soon as you've entered any data that's worth keeping.

◆ After the new document is saved, keep right on saving it as often as you can. When I'm writing a book, I typically save my work every 30 to 60 seconds (I'm paranoid!), but a reasonable schedule is to save your work every 5 minutes or so.

Saving a New Document

Saving a new document takes a bit of extra work, but after that's out of the way, subsequent saves require only a mouse click or two. To save a new document, use either of the following techniques:

- ◆ Select the **File, Save** command.

- ◆ Click the **Save** button in the program's toolbar (see Figure 4.1).

Most programs will display a Save As dialog box like the one shown in Figure 4.2.

From here, there's an easy road and a hard road you can take to get your document saved.

The easy road is when you see **My Documents** in the **Save in** list (as shown in Figure 4.2). As its name implies, My Documents is a built-in folder that Windows provides for storing your documents. If you want to use it (which I highly recommend), all you need to do is enter a name for the document in the **File name** text box, and then click **Save.** Note, however, that Windows places a few restrictions on file names; see step 3 in the steps that follow.

Figure 4.2

The Save As dialog box appears when you're saving a new document.

The ever-so-slightly-harder road is when you're working with images or music files. In this case, you first perform an extra step in the Save As dialog box:

- ◆ If you're saving an image, double-click the **My Pictures** icon to open the My Pictures folder, which is a special folder for storing graphics files. (I tell you more about it in Chapter 7.)

◆ If you're saving a music file or sound file, double-click the **My Music** icon to open the My Music folder, which is (as you've probably guessed by now) a special folder for storing music and sound files. (You learn about it in Chapter 9.)

The hard road is when you want to use some other folder to store your document. Here are the steps you need to walk through to get your document safely stowed somewhere else:

1. The **Save in** drop-down list tells you the name of the current folder. To choose a different folder, first drop down the list and choose the disk drive that contains the folder you want to use to store the file.

2. The Save As dialog box then shows you a list of the folders on the selected disk drive. Double-click the folder you want to open. You may need to repeat this several times to get to the folder you want.

3. Use the File name text box to enter a name for your document. Note that the name you choose must be different from any other document in the folder. Also, Windows XP lets you enter file names that are up to 255 characters long. Your names can include spaces, commas, and apostrophes, but not the following characters: \ , ? : * " < > .

4. Now use the **Save as type** drop-down list to choose the type of document you want to create. In the vast majority of cases you won't have to bother with this because the default type is best. Many programs can create different document types, however, and this capability often comes in handy.

5. Click the **Save** button. The program makes a permanent copy of the document on your hard disk.

Here are some notes about saving new documents:

◆ Happily, you won't have to go through the rigmarole of choosing a folder every time you save a new document. Most programs are smart enough to "remember" the most recent folder you worked with and will select it for you automatically the next time you're in the Save As dialog box. (Unfortunately, this only applies to the current session with the program. If you exit the program and then restart it, you have to reselect the folder.)

◆ If you want your new document to replace an existing document, open the folder that contains the document and then double-click the file name. The program will ask whether you want to replace the document, and you then click **Yes**.

◆ The rub with long file names is that DOS programs and programs meant to work with Windows 3.1 (now, thankfully, quite rare in the computing landscape) will scoff at your attempts to break through the old "8.3" file name barrier (eight characters for the file name and a three-character extension). What happens if you create a document with a long name, using a Windows XP program, and then try to open that document in an older program? Well, the document will probably open just fine, but you'll notice that the file name has been knocked down in size. You see, Windows XP actually keeps track of *two* names for each document: the long name and a shorter DOS-compatible name. The latter is just the first six characters of the long name (sans spaces), followed by a tilde (~), followed by a number. For example, a file named Fiscal 2005 - First Quarter Budget Spreadsheet would also use the DOS alias FISCAL~1.

> **Cross-Reference**
>
> Confused about folders? Don't worry, I tell you all about them in Chapter 5.

Saving an Existing Document

After all that hard work saving a new document, you'll be happy to know that subsequent saves are much easier. That's because when you select the **File, Save** command, the program simply updates the existing hard disk copy of the document. This takes just a second or two (usually) and no dialog box shows up to pester you for information. Because this is so easy, there's no excuse not to save your work regularly. If you're a fan of keyboard shortcuts, here's one to memorize for the ages: Press **Ctrl+S** to save your document. If you're a fan of toolbar buttons, click the **Save** toolbar button shown in Figure 4.1.

> **Cross-Reference**
>
> For more information about how to back up your documents, see the section in Chapter 22 titled "Step 6—Back Up Your Files."

Taking Advantage of the My Documents Folder

I mentioned earlier that I highly recommend you use the prefab My Documents folder, which is designed to be a central storage area for all your documents. Using this folder is a good idea for three reasons:

◆ It makes your documents easy to find because they're all stored in one place.

◆ When you want to back up your documents, you need to only select a single folder (rather than hunting around your hard disk for all your documents).

◆ It's easy to get to: Select **Start, My Documents.** (You can also get there by opening the My Documents folder within My Computer or Windows Explorer.)

Using the Save As Command to Make a Copy of a Document

As you slave away in Windows XP, you sometimes find that you need to create a second, slightly different, copy of a document. For example, you might create a letter and then decide that you need a second copy to send to someone else. Rather than re-creating the entire letter from scratch, it's much easier to make a copy of the existing document and then change just the address and salutation.

The easiest way to go about this is to use the Save As command. This command is a lot like Save, except that it enables you to save the document with a new name or to a new location. (Think of it as the don't-reinvent-the-wheel command.) To use Save As to create a new document, follow these steps:

1. Open the original document (not a new one). (If you're not sure how to go about this, skip ahead to section titled "Opening an Existing Document" to find out.)

2. Select the **File, Save As** command. The program displays the same Save As dialog box shown in Figure 4.2.

3. Either select a different storage location for the new document or enter a different name (or both).

4. Click **Save.** The program closes the original document, makes a copy, and then opens the new document.

5. Make your changes to the new document (see the next section).

Getting It Right: Text Editing for Beginners

As you create your document, you have to delete text, move text chunks to different locations, and so on. To make your electronic writing life easier, it's crucial to get these basic editing chores down pat. To that end, here's a summary of some editing techniques you can use in most any program that deals with text (including Notepad, WordPad, Outlook Express, and MSN Messenger):

Look Out!

If you highlight some text and then press a character on your keyboard, your entire selection will disappear and be replaced by the character you typed! (If you press the **Enter** key, the highlighted text just disappears entirely.) This is normal behavior that can cause trouble for even experienced document jockeys. To get your text back, immediately select the **Edit, Undo** command or press **Ctrl+Z.**

◆ **Highlighting text with the mouse**   Before you can do something to existing text, you need to *highlight* it. To highlight text with a mouse, click and drag the mouse over the characters you want. That is, you first position the mouse pointer a teensy bit to the left of the first character you want to highlight. Then you press and hold down the left mouse button and move the mouse to the right. As you do, the characters you pass over become highlighted. While you drag, you can also move the mouse down to highlight multiple lines. When you release the mouse button, the text remains highlighted.

◆ **Highlighting text with the keyboard**   To highlight text by using the keyboard, position the cursor to the left of the first character, hold down the **Shift** key, and then press the **right-arrow** key until the entire selection is highlighted. Use the **down-arrow** key (or even **Page Down** if you have a lot of ground to cover) when you need to highlight multiple lines.

◆ **Copying highlighted text**   To make a copy of the highlighted text, select the **Edit, Copy** command. (Alternatively, you can also press **Ctrl+C** or click the **Copy** toolbar button, shown in Figure 4.1). Then position the cursor where you want to place the copy, and select the **Edit, Paste** command. (Your other choices are to press **Ctrl+V** or click the **Paste** toolbar button; again, see Figure 4.1). A perfect copy of your selection appears instantly. Note that you can paste this text as many times as you need.

◆ **Moving highlighted text**   When you need to move something from one part of a document to another, you *could* do it by making a copy, pasting it, and then going back to delete the original. If you do this, however, your colleagues will certainly make fun of you, because there's an easier way. After you highlight what you want to move, select the **Edit, Cut** command (the shortcuts are pressing **Ctrl+X** or clicking the **Cut** toolbar button; see Figure 4.1). Your selection disappears from the screen, but don't panic; Windows XP saves it for you. Position the cursor where you want to place the text, and then select **Edit, Paste.** Your stuff miraculously reappears in the new location.

◆ **Deleting text**   Because even the best typists make occasional typos, knowing how to delete is a necessary editing skill. Put away the White-Out, though, because deleting a character or two is easier (and less messy) if you use either of the following techniques: Position the cursor to the right of the offending character and press the **Backspace** key; or position the cursor to the left of the character and press the **Delete** key. If you have a large chunk of material you want to expunge from the document, highlight it and press the **Delete** key or the **Backspace** key.

Windows Wisdom

All this cut, copy, and paste moonshine is a bit mysterious. Where does cut text (or whatever) go? How does Windows XP know what to paste? Does Windows XP have some kind of digital hip pocket that it uses to store and retrieve cut or copied data? Truth be told, that's not a bad analogy. This "hip pocket" is actually a chunk of your computer's memory called the *clipboard*. Whenever you run the **Cut** or **Copy** command, Windows XP heads to the clipboard, removes whatever currently resides there, and stores the cut or copied data. When you issue the **Paste** command, Windows XP grabs whatever is on the clipboard and tosses it into your document.

♦ **To err is human, to undo divine**   What do you do if you paste text to the wrong spot or consign a vital piece of an irreplaceable document to deletion purgatory? Happily, Notepad, WordPad, and many other Windows XP programs have an Undo feature to get you out of these jams. To reverse your most recent action, select the **Edit, Undo** command to restore everything to the way it was before you made your blunder. And, yes, there are shortcuts you can use: Try either pressing **Ctrl+Z** or clicking the **Undo** toolbar button (pointed out, as usual, in Figure 4.1).

It's important to remember that most of the time the **Undo** command usually only undoes your most recent action. So if you delete something, perform some other task, and then try to undo the deletion, chances are the program won't let you do it. Therefore, always try to run **Undo** immediately after making your error. Note, however, that some programs are more flexible and will let you undo several actions. In this case, you just keep selecting the **Undo** command until your document is back the way you want it.

Closing a Document

Some weakling Windows programs (such as WordPad and Paint) allow you to open only one document at a time. In such programs, you can close the document you're currently working on by starting a new document, by opening another document, or by quitting the program altogether.

However, most full-featured Windows programs let you open as many documents as you want (subject to the usual memory limitations that govern all computer work). In this case, each open document appears inside its own window—called a *document window*, not surprisingly. These document windows have their own versions of the **Minimize, Maximize, Restore,** and **Close** buttons. Also, the name of each document appears on the program's Window menu, which you can use to switch from one document to another.

Because things can get crowded pretty fast, though, you probably want to close any documents you don't need at the moment. To do this, activate the document you want to close and select the **File, Close** command, or click the document window's **Close** button. If you made changes to the document since last saving it, a dialog box appears asking whether you want to save those changes. Click **Yes** to save, **No** to discard the changes, or **Cancel** to leave the document open. In most programs that support multiple open documents, you also can close the current document by pressing **Ctrl+F4.**

Opening an Existing Document

After you've saved a document or two, you often need to get one of them back on-screen to make changes or review your handiwork. To do that, you need to *open* the document by using any of the following techniques:

♦ **Use the Open dialog box**   Select the program's **File, Open** command. (Alternatively, press **Ctrl+O** or click the **Open** toolbar button, shown in Figure 4.1.) The Open dialog box that appears is similar to the Save As dialog box you messed with earlier. Find the document you want to open, highlight it, and then click **Open.**

♦ **Use the My Documents folder**   If you're using the My Documents folder to store your stuff, you can open a document by displaying My Documents and then double-clicking the document's icon. You can also highlight the document and then select **File, Open.** If the appropriate application isn't running, Windows XP will start it for you and load the document automatically.

♦ **Use My Computer or Windows Explorer**   Along similar lines, you can also use My Computer or Windows Explorer (located under **Start, All Programs, Accessories**) to open a document. Again, find the document you want and launch its icon.

It's possible to convince the Start menu to display a list of the most recent documents you've worked on. I'll show you how to do this in Chapter 21.

Sending a Document to the Printer

The nice thing about printing in Windows XP is that the basic steps you follow are more or less identical in each and every Windows program. After you learn the fundamentals, you can apply them to all your Windows applications. Here are the steps you need to follow:

1. In your program, open the document you want to print.

2. Select the **File, Print** command. You see a Print dialog box similar to the one shown in Figure 4.3 for the WordPad word processor.

   If your fingers are poised over your keyboard, you may find that in most applications pressing **Ctrl+P** is a faster way to get to the Print dialog box. If you just want a single copy of the document, click the **Print** toolbar button (see Figure 4.1) to bypass the Print dialog box and print the document directly.

Figure 4.3

WordPad's Print dialog box is a typical example of the species.

3. The options in the Print dialog box vary slightly from application to application, but you almost always see three things:

   ◆ A list for selecting the printer to use. In WordPad's Print dialog box, for example, use the **Select Printer** list to select the printer.

   ◆ A text box or spin box to enter the number of copies you want. In the WordPad Print dialog box, use the **Number of copies** text box.

   ◆ Some controls for selecting how much of the file to print. You normally have the option of printing the entire document or a specific range of pages. (WordPad's Print dialog box also includes a **Selection** option button that you can activate to print only the currently highlighted text.)

> **Cross-Reference**
>
> Before you can print, you may need to tell Windows XP what type of printer you have. I tell you how to go about this in Chapter 6. See the section titled "Installing Specific Devices."

4. When you've chosen your options, click the **Print** button to start printing (some Print dialog boxes have an **OK** button, instead).

Keep watching the information area of the taskbar (the area to the left of the clock). After a few seconds (depending on the size of the document), a printer icon appears, as shown in Figure 4.4. This tells you that Windows XP is hard at work farming out the document to your printer. This icon disappears after the printer is finished with its job. If you have an exceptionally speedy printer, this icon may come and go without you ever laying eyes on it. If the printer icon shows up with a red question mark icon superimposed on it, it means there's a problem with the printer.

Figure 4.4

The printer icon tells you that Windows XP is printing.

The Least You Need to Know

- To forge a new document, select the **File, New** command, press **Ctrl+N,** or click the toolbar's **New** button.

- To save a document, select the **File, Save** command, press **Ctrl+S,** or click the toolbar's **Save** button. If you're saving a new document, use the Save As dialog box to pick out a location and a name for the document.

- You'll simplify your life immeasurably if you store all your files in the My Documents folder.

- Press **Backspace** to delete the character to the left of the cursor; press **Delete** to wipe out the character to the right; press **Ctrl+Z** to undo your most recent mistake.

- To open a document, select the **File, Open** command, press **Ctrl+O,** or click the toolbar's **Open** button.

- To print a document, select the **File, Print** command, press **Ctrl+P,** or click the toolbar's **Print** button.

Using My Computer to Fiddle with Files and Folders

In This Chapter

- ◆ Navigating your system using My Computer
- ◆ Creating, selecting, copying, moving, renaming, deleting, and searching for files and folders
- ◆ "Burning" files to a CD
- ◆ Changing the file and folder view
- ◆ Sorting files and folders
- ◆ A fistful of useful file and folder factoids

In Chapter 4, you learned that it's off-the-scale crucial to save your documents as soon and as often as you can. That way, you preserve your documents within the stable confines of your computer's hard disk. You also learned that it's best to use your hard disk's My Documents folder as a central storage location for your documents.

You learned, in other words, that your hard disk is a vital chunk of digital real estate. So, as a responsible landowner, it's important for you to tend your plot and keep your grounds well maintained. That's the purpose of this chapter, as it shows you how to use some of Windows XP's built-in tools to work with your hard disk's files and folders. You get the scoop on creating new folders, copying and moving files from one folder to another, renaming and deleting files and folders, and much more.

My, Oh, My: Learning About Your Computer Using My Computer

Windows XP has an annoying habit of appending the word "My" onto the front of things. On the Start menu alone you spy at least four of these exercises in self-absorption: My Documents, My Pictures, My Music, and My Computer (and possibly also My Network Places). This "My-opic" point of view is a bit cutesy, but it serves a more serious purpose: To remind you that what's truly important on your system is what you create yourself.

With that in mind, let's take a closer look at the main "My" machine: My Computer. From the name, you might be tempted to think that it represents your entire computer. Well, that's close, but there's no cigar for you. My Computer really represents only the areas of your computer where files can be stored: your hard disk, your floppy disk, your CD-ROM or DVD-ROM drive, "removable" disks such as those that work with Zip or Jaz drives, attached digital cameras, folders on a network, and so on.

You can prove this for yourself by opening the Start menu and then clicking the **My Computer** icon. You end up eyeballing a window that looks suspiciously like the one shown in Figure 5.1. (Your version of My Computer may look a bit different if your computer has a different configuration than mine.)

My Computer's job is to display the contents of a given folder so that you can check out what's in the folder or muck about with those contents in some way (such as renaming one of your files; see the "Renaming a File or Folder" section later in this chapter). So the My Computer window is set up to help you do just that. First, notice that the title bar shows you the name of the current folder that My Computer is displaying. (You always see "My Computer" at first, but the title changes as you jump from folder to folder.)

> **Windows Wisdom**
>
> Although my definition of a *folder* as a slice of a disk used for storage is accurate, Windows takes this idea of storage to great lengths. That is, in the Windows worldview, anything that can store anything is considered to be a folder. So even though My Computer isn't technically a slice of any disk, it's treated as a folder because it stores various icons.

> **Windows Wisdom**
>
> If your CD or DVD drive is empty, My Computer shows the icon with *CD Drive* or *DVD Drive*. However, if you insert a CD or DVD disc in the drive, then My Computer's display changes to show whatever title and icon the manufacturer assigned to the disc.

The name of the current folder

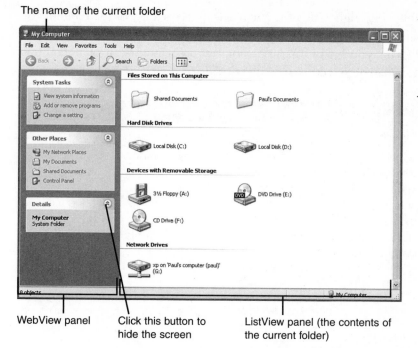

Figure 5.1

Click the Start menu's **My Computer** *icon to check out your computer's goodies.*

WebView panel   Click this button to hide the screen   ListView panel (the contents of the current folder)

Next, after you get below the usual window suspects (the title bar, the menu bar, and the toolbar), you see that the My Computer window is divided into two sections:

◆ **WebView panel**   The left side of the window offers a collection of icons that are related to the current folder. Depending on the folder that's currently displayed, these icons will be separated into three or four different sections. Here are the four most common sections that you'll stumble upon:

> **System Tasks**   The icons in this section initiate broad, system-level actions. For example, in My Computer, this section includes the **Add or remove programs** icon for installing or uninstalling software.

> **File and Folder Tasks**   The icons in this section run commands related to files and folders (such as renaming a folder or deleting a file).

> **Other Places**   The icons in this section represent other folders on your computer.

> **Details**   The text in this section gives you information about the current folder or about a file inside the folder (if you click the file to highlight it).

For the icons in the WebView panel, you can run the task or display the folder by clicking the icon. Note, too, that you can hide a section's icons (or the text in the Details section) by clicking the **double-arrow** button in the top-right corner (refer to Figure 5.1).

◆ **ListView panel**   The right side of the window displays a list of the contents of the current folder. The My Computer folder stores your computer's disk drives, so that's mostly what you see in this area. The text associated with each icon tells you what kind of disk drive you're dealing with.

Hacking Windows

By default, Windows XP doesn't show you the full name of each file. The actual file name consists of the *primary name*—the name you see in My Computer—followed by a dot (.) and an *extension*. This is a three-letter (usually) code that specifies what type of file you're dealing with. For example, a text file uses the *txt* (text) extension, while most WordPad files use the *doc* (document) extension. It's often easier to determine the file type from the extension than from the icon, so you might want to force Windows XP to show the file extensions. To do that, run My Computer and select **Tools, Folder Options**. In the Folder Options dialog box, click the **View** tab and then clear the **Hide extensions for known file types** check box. Click **OK** to put the setting into effect.

Navigating to a File

One of the most common chores associated with My Computer is navigating through various folders and subfolders to get to a particular file. How you go about this depends on whether the file you want is housed in My Documents (or one of its subfolders) or in some other part of your system.

The My Documents route is easiest, so let's start with that. If you're in the My Computer window, click **My Documents** in the Other Places section. (Remember, however, that you can bypass My Computer and go to My Documents directly by selecting **Start, My Documents.**) Figure 5.2 shows My Documents on my system, which is populated with a few of my files.

As you can see, this folder contains a couple of icons that represent subfolders, and the rest of the icons represent files. If the file you want is in one of the subfolders, double-click the subfolder's icon. Repeat this as often as necessary to reach the file you want.

If your file isn't in My Documents or one of its subfolders, then you need to hunt it down in some other part of your computer. To do that, follow these steps:

1. In My Computer, double-click the icon for the disk drive that contains the file you want. (If you plan on looking for your file on a floppy drive, CD or DVD drive, or a removable disk drive, be sure you have a disk inside the drive, or Windows XP will reprimand you with an error message.)

2. If Windows doesn't display the contents of the disk drive (for example, you might instead see the message **Looking for your programs?**), then in the System Tasks section, click the **Show the contents of this drive** icon.

3. If your file isn't in the current folder, double-click the icon for the subfolder that contains the file.

4. Repeat step 3 until you get to the file.

Look Out!

Certain drives and folders that contain Windows XP system files don't show their contents right away. Note that unless you're given specific instructions, under no circumstances should you play around with (rename, delete, move, and so on) any of the files in these system drives and folders.

Subfolders

Files

Figure 5.2

Opening a folder reveals the contents of that folder.

You may have noticed by now that the icons in the various folders have all kinds of different pictures. For example, most folders have a yellow icon that looks suspiciously like a file folder. Makes sense. Files are another story, however, because they have all kinds of different icons. The reason is that each icon tells you what kind of file you're dealing with and which program will run if you open (double-click) the file. In Figure 5.2, for example, the files named "A Few of My Favorite Words" and "Alignment Examples" are WordPad documents, and the files named "A Guy In a Bar" and "A Shaggy Dog Story" are Notepad documents.

Getting Around in My Computer

Getting from here to there in My Computer is often easiest using the program's tool-bar, which is chock-full of one-click wonders. However, it's sometimes difficult to tell which button does what. To help out, you can force My Computer to display the name of each button (see Figure 5.3). To do this, select **View, Toolbars, Customize** (or right-click the toolbar and then click **Customize**). In the Customize Toolbar dialog box, use the **Text options** list to choose **Show text labels,** and then click **OK**.

Figure 5.3

*The **Back** and **Forward** buttons maintain lists of the places you've been.*

Click this arrow to display the Back list

Here are a few pointers for navigating from folder to folder in My Computer:

- To go back to the previous folder, either click the **Back** button in the toolbar or select **View, Go To, Back.** (There's also a keyboard shortcut that you can use: **Alt+Left Arrow.**)

- After you've gone back to a previous folder, you can move forward again either by clicking the **Forward** button or by selecting **View, Go To, Forward.** (The keyboard shortcut for this is **Alt+Right Arrow.**)

- Rather than stepping back and forward one folder at a time, you can leap over multiple folders in a single bound. To do this, click the **downward-pointing arrow** beside either the **Back** or **Forward** toolbar button. In the list that appears (see Figure 5.3), click the folder you want to visit. (You also can do this by selecting **View, Go To** and then choosing the folder from the list at the bottom of the menu.)

- If a folder has subfolders, the folder is called the *parent* and each subfolder is called a *child*. (Strange terms, I know.) If you're viewing a child folder, you can go to its parent folder either by clicking the **Up** button in the toolbar or by selecting **View, Go To, Up One Level.** (Keyboard fans can press **Backspace** instead.)

Taking Advantage of the Handy Folders List

The thing I dislike the most about My Computer is that it shows only one folder at a time, so you often end up "drilling down" through a series of subfolders to get where you want to go. Too slow! To speed things up, activate My Computer's Folders list either by clicking the **Folders** toolbar button or by selecting **View, Explorer Bar, Folders.** (To get rid of the Folders list, repeat the same procedure.)

As you can see in Figure 5.4, the result is that the WebView panel is replaced by a list of folders. When you highlight a folder in this list, the folder's contents appear in the ListView panel on the right. To view subfolders within the Folders list, use the following techniques:

Windows Wisdom

When you combine My Computer with the Folders list, the resulting window is exactly the same as the one you see when you launch another Windows XP program: Windows Explorer. You fire up the latter by selecting **Start, All Programs, Accessories, Windows Explorer.**

◆ **To view subfolders**   Click the **plus sign** (+) beside the folder name. The plus sign changes to a minus sign (–).

◆ **To hide subfolders**   Click the **minus sign** (–) beside the folder name. The minus sign changes to a plus sign (+).

Click a plus sign (+) to open a branch

Figure 5.4

My Computer modified to show the handy Folders list.

Click a minus sign (–) to close a branch

Workaday File and Folder Maintenance

Now that you and My Computer are getting acquainted, it's time to put this digital domestic to good use. Specifically, the next few sections show you how to use My Computer to perform no fewer than six workaday chores for files and folders: creating, copying, moving, renaming, deleting, and compressing.

Creating a New File or Folder

If you want to manufacture a shiny, new file for yourself, the best way to go about it is to run the appropriate application and select that program's **File, New** command. (Note, too, that most programs—including Windows XP's WordPad and Notepad accessories—create a new file for you automatically when you start them.) You then select the **File, Save** command to save the file to your hard disk.

However, it *is* possible to create a new file within My Computer. Here's how:

1. Open the folder in which you want to create the file. If you're not sure which folder to use, open the handy My Documents folder.

2. Select the **File, New** command. This displays another menu with at least the following file flavors (your system may have more):

   ◆ **Folder**   This command creates a new subfolder.

   ◆ **Shortcut**   This command creates a shortcut, which acts as a pointer to a program or document. (I tell you more about shortcuts in Chapter 21.)

   ◆ **Briefcase**   This command creates a Briefcase, which is a special folder you use for transferring files between two computers. (See Chapter 13.)

   ◆ **Bitmap Image**   This command creates an image file of the same type as those you create using Windows XP's Paint program. (See Chapter 7.)

   ◆ **WordPad Document**   This command creates a file of the same type as those you create using the WordPad program in Windows XP. (See Chapter 11.)

   ◆ **Rich Text Document**   This command creates a slightly different type of WordPad file. (Again, head for Chapter 11 to get more info.)

   ◆ **Text Document**   This command creates a plain text file that's the same as what you create using the Notepad program. (See Chapter 11.)

   ◆ **Wave Sound**   This command creates a sound file. (I tell you more about sound files in Chapter 9.)

◆ **Compressed (Zipped) Folder**   This command creates a special folder that compresses multiple files into a smaller package suitable for sending over the Internet. I talk more about this type of file later in this chapter in the section "Creating a Compressed Folder."

3. Select the type of file you want. Windows XP creates the new file and displays a generic (read: boring) name—such as "New Text Document"—in a text box.

4. Edit the name and then press **Enter** or click some of the blank real estate inside the window.

If you misspell the file name or simply change your mind, just hold tight and I'll teach you how to change the file name later in this chapter. If Windows XP complains about a particular character that you try to use, leave it out for now. I'll tell you about the rules for file names a bit later. (In both cases, see the "Renaming a File or Folder" section later in this chapter.)

Selecting Files and Folders

Before getting to the rest of the file-maintenance fun, you need to know how to select the files or folders that you want to horse around with.

Let's begin with the simplest case: selecting a single file or folder. This is a two-step procedure:

1. Open the folder that contains the file or subfolder you want to horse around with.

2. In the ListView panel, click the file's icon.

So far, so good. However, there will be plenty of times when you need to deal with two or more files or folders. For example, you might want to herd several files onto a floppy disk. Rather than doing this one item at a time, you can do the whole thing in one fell swoop by first selecting all the items and then moving (or copying, or whatever) them as a group. Windows XP offers the following methods:

◆ **Selecting consecutive items**   If the files or folders you want to select are listed consecutively, say "Ooh, how convenient!" and then do this: Select the first item, hold down the **Shift** key, select the last item, and then release **Shift.** Windows XP kindly does the dirty work of selecting all the items in between.

◆ **Selecting nonconsecutive items**   If the files or folders you want to select are listed willy-nilly, say "Oy!" and then do this: Select the first item, hold down the **Ctrl** key, select each of the other items, and then release **Ctrl.**

♦ **Selecting all items** If you want to select everything inside a folder, choose the **Edit, Select All** command, or press **Ctrl+A.**

Copying and Moving a File or Folder

A copy of a file or folder is an exact replica of the original that you store on another part of your hard disk or on a removable disk (such as a floppy disk). Copies are useful for making backups or if you want to transport a file or folder to another computer.

Note, too, that the location of the files and folders you create isn't set in stone. If you're not happy with the current location, there's no problem moving a file or folder somewhere else.

Windows XP offers two basic methods for copying and moving files and folders: the **Copy to Folder** and **Move to Folder** commands, and the "drag-and-drop" mouse technique.

To use the **Copy to Folder** or **Move to Folder** command, follow these steps:

1. Select the files or folders you want to transport.

Windows Wisdom

Windows XP has a special Send To menu that contains commonly used destinations, such as your floppy disk or your My Documents folder. To see this menu, either select **File, Send To** or right-click an item and then click **Send To**. Now select the destination you want, and Windows XP copies the selected items lickety-split.

2. Pull down the **Edit** menu and choose one of the following commands:

> **Copy to Folder** This is the command to choose if you're copying files or folders. Alternatively, click **Copy this file** (or **Copy the selected items** if you have multiple files or folders selected) in the WebView panel's File and Folder Tasks section.
>
> **Move to Folder** This is the command to choose if you're moving files or folders. Alternatively, click **Move this file** (or **Move the selected items** if you have multiple files or folders selected) in the WebView panel's File and Folder Tasks section.

3. Either way, you end up with a version of the Browse for Folder dialog box on-screen. Use the folder "tree" to locate and select the destination folder or disk drive.

4. Click **Copy** or **Move** (depending on which **View** menu command you chose).

Mouse fans will enjoy the alternative drag-and-drop method:

1. Display the Folders list, as described earlier.

2. Use the ListView panel to select the files or folders you want to copy or move.

3. Move the mouse pointer over any selected item and hold down the right mouse button (yes, you read that correctly: the *right* mouse button).

4. With the button held down for dear life, move the mouse pointer toward the destination folder in the Folders list (this is the "dragging" part).

5. Position the mouse pointer over the destination folder (wait until you see it highlighted) and then release the mouse button (this is the "dropping" part). Windows XP displays a shortcut menu.

6. Click **Copy Here** or **Move Here,** as appropriate.

To get the most out of this drag-and-drop method, you need to first set up the My Computer window so that your destination folder is visible in the Folders list. If you're in mid-drag and you realize you forgot to do this, here are two tips that can help:

♦ If you need to scroll down the Folders list, drag the mouse and highlight the bottom item in the Folders list; similarly, you can scroll up the list by dragging the mouse so that it highlights the top item in the list.

♦ If the destination is a subfolder in an unopened folder, drag the mouse into the Folders list and place it over the folder. After a few seconds, Windows kindly opens the folder.

Renaming a File or Folder

Windows XP supports file and folder names up to about 255 characters long, so you don't have to settle for boring monikers on the files and folders you create. If you don't like a name, feel free to rename it. Follow these simple steps to rename a file or folder:

1. Select the file or folder you want to rename. (You can work with only one item at a time for this.)

2. Run the **File, Rename** command. (You can also press **F2** or click **Rename this file** in the WebView panel's **File and Folder Tasks** section.) Windows XP creates a text box around the name.

3. Edit the name as you see fit.

4. When you're done, press **Enter.**

Bear in mind that although Windows XP likes long filenames and accepts most keyboard characters (including spaces), there are nine characters that are strictly verboten: *, \ : " < > ? / .

Deleting a File or Folder

Although most of today's hard disks boast a mammoth amount of real estate, you could still run out of room one day if you don't delete the debris that you no longer use. Deleting unwanted files and folders is fairly easy:

1. Select the files or folders you want to blow away.

2. Run the **File, Delete** command. (Alternatively, press **Delete** or click **Delete this file** or **Delete the selected items** in the WebView panel's **File and Folder Tasks** section.) Windows XP asks whether you're sure you want to consign these poor things to the cold, cruel Recycle Bin.

3. Say "But of course, my good fellow!" and click **Yes.**

What happens if you nuke some crucial file or folder that you'd give your right arm to have back? Assuming you need your right arm, Windows XP offers an alternative method to save your bacon: the *Recycle Bin.*

Jargon Jar

The **Recycle Bin** is a special storage area that Windows XP has set aside for deleted files and folders.

You should know, first off, that if the deletion was the last thing you did, you don't have to bother with the Recycle Bin. Just pull down the **Edit** menu and select the **Undo Delete** command (or press **Ctrl+Z**) to salvage the file. Note that it will be placed back in the folder where you originally deleted it, not necessarily in the folder you are currently in.

Windows Wisdom

Another way to delete a file or folder is to drag it from My Computer and drop it on the desktop's Recycle Bin icon.

In fact, Windows XP is only too happy to let you reverse the last *10* actions you performed. Again, you pull down the **Edit** menu and select the **Undo Whatever** command (where *Whatever* is the name of the command, such as **Delete**).

Otherwise, you have to trudge through these steps:

1. Double-click the desktop's **Recycle Bin** icon. The folder that appears contains a list of all the stuff you've expunged recently.

2. Select the files or folders you want to recover.

3. Select the **File, Restore** command (or click **Restore this item** or **Restore the selected items** in the WebView panel). Windows XP marches the items right back to where they came from. Whew!

How the heck can the Recycle Bin restore a deleted file?

Good question. You can get part of the answer by looking at the Recycle Bin icon on your Windows XP desktop. It looks like a garbage can, and that's sort of what the Recycle Bin is. Think about it: If you toss a piece of paper in the garbage, there's nothing to stop you from reaching in and pulling it back out. The Recycle Bin operates the same way: It's really just a special hidden folder (called Recycled) on your hard disk. When you delete a file, Windows XP actually moves the file into the Recycled folder. So restoring a file is a simple matter of "reaching into" the folder and "pulling out" the file. The Recycle Bin handles all this for you (and even returns your file without wrinkles and coffee grounds). However, just like when you hand your trash out to the garbage man, after you empty the Recycle Bin (by right-clicking the desktop's **Recycle Bin** icon and then clicking **Empty Recycle Bin**), there is no retrieving the lost files.

Creating a Compressed Folder

When you download files from the Internet, they often arrive as Zip files. These are compressed archive files that contain one or more files that have been compressed for faster downloading. In Windows XP, a Zip file is called a *compressed folder*. Why a "folder"? Because a Zip file contains one or more files, just like a regular folder. As you'll see, this makes it easy to deal with the files within the Zip, and it enables Windows XP to offer a few useful compression and decompression features.

To create a Zip file, there are two methods you can use:

◆ Select the items you want to store in the Zip file and then run the **File, Send To, Compressed (Zipped) Folder** command. Windows XP creates a Zip file with the same name as the first selected file.

◆ Create a new, empty Zip file by running the **File, New Compressed (Zipped) Folder** command. Windows XP creates a new Zip file with an active text box. Edit the name and press **Enter.** You can then drag the files you want to archive and drop them on the Zip file's icon.

To see what's inside a Zip file, double-click it. Windows XP opens the file as a folder that shows the files within the Zip in the ListView panel. From here, use the following techniques to work with the archived files:

- ◆ To extract some of the files, select them, drag them out of the compressed folder, and then drop them on the destination folder.

- ◆ To extract all of the files, select them and then drag and drop them on the destination. Alternatively, select **File, Extract All** (or click the WebView panel's **Extract all files** icon) to launch the Extraction Wizard. Click **Next** and then click **Browse** to select a destination for the extracted files. Finally, click **Next** to extract the files. In the next wizard dialog box, activate the **Show extracted files** check box to open a window for the destination folder (this is optional), and then click **Finish.**

"Burning" Files to a CD-R or CD-RW Disc

CD-ROM drives are great, but the ROM part stands for "read-only memory," which means that you can't use them to, say, create your own audio CDs or make a backup copy of a CD-ROM. If you're interested in doing these things, then what you need is a CD-R drive. Unlike a CD-ROM, a CD-R disc can accept new data (the "R" stands for "recordable"). Since this process is called *burning* data to the disc, these drives are also called *CD burners.*

The problem with a CD-R disc is that you can only write to it once. So even though the disc is capable of holding about 600MB of data, if you write just 1MB and stop, that's all you'll be able to write to the disc. A better system is the newer CD-RW drive. The "RW" is short for "ReWritable" and it means that you can write to a CD-RW disc, stop, and then come back later and write some more. This makes CD-RW drives great for making backups of your work. Note, however, that most CD-ROM and CD-R drives can't understand CD-RW discs.

The fun news is that Windows XP supports burning files and folders to both CD-R and CD-RW discs right out of the box. If you have a CD burner attached to your computer, Windows XP should recognize it and be ready to burn at will. To try this out, follow these steps:

1. Insert a CD-R or CD-RW disc in your CD burner.

2. In My Computer, highlight the files or folders you want to burn to the disc.

3. Select **File, Send To, CD Drive (D:)** (where D is the drive letter of your CD burner). Windows XP "copies" the file, but nothing is being burned to the disc just yet. Windows XP is just storing the files in a temporary location.

4. Repeat steps 3 and 4 until you've finished copying the files and folders you want to burn. (Remember: You only get one chance to burn data to a CD-R disc.)

5. Use My Computer to open the CD burner drive. You'll see a section titled **Files Ready to Be Written to the CD.** Feel free to delete or rename these files.

6. In the **CD Writing Tasks** section, click **Write these files to CD.** Windows XP asks the CD Writing Wizard to take over from here.

7. The first thing the wizard does is ask you to name the CD and it suggests today's date. If you can think of something more useful (there's a no-brainer), enter it in the box and click **Next.** The wizard then busies itself writing the data to the disc.

8. When the wizard's work is done, it spits out the disc and asks if you want to copy the selected files to another disc. If you do, activate the **Yes, write these files to another CD** check box and click **Next.** Otherwise, click **Finish.**

Finding a File in That Mess You Call a Hard Disk

Bill Gates, Microsoft's Big Cheese, used to summarize his company's mission of easy access to data as "information at your fingertips." We're still a long way off from that laudable goal, but there are a few things you can do to ensure that the info you need is never far away:

◆ **Use the My Documents folder**   The most inefficient way to store your documents is to scatter them hither and yon around your hard disk. A much better approach is to plop everything in a single place so that you always know where to look for things. The perfect place for this is the My Documents folder that Windows XP provides for you.

◆ **Use subfolders to organize your documents**   Using My Documents is a good idea (if I do say so myself), but you shouldn't just cram all your stuff into that one folder. Instead, create subfolders to hold related items. Windows XP starts you off with subfolders named My Pictures and My Music, which are the ideal places for your graphics and music files. Feel free to add other subfolders for things such as letters, memos, projects, presentations, spreadsheets, and whatever other categories you can think of.

◆ **Give your files meaningful names**   Take advantage of Windows XP's long file names to give your documents useful names that tell you exactly what's inside each file. A document named "Letter" doesn't tell you much, but "Letter to A. Gore Re: Inventing the Internet" surely does.

◆ **Dejunk your folders**   Keep your folders clean by deleting any junk files that you'll never use again.

If you're like most people, then you'll probably end up with hundreds of documents, but if you follow these suggestions, finding the one you need shouldn't be a problem. Even so, there will be times when you don't remember exactly which document you need, or you might want to find all those documents that contain a particular word or phrase. For these situations, Windows XP offers a Search feature that can help you track down what you need.

To get started, you have two choices:

◆ To search within the current folder in My Computer, either select the **View, Explorer Bar, Search** command, or click the **Search** toolbar button. (Pressing **Ctrl+E** also works.)

◆ To search all of My Computer (that is, all your hard disk drives), select **Start, Search.**

Figure 5.5 shows the window that appears if you use the former technique.

Figure 5.5

Windows XP's Search Companion helps you find AWOL files.

What happens from here depends on which link you click in the WebView panel.

If you want to search for multimedia files, click the **Pictures, music, or video** link and then follow these steps:

1. The WebView panel now displays three check boxes: **Pictures and Photos, Music,** and **Video.** Activate the check boxes that correspond to the type of file (or files) you want to find.

2. Use the **Find files named** text box to type in the name of the file you want. Note that you don't have to enter the entire name of the file; just a word or even a few letters will do.

3. If you want to use some fancier search options (explained a bit later), click the **Use advanced search options** link.

4. Click **Search.**

If you want to search through all the documents you've created, click the **Documents (word processing, spreadsheet, etc.)** link and then follow these steps:

1. The WebView panel now displays four **Last time it was modified** option buttons. Select the option that best represents the last time you made changes to the file (or select **Don't remember** if you have no idea).

2. Use the **All or part of the document name** text box to type in the name of the file you want. (Again, you can enter just a word or even a few letters from the name.)

3. If you want to use some fancier search options (explained a bit later), click the **Use advanced search options** link.

4. Click **Search.**

If you want to search through all the files on your system, click the **All Files and Folders** link and then follow these steps:

1. Use the **All or part of the file name** text box to enter some or all of the file name.

2. Use the **A word or phrase in the file** text box to search for a file by content. Enter a word or part of a word that the desired file contains.

3. Use the **Look in** list to select the folder or disk drive in which you want to search (if the displayed folder isn't the one you want).

4. Use the **When was it modified?** options to refine the search according to the date the file was last edited.

5. If you click **What size is it?** the Search Companion provides a few controls that enable you to locate a file according to its size.

6. If you want to use the advanced search features, click the **More advanced options** link.

7. Click **Search.**

You can refine each of these search techniques even further by using the following advanced options:

- **Search system folders**   Activating this check box extends the search to include the Windows XP folders. You probably won't ever need to include these sub-folders in your search.

- **Search hidden files and folders**   Activating this check box extends the search to include those files and folders that have been hidden by Windows XP. Again, you shouldn't ever need to search these files.

- **Search subfolders**   Activating this check box tells the Search Companion to examine not only the current folder, but also all of its subfolders.

- **Case sensitive**   Activating this check box tells the Search Companion to match the exact uppercase and lowercase letters you entered for the file name.

- **Search tape backup**   Activating this check box forces the Search Companion to extend its search to a tape drive on your system. If you have a tape drive, activating this feature can seriously slow down your searches.

Launching a Program with the Run Command

In rare cases, the program you want to run might not appear on any of the Start menus. This is particularly true of older DOS programs that don't do Windows. For the time being, you can use the Run command to get these old geezer programs under way.

This isn't for the faint of heart, however, because it requires a bit more work, as the following steps show:

1. Select **Start, Run.** Windows XP displays the Run dialog box.

2. In the **Open** text box, type the name of the disk drive where the program resides (for example, **d:**), its folder (such as **\install**), and then the name of the file that starts the program (for example, **setup.exe**). With these examples used, you'd enter **d:\install\setup.exe.**

3. Click **OK** to run the program.

Whew! Compared to the Start menu, that's true, calluses-on-the-fingertips manual labor. Bear these points in mind when you're working with the Run dialog box:

- Instead of typing the command, you can click the **Browse** button and choose the program from the Browse dialog box that appears.

- If any part of the file name or folder name contains spaces or is longer than eight characters, you have to surround the whole thing with quotation marks. If you're not sure about this, go ahead and add the quotation marks anyway.

- Although you normally use Run to enter program files, you can also use Run to enter the name and location of documents, folders, and even World Wide Web addresses. In each case, Windows XP launches the appropriate program and loads the item you specified.

- Windows XP "remembers" the last few commands you entered in the Run dialog box. If you need to repeat a recent command, drop down the **Open** list and select the command.

- If you have a keyboard with the Windows logo key on it, press that **+R** to display the Run dialog box.

Points of View: Changing the My Computer View

In the standard My Computer view, each file and folder is displayed using a big, fat icon. However, there are also several other views you can try on for size. You access these views either by pulling down the **View** menu or by clicking the **Views** button in the toolbar (see Figure 5.6). There are five possibilities:

- **Thumbnails** This view displays previews—called *thumbnails*—of all the image files in the current folder. If you have any HTML files in the folder (these are files that contain web page data), a thumbnail of the web page is shown. I tell you more about this view in Chapter 7. For an example, see Figure 7.1.

- **Tiles** This is the default icon view that displays the files in columns.

- **Icons** This view displays files and folders using smaller, cuter versions of the icons arranged in rows (see Figure 5.6).

- **List** This view also displays the files and folders using even smaller icons, and everything is arrayed in multiple columns (see Figure 5.6).

- **Details** This view displays the files and folders using a four-column list (see Figure 5.6). For each file and folder, you see its Name, its Size, its Type (such as WordPad Document), and Date Modified (the date and time it was last changed). However, these aren't the only columns available. There's actually a truckload of them, and you can see the complete list by selecting **View, Choose Details**. (This command is around only when you're in Details view.) In the Column Details dialog box, use the check boxes to toggle columns on and off.

Figure 5.6

Three separate My Computer windows demonstrating the Icons, List, and Details views.

Ordering My Computer Around: Sorting Files

To complete your reading of My Computer's views news, let's see how you sort the files and subfolders in the current folder. By default, file and subfolders are sorted alphabetically by name, with the subfolders displayed first, and then the files. You can change this by selecting the **View, Arrange Icons by** command, which reveals a submenu with seven choices:

Windows Wisdom

Some of the special folders in Windows XP have their own sorting options. For example, in the My Music folder you can sort music files by Artist and Album Title. Similarly, in the My Pictures folder you can sort by the Picture Taken On date and by the Dimensions of the image.

◆ **Name**　This is the default sort order.

◆ **Size**　This command sorts the folders numerically by the size of each file.

◆ **Type**　This command sorts the folders alphabetically by the type of document.

◆ **Modified**　This command sorts the folders according to the date and time when each item was last modified.

◆ **Show in Groups**   When this command is activated (it's not available in the List view), Windows XP arranges the folder contents into categories. The actual categories you see depend on which of these four sort commands is active:

Name   The contents are grouped by the letters of the alphabet (items with names that begin with "A" are in the **A** group, those that begin with "B" are in the **B** group, and so on).

Size   The contents are grouped into general size categories: **Tiny, Small, Medium, Large, Gigantic,** and so on.

Type   The contents are grouped into file type categories (for example, WordPad Document and Wave Sound).

Modified   The contents are grouped into general date categories: **Today, Last Week, Last Month, Last Year, A long time ago,** and so on.

> **Windows Wisdom**
>
> If you're in Details view, you can sort a folder by clicking the column headers (**Name, Size,** and so on). For example, clicking the **Size** column header sorts the folder by size. Clicking the header again switches the sort between ascending and descending.

◆ **Auto Arrange**   Activating this command (it's not available in the List and Details views) toggles the Auto Arrange feature on and off. When it's on, My Computer automatically resorts the folders (using the current sort choice) whenever you add, rename, or delete a file or folder.

◆ **Align to Grid**   Activating this command (it's not available in the List and Details views) tells My Computer to herd the files that you move into their proper rows or columns.

Start Spreading the Views: Applying a View to All Folders

The view options—specifically, the icon view (Tiles, Icons, and so on) and the sort order—you set for one folder are immediately jettisoned when you leap to another folder. If you'd like to use one set of options for *all* your folders, you can tell Windows XP to make it so. Here are the steps to follow:

1. Set up a folder just the way you like it.

2. Select **Tools, Folder Options.** The Folder Options dialog box skids onto the screen.

3. Display the **View** tab.

4. Click **Apply to All Folders.** Windows XP asks you to confirm.

5. Click **Yes** to get back to the Folder Options dialog box.

6. Click **OK.**

If you grow tired of these view options and you want to go back to the original look and feel, display the **View** tab once again and click **Reset All Folders.**

A Few More Folder Options

The Folder Options dialog box you visited briefly in the previous section is loaded with settings that change the way My Computer displays folders. Most of the settings in the **View** tab and all the settings in **File Types** tab are obscure and can be safely ignored by normal people. However, the options in the **General** tab are relatively useful.

Let's start with the **Tasks** group. Earlier in this chapter, I told you about Windows XP's WebView panel that offers links to common tasks related to whatever type of folder or file you're working with. The **Tasks** group controls the display of this panel:

 ◆ **Show common tasks in folders**   Activate this option to display the WebView panel.

 ◆ **Use Windows classic folders**   Activate this option to do away with the WebView panel.

The **Browse folders** groups also gives you two options:

 ◆ **Open each folder in the same window**   When this option is activated and you double-click a folder icon to open it, My Computer displays that folder in the same window.

 ◆ **Open each folder in its own window**   When this option is activated and you double-click a folder icon to open it, My Computer displays that folder in a separate window. This option can lead to some serious desktop overcrowding as the folder windows multiply, so I don't recommend using it.

The options in the **Click items as follows** group determine how you launch and select icons:

 ◆ **Single-click to open an item (point to select)**   To activate this option means that you can launch an icon by single-clicking it instead double-clicking it. It also means that you can select a file just by pointing your mouse at it. Note, too, that the following two option buttons also arise from their slumbers:

> **Underline icon titles consistent with my browser**   Activate this option to tell Windows XP to underline all the file names and icon titles using the same style as defined within Internet Explorer. This usually means that file and folder names and icon titles appear in a blue, underlined test. This is a good idea because it gives you a visual reminder that this single-click feature is turned on.

> **Underline icon titles only when I point at them**   Activate this option to have Windows XP underline file names and icon titles only when you point at them. This is a bit tidier-looking than having everything underlined.

◆ **Double-click to open an item (single-click to select)**   Activate this option to use the old-fashioned mouse techniques for launching and selecting stuff.

The Least You Need to Know

◆ You select a file or folder by clicking it. To select multiple files or folders, hold down **Ctrl** and click each one.

◆ To drag and drop a file or folder, move the mouse pointer over the item, hold down the right mouse button, move the mouse pointer over the destination, and then release the button. In the shortcut menu that pops up, click either **Copy Here** or **Move Here.**

◆ To burn data to a CD, select the files and folders and then select **File, Send To, CD Drive (D:)** (where D is the drive letter of your CD burner). Then open the CD drive and click **Write these files to CD.**

◆ To search for a file in My Computer's current folder, either select the **View, Explorer Bar, Search** command, or click the **Search** toolbar button. To search all of My Computer (that is, all your disk drives), select **Start, Search.**

◆ To display the Folders bar, activate the **View, Explorer Bar, Folders** command, or activate the **Folders** button in the toolbar.

◆ To change the icon view, choose one of the following commands on the **View** menu (or the toolbar's **Views** button): **Thumbnails, Tiles, Icons, List,** or **Details.**

Chapter 6

Installing and Uninstalling Programs and Devices

In This Chapter

◆ Installing and uninstalling chunks of Windows XP

◆ Installing and uninstalling software programs

◆ Step-by-step procedures for installing all kinds of devices

◆ Installing specific devices such as printers, modems, joysticks, and scanners

◆ Saying *adios* to devices you no longer need

It's one thing to understand that the PC is a versatile beast that can handle all kinds of different programs and devices, but it's quite another to actually install the stuff. This chapter will help by showing you exactly how to install Windows XP components, software programs, and devices on your machine. For good measure, you also learn how to uninstall all those things, just in case they don't get along with your computer.

The Welcome Wagon: Installing a Program

As you work through this book, you'll see that Windows XP comes stocked with a decent collection of programs, some of which are first-rate (such as Internet Explorer and Outlook Express) and some of which are merely okay (such as Paint and WordPad). Also, most PC manufacturers are kind enough to stock their machines with a few extra programs.

However, it's a rare computer owner who's satisfied with just these freebies (or even wants them in the first place). Most of us want something better, faster, cooler. If you decide to take the plunge on a new program, this section shows you how to install it in Windows XP. To get you started, the next section shows you how to install new Windows XP components.

Installing a Windows XP Component

Like a hostess who refuses to put out the good china for just anybody, Windows XP may not have installed all of its components automatically. Don't feel insulted; Windows is just trying to go easy on your hard disk. The problem, you see, is that some of the components that come with Windows XP are software behemoths that will happily usurp acres of your precious hard disk land. In a rare act of digital politeness, Windows bypasses these programs (as well as a few other nonessential tidbits) during a typical installation. If you want any of these knickknacks on your system, you have to tell Windows XP to install them for you.

The good news is that Windows XP comes with a handy Windows Components Wizard that enables you to add any of those missing pieces to your system without having to trudge through the entire Windows installation routine. Here are the steps to follow:

1. Select **Start, Control Panel** to rustle up the Control Panel window.

2. Click the **Add or Remove Programs** icon. Windows XP tosses the Add or Remove Programs window onto your screen.

3. Click the **Add/Remove Windows Components** link to launch the Windows Components Wizard shown in Figure 6.1. (Note that Windows XP takes inventory of the currently installed components, so the wizard takes a few seconds to appear.)

Figure 6.1

The Windows Components Wizard helps you add the bits and pieces that come with Windows XP.

4. The **Components** box lists the various chunks of Windows XP that are already installed as well as those you can add.

   Here's a translation of what the various check box states mean in the Components list: **Unchecked** means the component is not installed. If the component comes in several pieces, none of those pieces is installed. **Checked with a gray background** means the component is partially installed. That is, the component has multiple chunks, but only some of those chunks reside on your system. **Checked with a white background** means the component is installed. If the component comes in several pieces, all of those pieces are installed.

   You have two ways to proceed:

   ◆ To add an entire component, activate its check box.

   ◆ To add only part of a component (assuming that it has multiple parts), click the component name to highlight it and then click **Details.** In the new dialog box that appears, activate the check boxes for the subcomponents you want to install, and click **OK.**

5. Click **Next.** The wizard takes a few moments to gather its thoughts before moving on to the next step.

6. It's likely that the wizard will prompt you to insert your Windows XP CD-ROM. If so, insert the CD-ROM, wait about five seconds, and then click **OK.** The wizard installs the necessary files on your computer.

7. Click **Finish.** The wizard drops you off back at the Add or Remove Programs window.

8. Click **Close.**

9. Depending on the components you add, Windows XP might ask you to restart your computer. If it does, remove the Windows XP CD and then click **Yes** to let Windows XP handle this for you. When the restart is complete, the new components are ready to roll.

Bringing a New Program into Your Computer Home

The built-in Windows XP programs do the job as long as your needs aren't too lofty. However, what if your needs *are* lofty, or if you're looking to fill in a software niche that Windows XP doesn't cover (such as a spreadsheet program, a database, or an action game)? In that case, you need to go outside the Windows box and purchase the appropriate program.

After you have the program, your next chore is to install it. This means you run a "setup" routine that makes the program ready for use on your computer. Most setup procedures perform the following tasks:

◆ Create a new folder for the program.

◆ Copy any files that the program needs to run to the new folder and to other strategic folders on your hard disk.

◆ Adjust Windows XP as needed to ensure that the program runs properly.

Windows Wisdom _____

I recommend that you accept the default values offered by the install program (unless you *really* know what you're doing). In particular, if the program gives you a choice of a "typical" or a "custom" installation, go the "typical" route to save yourself time and hassle. You can always go back and install additional components for the specific program later. (See "Changing a Program's Installed Components," later in this chapter.)

Jargon Jar _____

AutoRun is a feature that automatically launches a program's setup routine (or, later, the program itself) after you insert its CD-ROM or DVD-ROM disc.

How you launch this setup routine depends on how the program is distributed:

◆ **If the program is on a CD** In this case, you might not have to do much of anything. Most computer CDs support a feature called *AutoRun*. This means when you insert the disc into your CD-ROM (or DVD-ROM) drive for the first time, the setup routine gets launched automatically.

◆ **If you downloaded the program from the Internet**   In this case, you end up with the downloaded file on your hard disk. Be sure this file resides in an otherwise-empty folder and then double-click the file. This either launches the setup routine or it "extracts" a bunch of files into the folder. If the latter happens, look for an application file named **Setup** (or, more rarely, **Install**), and then double-click that file.

For all other cases—a CD-based program that doesn't start automatically or a program distributed on floppy disks—your best bet is to get Windows XP to launch the setup routine for you. Here's how:

1. Select **Start, Control Panel** to fire up the Control Panel window.

2. Click the **Add or Remove Programs** icon to get to the Add or Remove Programs window.

3. Click the **Add New Programs** link.

4. Click the **CD or Floppy** button. The dialog box that appears asks you to insert the first installation disk or the program's CD-ROM.

5. Insert the CD (or DVD) disc or the floppy disk that came with the program. (Some older programs ship with multiple floppy disks. In this case, look for the disk labeled "Disk 1" or "Setup.")

6. Click **Next.** Windows XP checks your floppy drive and CD (or DVD) drives, searching desperately for any installation program it can find:

   ◆ If the wizard locates a likely candidate, it displays it in the **Open** text box, as you can see in Figure 6.2.

Figure 6.2

Windows XP can hunt down your software's installation program automatically.

◆ If it doesn't find an installation program, the wizard asks you to enter the appropriate command in the **Open** text box. If you know where the installation program is located, type the drive, folder, and file name (for example, e:\install\setup). You can also click **Browse** to use a dialog box to pick out the program.

7. Click **Finish.** Windows XP launches the installation program.

From here, follow the instructions and prompts that the setup routine sends your way. (This procedure varies from program to program.)

Hacking Windows

Sometimes installing a program can wreak havoc on your system. The quickest way to recover from a bad installation is to restore your system to the way it was before you ran the setup program. The only way to do that is to set a *restore point* just before you run the setup program. A restore point is a kind of digital snapshot of your computer's current configuration. If things go awry, you can tell Windows XP to consult that snapshot and revert the system to what it was before the rogue program did its damage. To learn how to set and use restore points, see Chapter 23.

Changing a Program's Installed Components

When you install most programs, the setup software puts the entire program onto your computer. However, some larger programs (such as Microsoft Office) will only install some of their components. If you find you're missing something when working with the program, follow these steps to install the component you need:

1. Select **Start, Control Panel, Add or Remove Programs** to display the Add or Remove Programs window.

2. You should be in the **Change or Remove Programs** section. If not, click **Change or Remove Programs.**

3. In the **Currently Installed Programs** list, click the item for the program you want to work with.

4. Click the **Change** button (it might be called **Change/Remove,** instead).

5. What happens from here depends on the program. For example, you may be asked to insert the program's CD. Eventually, you should see an option that says something like **Add or Remove Features.** Make sure you select that option, which means you'll eventually see a list of features that you can add to the program. Look for the feature you want and select it.

That last step is detail-challenged, I know, but every program has its own way of doing things, so you'll just have to see what the program throws your way.

The Bum's Rush: Uninstalling a Program

Most programs seem like good ideas at the time you install them. Unless you're an outright pessimist, you probably figured that a program you installed was going to help you work harder, be more efficient, or have more fun. Sadly, many programs don't live up to expectations. The good news is that you don't have to put up with a loser program after you realize it's not up to snuff. You can *uninstall* it (completely remove a program from your computer) so that it doesn't clutter up your Start menu, desktop, hard disk, or any other location where it might have inserted itself.

Uninstalling a Windows XP Component

You've seen how the Windows Component Wizard makes it easy to bring Windows XP components in from the cold of the CD-ROM to the warmth of your hard drive. What happens, however, if you grow tired of a particular component's company? For example, the artistically challenged might want to get rid of that Paint program they never use.

Happily, showing these and other Windows XP components to the door is even easier than installing them. And as an added bonus, lopping off some of Windows' limbs serves to free up hard disk space, giving you more room for *really* important games—uh, I mean, applications. As you might expect, removing Windows XP components is the opposite of adding them:

1. Select **Start, Control Panel, Add or Remove Programs.**

2. Click the **Add/Remove Windows Components** link to once again meet up with the Windows Components Wizard.

3. Deactivate the check boxes for the components you want to blow away. For multiprogram components, click **Details** to see the individual programs, deactivate the check boxes for those you want to nuke, and then click **OK** to return the Windows Setup tab.

4. Click **Next.** Windows XP removes the components you specified without further delay.

5. Click **Finish.**

6. Depending on the components you removed, Windows XP may ask to restart your computer. If so, click **Yes** to make it happen.

Giving a Program the Heave-Ho

If you have a Windows application that has worn out its welcome, this section shows you a couple of methods for uninstalling the darn thing so that it's out of your life forever. The good news is that Windows XP has a feature that enables you to vaporize any application with a simple click of the mouse. The bad news is that this feature is only available for some programs.

To check whether it's available for your program, follow these steps:

1. Display the Control Panel by selecting **Start, Control Panel** and then click the **Add or Remove Programs** icon.

2. Make sure that the **Change or Remove Programs** link is active.

3. As shown in Figure 6.3, the **Currently installed programs** list shows the programs that have been installed on your computer and that Windows XP knows how to remove automatically. If the program you want to blow to kingdom come is on this list, highlight it and then click its **Change/Remove** button. (Note that some programs have separate Change and Remove buttons. In this case, you need to click the **Remove** button.)

Figure 6.3

The Change or Remove Programs link maintains a list of programs that you can annihilate automatically.

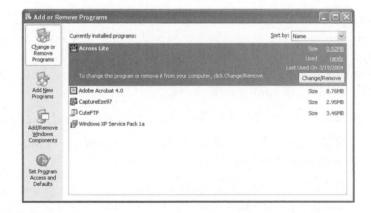

4. What happens next depends on the program. You may see a dialog box asking you to confirm the uninstall, or you may be asked whether you want to run an "Automatic" or "Custom" uninstall. For the latter, be sure to select the **Automatic** option. Whatever happens, follow the instructions on the screen until you return to the Add or Remove Programs window.

5. Click **Close** to wrap things up.

Didn't see the program in the **Currently installed programs** list? All is not lost because there's still one more place to check: the program's home base on the Start menu. Select **Start, All Programs** and then open the program's menu (if it has one). Look for a command that includes the word "Uninstall" (or, less likely, "Remove"). If you see one, great—click it to launch the uninstall procedure.

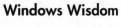 **Windows Wisdom**

Don't be surprised if the uninstall routine doesn't wipe out absolutely everything for a program. If you created any documents, customized the program, or moved its Start menu items to a new location, the uninstall program leaves behind a few scraps.

For those applications that can't be uninstalled automatically, you need to roll up your sleeves and do the whole thing by hand. Here's what to do:

1. Use My Computer to display the program's folder. (Hint: Most programs store their files in a subfolder of the **Program Files** folder on drive C.)

2. Check to see whether the folder contains any data files you want to preserve. If you spent any time at all creating documents (or whatever) in the application, it's a wise precaution to save them for posterity. For one thing, you might want to use them in another application; for another, you might change your mind six months from now and decide to reinstall the application. If you want to save your data, highlight the files and then *move* (not copy) them to another folder (that you can use for storage), or to a floppy disk.

3. With that out of the way, go ahead and delete the application's folder.

4. Erase any traces of the program from your Start menu.

5. If the program added any shortcuts to the desktop, delete them, too.

6. To be safe, exit and then restart Windows XP.

Cross-Reference

Not sure how to delete a folder? Head for Chapter 5, and see the "Deleting a File or Folder" section. To learn how to delete items from the Start menu, go to Chapter 21.

Device Advice I: Installing Hardware

Software installation is usually a painless operation that often requires just a few mouse clicks on your part. Hardware, however, is another story altogether. Not only must you attach the device to your machine (which might even require that you remove the cover to get inside the computer), but you also have to hope that the new device doesn't conflict with an existing one.

The latter is less of a problem thanks to the support Windows XP has for something called Plug and Play. This enables Windows XP to immediately recognize a new device and to configure that device automatically. It's a kind of hardware nirvana that makes it easy for the average bear to upgrade the physical side of their computers. To make it work, however, you need two things:

♦ **Devices that support Plug and Play** Most new hardware doodads are Plug and Play-friendly. However, to be safe, check the box to be sure it says "Plug and Play" before buying anything. Note that the newfangled USB (Universal Serial Bus) devices support Plug and Play. However, your computer needs to have one or more USB ports to use them.

♦ **Devices that are compatible with Windows XP** Windows XP, finicky beast that it is, won't work with just any old device. Again, before buying a device, check the box to see whether it says anything about being compatible with Windows XP. (Devices that are compatible with Windows 98, Me, or 2000 ought to work fine, as well.)

Understanding Hardware Types

Although thousands of devices are available, and dozens of device categories, I like to organize devices according to how you attach them to the computer. From this point of view, there are four types to worry about:

♦ **External plug-in devices** These are devices that use some kind of cable to plug into a *port* in the back of the PC. These devices include keyboards, mice, joysticks, modems, printers, speakers, and monitors. These kinds of devices are easy to install if you remember one thing: The computer's ports each have a unique shape, and the cable's plug has a shape that matches one of those ports. So, there's usually only one possible place into which any cable can plug. The exception to this is if the back of the computer has two ports with identical configurations. That just means your machine offers two of the same port type, so you can plug your device into either one.

> **Jargon Jar**
>
> A **port** is a computer receptacle into which you plug in the cable for a device.

♦ **PC Card (PCMCIA) devices** These types of devices are the easiest to install because they simply slip into any one of the computer's PC card slots (or *sockets*, as they're called). Note, however, that these slots are almost always found only on notebook computers.

◆ **Internal disk drives** These are the toughest devices to install not only because you have to get inside your computer, but also because there are many steps involved. Your best bet here is to take the machine to a computer service center or cajole a nearby computer geek into doing the job for you.

◆ **Internal circuit boards** These are cards that plug into slots inside your computer. There are circuit boards for all kinds of things, including sound cards, graphics cards, network cards, and video decoder cards (which usually come with DVD-ROM drives nowadays). Again, you should get someone who knows what he or she is doing to install these kinds of devices for you.

Running the Add Hardware Wizard

Your device and your computer are now shacked up, but they're not married yet. To get a full relationship going, Windows XP has to install a tiny bit of software called a *device driver.* This miniprogram has the code that operates (drives) the device, so it acts as a kind of middleman between the device and Windows XP.

In the best of all possible worlds, after you've attached the device (and, if necessary, restarted your computer), Windows XP recognizes the new limb and displays the New Hardware Found dialog box. (This is my favorite dialog box because it means I have little if any work to do from here. An under-your-breath "Yes!" is the appropriate reaction to seeing this dialog box.) Windows XP then proceeds to install the device driver and any other software required to make the device go. This is automatic, for the most part, but you may occasionally be asked a few simple questions to complete the setup. In particular, you might see the Found New Hardware Wizard, which leads you through the installation of a device driver. (The process is similar to upgrading a driver.)

If, for some reason, Windows XP doesn't automatically recognize your new device, all is not lost. That's because Windows XP comes with a hardware helper called the Add New Hardware Wizard, which scours every nook and cranny of your system to look for new stuff. Here's how it works:

1. Select **Start, Control Panel** to crack open the Control Panel window.

2. Click **Printers and Other Hardware,** and then click the **Add Hardware** link in the WebView panel's **See Also** section. The Add Hardware Wizard wipes the grease from its hands and comes out to meet you.

3. The initial dialog box just tells you some things you already know, so click **Next.** The wizard then checks for new Plug and Play devices that you've connected recently but that haven't been installed. If it finds any, you'll see the Found New Hardware message and the wizard will install the necessary device driver. In this case, skip to step 8.

4. If the wizard didn't find any new Plug and Play devices, it asks if the hardware is connected. Make sure the **Yes, I have already connected the hardware** option is activated and then click **Next.**

5. Now the wizard displays the **Installed hardware** list with all of your computer's devices. Click **Add a new hardware device** at the bottom of the list and then click **Next.**

6. The next wizard dialog box asks whether you want Windows to detect your new hardware automatically. This is the best way to go; make sure to activate the **Search for and install the hardware automatically (Recommended)** option, and then click **Next.** (I tell you a bit later how to specify hardware yourself.)

7. If the Add New Hardware Wizard doesn't find any new hardware, it tells you so. If that happens, click **Cancel,** shut down your computer (make sure that you use the **Start, Turn Off Computer** or **Start, Shut Down** command), check to see whether you attached the new device correctly, and then try again. If it's still a no-go, try installing the hardware by using the instructions given later in this section.

8. More likely, however, the wizard will tell you that it's finished detecting and is ready to install the support files for the device. It will then display a list of the installed devices. Click **Finish.**

If the wizard failed in its quest to find your device, you can stick Windows XP's nose in it, so to speak, by specifying exactly which device you added. To get started, you have two choices:

♦ If you're starting the Add Hardware Wizard from scratch, follow the preceding steps 1 through 4.

♦ If you're still in the wizard at the dialog box that tells you Windows didn't find any new devices, click **Back.**

You now follow these steps:

1. Activate the **Install the hardware that I manually select from a list (Advanced)** option, and click **Next.**

2. The wizard displays a whack of device categories in the **Common hardware types** list. Highlight the category that applies to your device. If you don't see the appropriate category, click **Show All Devices.** When you're ready to proceed, click **Next.**

3. The wizard takes a few seconds to gather its thoughts, and then it displays a list of device manufacturers and devices. For example, Figure 6.4 shows the dialog box that appears for the Imaging devices category. You have two ways to proceed from here:

Figure 6.4

Use this dialog box to pick out the device manufacturer and model.

◆ Highlight the device maker in the **Manufacturer** list, then highlight the name of your device in the **Model** list.

◆ If your device is nowhere to be found, it's likely that you received a disk inside the device package. Insert the disk and then click **Have Disk.** In the Install from Disk dialog box, enter the location of the disk (type the drive letter followed by a colon [:] and a backward slash [\], such as **A:**) and click **OK.** (If Windows XP complains about not being able to find anything on the disk, click **Browse** and look for a subfolder on the disk, usually with some form of "Windows" label.) You'll eventually see a list of models that can be installed. Highlight your model.

◆ If you don't have a disk from the manufacturer, you can still download the specific device driver for your hardware from the manufacturer's website. (See Chapter 25 for more on this.) Once you've done that, you'd then click **Have Disk** and enter the location of the downloaded device driver file.

4. Click **Next.** The wizard tells you that it will now install the drivers for the device.

5. Click **Next.** The wizard, true to its word, installs the device drivers. Note that you might need to insert your Windows XP CD at this point.

6. When all is said and done, click **Finish** to close the wizard. If Windows XP asks if you want to restart your computer, click **Yes.**

Installing Specific Devices

Just to keep everyone thoroughly confused (which a cynic might describe as Windows' *real* job), Windows XP offers different installation routes for certain types of devices. These include perennially popular items such as printers, modems, joysticks, scanners, and digital cameras. Here's a quick look at what you have to do to install these types of devices:

♦ **Installing a printer**   Select **Start, Control Panel,** click **Printers and Other Hardware** and then click the **Add a printer** icon. This conjures up the Add Printer Wizard to take you through the process. Along the way, you get asked how your printer is attached (choose **Local printer,** the manufacturer and model, and the printer port (this is almost always **LPT1**).

♦ **Installing a modem**   Select **Start, Control Panel,** click **Printers and Other Hardware,** and then click **Phone and Modem Options.** This unleashes the Install New Modem Wizard. (If, instead, you see the Phone and Modem Option dialog box, it means your modem is already installed and should be shown in the Modems tab. If it's not, or if you want to install a different modem, click **Add.**) This wizard scours your computer's ports to see if a modem is attached to one of them.

♦ **Installing a game controller**   To Windows XP, a joystick or other device you use for gaming is called a *game controller.* To install one, Select **Start, Control Panel,** click **Printers and Other Hardware,** and then click the **Game Controllers** icon. In the Game Controllers dialog box, click **Add.**

♦ **Installing a scanner or digital camera**   Select **Start, Control Panel,** click **Printers and Other Hardware,** and then click the **Scanners and Cameras** icon. In the Scanners and Cameras window, click the **Add an imaging device** link to send in the Scanner and Camera Installation Wizard.

Device Advice II: Removing Hardware

If a device suddenly becomes tiresome and boring, or if you get a better device for your birthday, you need to remove the old device from your computer and then let Windows XP know that it's gone. The exception to this is if the device supports Plug and Play. If it does, then Windows XP recognizes that the device is gone and it adjusts itself accordingly. Otherwise, you need to do it by hand:

1. Select **Start, Control Panel,** click **Printers and Other Hardware,** and then click the **System** link. Windows XP arranges a meeting with the System Properties dialog box.

2. Display the **Hardware** tab and then click **Device Manager.**

3. Click the plus sign (+) beside the hardware category you want to work with. For example, if the soon-to-be-toast device is a network adapter, open the **Network adapters** branch.

4. Click the device and then select the **Action, Uninstall** command. Windows XP states the obvious and tells you that you're about to remove the device.

Windows Wisdom

An easier way to get to the System Properties dialog box is to click **Start,** right-click the **My Computer** icon, and then click **Properties** in the shortcut menu.

5. Say "Duh!" and click **OK.** Windows XP wastes no more of your time and removes the device from the list.

6. Click **Close.**

7. If the device is an internal component, shut down your computer (use **Start, Turn Off Computer** or **Start, Shut Down**) and then remove the device. Otherwise, just unplug the device.

The Least You Need to Know

- Most computer CD-ROM (and DVD-ROM) discs support AutoRun, so the installation program runs automatically after you insert the disc.

- Use Control Panel's **Add or Remove Programs** icon to help you install and uninstall Windows XP components and third-party programs.

- To ensure the easiest hardware configuration, buy only devices that are both Plug and Play–compatible and Windows XP–compatible.

- When installing an external device, remember that its cable can plug into only a single, complementary port on the back of the computer.

- If Plug and Play doesn't work, launch Control Panel, click **Printers and Other Hardware,** and then click the **Add Hardware** link to help you install and uninstall devices.

Part 2

Windows XP at Home

It wasn't all that long ago when computers were viewed as "business only" beasts, and only the most geeklike among us actually had a PC at home. Now, this being the twenty-first century and all, the digital domicile is a reality and computers in the home are as common as the weeds in your neighbor's yard. Just think: All that cursing and fuming you direct toward your work computer can now be continued in the privacy of your own home. But that's not the only advantage to having a home machine. Now you can perform many personal tasks that aren't appropriate at the office: making drawings, manipulating photos, playing and copying music, and making digital movies. And the best news is that Windows XP is set up to handle all of those leisure-time activities right out of the box. The chapters in Part 2 show you how to perform these and other home-sweet-home tasks.

Chapter 7

Playing with Pictures

In This Chapter

♦ GIF, JPEG, and other image format acronyms

♦ Working with image thumbnails, filmstrips, and slide shows

♦ Converting an image from one format to another

♦ Ordering prints online

♦ Printing images

♦ Creating images with the Paint program

Windows has enabled us to go beyond the workaday world of letters and memos to documents that positively cry out for image enhancement: business presentations, flyers, newsletters, and web pages, to name only a few. Again, Windows has various tools that let you create images from scratch, mess around with existing images, and capture digital images from an outside source (such as a scanner). None of these tools are good enough for professional artists, but they're more than adequate for amateur dabblers whose needs aren't so grandiose. This chapter gives you a bit of background about images, tells you how to work with image files, and shows you how to create and modify images using the Paint program.

The Alphabet Soup of Picture File Formats

There's certainly no shortage of ways that the world's computer geeks have come up with over the years to confuse users and other mere mortals. But few things get the man (or woman) on the street more thoroughly bamboozled than the bewildering array of file formats (also known as file types) that exist in the digital world. And perhaps the worst culprit is the picture file category, which boasts an unseemly large number of formats. My goal in this section is to help you get through the thicket of acronyms and minutiae that characterize picture file formats, and to show you how to simplify things so that they actually make sense.

Before you go any further into this file format business, you might enjoy taking a step or two in reverse to consider the bigger picture: What is a file format and why do we need so many of them? I like to look at file formats as the underlying structure of a file that's akin to a car's underlying structure. The latter is a collection of metal and plastic bits that form the frame, axles, suspension, engine, and other innards that determine how the car performs. A file format is similar in that it consists of a collection of bits and bytes that determines how the picture is viewed. As you'll see, some formats are better suited for displaying photos, while others have a better time with line drawings.

Windows Wisdom

Throughout this chapter and in other parts of the book I'll use the terms *picture, image,* and *graphic* interchangeably.

The sigh-of-relief-inducing news is that even though the computing world is on speaking terms with dozens of different image formats, Windows XP is conversant with only five:

- **Bitmap**   This is the standard image file format used by Windows XP. It's good for color drawings, although its files tend to be on the large side. Bitmap image files use the .bmp extension, so these files are also referred to sometimes as BMP files.

- **GIF**   This is one of the standard graphics file formats used on the Internet's World Wide Web. It's only capable of storing 256 colors, so it's only suitable for relatively simple line drawings or for images that use only a few colors. The resulting files are compressed, so they end up quite a bit smaller than bitmap files.

- **JPEG**   This is the other standard graphics file format that you see on the World Wide Web. This format can reproduce millions of colors, so it's suitable for photographs and other high-quality images. JPEG (it's pronounced JAY-peg) stores images in a compressed format, so it can knock high-quality images down to a manageable size while still retaining some picture fidelity. (However, the more you compress the image, the poorer the image quality becomes.)

◆ **PNG**   This is a relatively new file format that's becoming more popular on the Internet (although it's still not supported by all browsers). It's a versatile format that can be used with both simple drawings and photos. For the latter, PNG supports compression to keep images relatively small. (And, unlike JPEG, the PNG compression doesn't reduce the quality of the image.)

◆ **TIF**   This format is often used with image scanners and digital cameras because it does a great job of rendering photos and other scanned images. The downside is that this format doesn't usually compress the images in any way, so it creates *huge* files. (Note that this file format sometimes goes by the name of TIFF instead of just TIF.)

So which one should you use when creating your own image files? That depends:

◆ If you're creating a drawing that you'll print out or work with only on your computer, use the bitmap format.

◆ If you're creating a simple drawing that you'll be publishing to the World Wide Web, use GIF.

◆ If you're creating a more complex drawing that you'll be publishing to the web, use PNG.

◆ If you're scanning in an image or downloading a photo from a digital camera for printing or for editing only on your computer, use TIF.

◆ If you're scanning in an image or downloading a photo from a digital camera for e-mailing or publishing to the web, use JPEG.

Hacking Windows

The features available with the My Pictures folder can also be applied to other folders where you store images. To do this, launch My Computer and open the folder you want to work with. Select **View, Customize This Folder** to display the Properties dialog box. In the Customize tab, the **What kind of folder to you want?** group enables you to apply a template to the folder. This means that you can convert your folder into a special folder that uses the same features as My Pictures (as well as other special folders, such as My Music). In the **Use this folder type as a template** list, choose the template type that best suits the content of your folder. For example, if your folder contains mostly images, choose the **Pictures** template or the **Photo Album** template. Note, too, that you can tell Windows XP to use the template with all the folder's subfolders by activating the **Also apply this template to all subfolders** check box.

A Tour of the My Pictures Folder

Back in Chapter 4, I told you about the My Documents folder and mentioned that it's the perfect spot to store the documents you create. If you've been doing that, then you no doubt have noticed that My Documents includes a subfolder named My Pictures, and you probably guessed that this subfolder is where you ought to be hoarding your picture files. That's certainly true, but not just because of the folder's name. No, My Pictures is the place to squirrel away your images because it's a special folder that "understands" picture files and so offers you some extra features that are designed specifically for messing around with images:

♦ It has a "thumbnail" view that shows you not only the name of each file, but also gives you a miniature preview of what each image looks like.

♦ It enables you to see a "preview" of any image, from which you can then rotate the image, print it, and perform a few other tasks.

♦ It enables you to view all your images one-by-one in a kind of "slide show."

♦ It enables you to set up a particular image as your Windows XP desktop background.

♦ It enables you to order prints of your digital photos from an Internet-based printing service.

The rest of this chapter takes you through the specifics of these features. Before getting to that, however, it's probably a good idea to review just how you get to the My Pictures folder. Windows XP offers two methods:

♦ Select **Start, My Pictures.**

♦ If you're currently in the **My Documents** folder, double-click the icon for the **My Pictures** subfolder.

All Thumbs: Using the Thumbnail View

When you arrive at the My Pictures folder, you'll probably see the files arranged something like those shown in Figure 7.1. That is, instead of a boring (and only marginally useful) icon, each file shows a minipreview of the image contained in the file.

Figure 7.1
By default, Windows XP displays a small preview of each graphics file in the My Pictures folder.

This handy way of looking at things is called the Thumbnail view, and it's the default view used by the My Pictures folder. If you just see file names instead of thumbnails, you can turn on the latter by activating the **View, Thumbnails** command.

If you want to know details about an image—such as its height and width in pixels, its file type, and its size—move your mouse pointer over the file. After a second or two, a banner appears with that image info written on it.

You should also note at this point that when you click an image file to highlight it, the WebView panel's **Picture Tasks** section offers several image-related links, including **View as slide show** and **Order prints online.** I'll talk about these links as you work through this chapter.

If you have a slow computer, you may find that Windows XP takes quite a bit of time to display each of the thumbnails. In that case, a faster alternative would be to switch to one of the regular views (such as **Icons, List,** or **Details**) and then click an image file to highlight it. Then, in the **WebView** area, click the **downward-pointing arrow** in the **Details** section to open it up. This shows you not only a thumbnail of the selected image, but also its type, dimensions, size, and the date it was created or last modified.

Attending a Strip Show: Using the Filmstrip View

The thumbnail view is a great way to find the image you're looking for, but it isn't a great way to view that image once you've picked it out from the herd. To see the bigger

Windows Wisdom

You can also activate the Previous Image icon by pressing the **left-arrow key** on your keyboard. For the Next Image icon, press the **right-arrow key**. Note, too, that you can also rotate the image by pulling down the **File** menu and selecting the **Rotate Clockwise** or **Rotate Counterclockwise** commands.

picture (literally), Windows XP gives you two choices: the Filmstrip view (which I discuss in this section) and the image preview (which I discuss in the next section).

The Filmstrip view is a new Windows XP feature, and you start it up by selecting the **View, Filmstrip** command. When you do that, the My Pictures window converts itself into the configuration shown in Figure 7.2. The bulk of the window displays the currently highlighted picture file, which is shown full-size or as large as possible. At the bottom of the window you see all your picture files arranged in a strip from left to right. In between, you see four icons:

◆ **Previous Image**   Click this icon to display the previous image in the strip (that is, the image to the left of the current image).

◆ **Next Image**   Click this icon to display the next image in the strip (that is, the image to the right of the current image).

Figure 7.2

Select **View, Filmstrip** *to see your picture files one-by-one in a kind of filmstrip.*

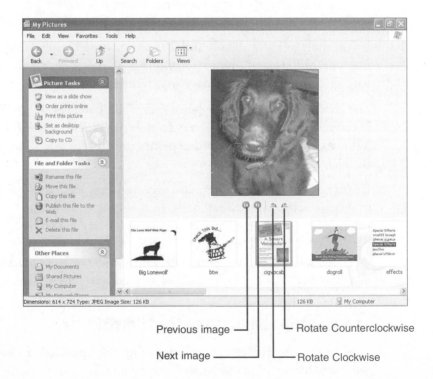

Previous image ———

Next image ———

——— Rotate Counterclockwise

——— Rotate Clockwise

◆ **Rotate Clockwise**   Click this icon to rotate the image clockwise by 90 degrees. Note that this rotation doesn't apply only to the Filmstrip view; Windows XP applies it to the file itself.

◆ **Rotate Counterclockwise**   Click this icon to rotate the image counterclockwise by 90 degrees. Again, this change is applied to the file itself.

A Closer Look: Previewing a Picture

If you prefer to work with one image at a time, the image preview feature might be just what you're looking for. To activate it, highlight the image you want to work with and then select **File, Preview** (an alternative method is to right-click the image and then click **Preview** in the shortcut menu that shows up). This loads the picture into the Image Preview window, shown in Figure 7.3.

This new window shows you a larger version of the image and is also festooned with a few icons at the bottom. You'll recognize our old friends Previous Image, Next Image, Rotate Clockwise, and Rotate Counterclockwise from the Filmstrip view. Here's what the other icons do:

◆ **Best Fit**   Click this icon (or press **Ctrl+B**) to display the image in the largest possible size that will still fit entirely within the Image Preview window.

◆ **Actual Size**   Click this icon (or press **Ctrl+A**) to see a life-sized version of the image.

◆ **Start Slide Show**   Click this icon (or press **F11**) to start a slide show of the files in the My Pictures folder (more on this later in the chapter).

◆ **Zoom In**   Click this icon (or press **+** on the numeric keypad only) to get a closer look at the picture.

◆ **Zoom Out**   Click this icon (or press **–** on the numeric keypad only) to pull back from the picture.

◆ **Delete**   Click this icon (or press **Delete**) to send the image to the Recycle Bin.

◆ **Print**   Click this icon (or press **Ctrl+P**) to start the Photo Printing Wizard (which I discuss in the section "Printing Pictures" later in this chapter).

◆ **Copy To**   Click this icon (or press **Ctrl+S**) to make a copy of the image in another folder.

◆ **Open for Editing**   Click this icon (or press **Ctrl+E**) to close the image and then reopen it in Paint.

Note that if you cue up a TIF file in the Image Preview window, you see a lot of other icons in addition to the ones shown in Figure 7.3. These extra icons are for *annotating* the image, which means adding your own notes and comments. This feature is used most often with faxes (which are often saved in TIF format), so I discuss annotation when I discuss faxing in Chapter 12.

Figure 7.3

Select **File, Preview** *to display the highlighted file in the Image Preview window.*

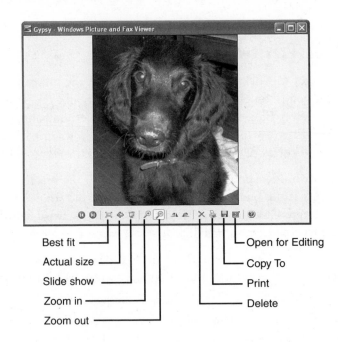

Best fit ——————
Actual size ——————
Slide show ——————
Zoom in ——————
Zoom out ——————

—— Open for Editing
—— Copy To
—— Print
—— Delete

Converting an Image to Another Format

One of the most common image chores is converting a file from one format to a different format. For example, I mentioned earlier that the GIF and JPEG formats are the ones most commonly used on the World Wide Web. If you've scanned in an image or digital photo to the TIF format (see Chapter 8) and you want to place it on a website, then you need to convert the image to JPEG. Similarly, if you've created a drawing in Paint (see "Giving Your Right Brain a Workout with Paint," later in this chapter) and saved it in the bitmap (BMP) format, then you need to convert it to GIF.

Here are the steps to trudge through to perform these and other image format conversions:

1. Display the picture in the Image Preview window.

2. Click the **Copy To** icon.

3. In the Copy To dialog box that comes by, use the **Save as type** list to choose the new file format you want.

4. (Optional) Select a new destination folder and change the **File name.**

5. Click **Save.**

Setting Up an Image Slide Show

For its next trick, the My Pictures folder also offers a "slide show" view. This means that Windows XP displays a full-screen version of the first file, waits about five seconds, displays the second file, and so on. To activate the slide show, you have two choices:

♦ In the My Pictures folder, click the **View as slide show** link in the WebView panel's Picture Tasks section.

♦ In the Image Preview window, click the **Start Slide Show** icon.

Note that you can also control the slide show by hand by using the following techniques:

♦ **To display the slide show controls**   Press **Tab.** This displays five icons in the upper-right corner of the screen. The first two icons enable you to restart and pause the slide show.

♦ **To show the next slide**   Click the mouse, press the **right-arrow key,** or click **Next Picture** in the slide show controls.

♦ **To show the previous slide**   Press the **left-arrow key** or click **Previous Picture** in the slide show controls.

♦ **To stop the slide show**   Press **Esc** or click **Close the window** in the slide show controls.

No Film? No Problem: Ordering Prints Online

If you have a digital camera, getting your photos from pixels to prints is often a challenge. It's not so bad if you have a fancy printer, but they tend to be expensive beasts (both to buy and to maintain). Recently, however, a far less expensive solution has been developed (take that as a pun, if you dare): the online printing service. The basic idea is straightforward: you send your digital photo to the online printing service, which then uses its fancy-schmancy printing equipment to convert your digital image into a real-world print. Once that's done, the service then mails the print to your home or business.

Support for this kind of service is built into Windows XP. Here's how it works:

1. Open the My Pictures folder.

2. Select the pictures you want to print online.

3. In the WebView panel's Picture Tasks section, click **Order prints online.** Windows XP gets the Online Print Order Wizard on the job.

4. The first wizard dialog box isn't much use, so click **Next.** The Select a Printing Company dialog box appears.

5. Use the **Companies** list to highlight which online printing company you prefer and then click **Next.** The wizard then connects to the Internet and downloads the appropriate data for the company you chose.

6. From here, follow the instructions that come your way for choosing print sizes and quantities, billing information, and so on. (The specific instructions vary depending on which printing company you use.)

Printing Pictures

Printing a picture—particularly a digital photo—is a bit different from printing a text document because in most cases you want to choose a different print layout depending on the size of the image and the size of the print you want. For that reason, Windows XP includes the Photo Printing Wizard that takes you step-by-step through the photo printing process. Here's how it works:

1. You can choose the files you want to print in advance or via the wizard:

    ◆ If you don't want to select any files now, go ahead and click the WebView panel's **Print pictures** link.

    ◆ If you want to print only a single file, select it and then click the WebView panel's **Print this picture** link. Note that if you change your mind about which picture or pictures to print, you can modify your selection using the wizard.

    ◆ If you want to print two or more files, select them and then click the WebView panel's **Print the selected pictures** link. The wizard assumes these are the files you want to print, so it won't give you any opportunity to add to your selections. (However, it does allow you to deselect one or more of the files.)

2. In the initial wizard dialog box, click **Next.** The Photo Selection dialog box appears.

3. For each image you want to print, activate the check box in the upper-right corner of the image. (Click **Select All** to activate the check box for every image; click **Clear All** to deactivate the check box for every image.) When you've made your choices, click **Next.** The Printing Options dialog box appears.

4. If you have more than one printer, use the **What printer do you want to use?** list to select a printer. You should also click the **Printing Preferences** button to adjust the settings on your printer. These settings depend on the printer, but they generally include selecting the type of paper you'll be using and whether you want to print in color or black and white. When you're ready to move on, click **Next.** The Layout Selection dialog box appears.

5. Use the **Available layouts** list to select the print size you want. When you select a different layout, the **Print preview** box shows you what your printed image will look like. When you've made your choice, click **Next.** The wizard sends your image (or images) to the printer.

6. Click **Finish.**

Setting a Picture as the Desktop Background

Windows XP's desktop comes with a fairly spiffy background image. However, you may find that you get bored with it after a while or that you have a picture of your own that you'd prefer to use. Either way, it's no problem to change the desktop background to any picture in your My Pictures folder. In fact, it takes just two measly steps:

1. In the **My Pictures folder,** select the file that contains the image you want to use.

2. In the WebView panel's Picture Tasks section, click the **Set as desktop background** link.

Capturing a Picture of the Screen

In the next chapter you'll learn how to get images into your computer by using a scanner or digital camera. Another way to get an image without having to draw anything is to "capture" what's on your screen. You have two ways to go about this:

♦ To capture the entire screen, lock, stock, and taskbar, press your keyboard's **Print Screen** key. (Depending on your keyboard, this key may be labeled **Print Scrn, PrtScn, PrtSc,** or some other variation on this theme.)

◆ If you want to capture only whatever is in the active window, press **Alt+Print Screen.**

Either way, you can then toss the captured image onto your hard disk by launching Paint (select **Start, All Programs, Accessories, Paint**) and selecting **Edit, Paste.** If Paint complains that the image you're pasting is too large, click **Yes** to enlarge your drawing to fit the image.

Giving Your Right Brain a Workout with Paint

Scientists tell us that, for most people, the left side of the brain is verbal, analytic, abstract, rational, and linear, while the right side of the brain is nonverbal, synthetic, analogical, intuitive, and holistic. The left brain enjoys words, but the right brain revels in images, so it's the latter that will get a kick out of Paint, Windows XP's main graphics program.

Even if you're a nonartist (that is, someone who hears "Leonardo" and thinks *Titanic*), Paint has plenty of easy-to-use tools that can help you get the job done. This section gives you a brief explanation of Paint's basic drawing techniques.

A Tour of the Paint Studio

To open your Paint studio, select **Start, All Programs, Accessories, Paint.** Figure 7.4 shows the Paint window that materializes.

Figure 7.4

A few key facts about the Paint window.

Tool box

Drawing area

Styles for the selected tool

Current colors

Color box

The Paint window is loaded with interesting-looking buttons and lots of color. Here's a rundown of the major features:

- ◆ **Tool Box**   This box holds the various tools you use to create or edit your artwork. There's a "pencil," a "brush," an "eraser," and all sorts of utensils for drawing lines and shapes. I describe the individual Tool Box tools in more detail in the next section.

- ◆ **Tool styles**   This box shows the styles that are available with the currently selected tool. You use these styles to add some variety to your drawings. For example, the Brush tool offers a selection of brush sizes and shapes.

- ◆ **Color Box**   This box holds all the colors and patterns you can use for drawing or filling shapes. It's just like having your own personal 28-crayon box of Crayolas, except these never need sharpening.

- ◆ **Current colors**   This area contains two boxes that display the currently selected foreground color (the top box) and background color (the bottom box). Selecting a new foreground color is a simple matter of clicking one of the color rectangles in the Color Box. If it's a new background color you're after, right-click a color swatch. (Confusingly, the definition of "foreground color" and "background color" varies depending on which tool you're using. I'll give you the details when I discuss each tool.)

- ◆ **Drawing area**   This white expanse is your Paint canvas. It's where you perform the mouse moves that lead to the creation of your digital drawings. It is, in other words, the place where all the fun happens.

Tool Time: How to Use the Paint Tools

The best way to tackle Paint is simply to enjoy yourself by experimenting with various tools, styles, and colors. Just let yourself go, toss off those inhibitions, and free yourself from the shackles of adult responsibilities. Give yourself permission to regress to an immature, to-heck-with-it-I'm-going-to-be-at-one-with-my-inner-child state. (It might be a good idea to close the door for this.)

When you're ready to go, roll up your sleeves, pick out a tool, and just start playing. However, just so you know, there *is* a basic four-step method you use for each tool:

1. In the Tool Box, click the tool you want to play with.

2. Click a tool style (if the tool has any).

3. In the Color Box, left-click a foreground color and right-click a background color.

4. Move the mouse pointer into the drawing area and then draw the shape you want. (The specifics of the drawing process vary from tool to tool, as you'll see in a second.)

Paint's Drawing Tools

Here's a review of the drawing-related tools you can grab from the Tool Box:

♦ **Pencil**   You use this tool to draw freehand lines. After selecting this tool, move the mouse pointer into the drawing area, hold down the left mouse button, and then wiggle the mouse around. Paint draws a freehand line that follows your every twitch and shimmy.

♦ **Brush**   This is another tool for drawing freehand lines. It differs from the Pencil tool in that it gives you a selection of brush shapes and sizes (in the tool styles area).

♦ **Line**   You use this tool to draw straight lines (the tool styles offer five different widths for your line-drawing pleasure). To create a line, drag the mouse pointer within the drawing area. You can make Paint draw a perfect horizontal or vertical line, or a line pitched at a 45-degree angle, by holding down the **Shift** key while you drag the mouse.

♦ **Rectangle**   This tool draws rectangles. The point where you hold down the mouse button defines one corner of the rectangle, and you create the rest of it by dragging the mouse. Need to draw a perfect square? No problem: Just hold down the **Shift** key while dragging. The Rectangle tool offers three styles: a "border only" style that draws only the border of the shape; a "border and fill" style that draws a border (using the foreground color) and fills it with a color (the background color); and a "no border" style that omits the shape's border and draws only the fill.

♦ **Ellipse**   You use this tool for drawing ovals. Again, you do this by dragging the mouse inside the drawing area. If what you really need is a perfect circle, hold down the **Shift** key while doing the dragging thing.

◆ **Rounded Rectangle**   This tool combines the Rectangle and Ellipse tools to produce a rectangle that has rounded corners.

◆ **Curve**   Use this tool when you need a wavy line. This one works a little differently from the others you've seen so far. You begin by dragging the mouse pointer until the line is the length you want, and you then release the button. To curve the line, drag the mouse again and then release the button. If you're feeling spunky, you can add a second curve to the line by dragging the mouse once again and then releasing the button when you're done.

◆ **Polygon**   You use this tool to create a polygon. (In case you can't remember back to high school geometry, a *polygon* is a succession of straight lines that forms an enclosed object. A triangle and a rectangle are examples of polygons.) To wield this tool, begin by dragging the mouse pointer until the first side is the length and angle you want, and then release the mouse button. To create the next side, move the pointer to where you want the side to end, and then click. Paint dutifully draws a line from the end of the previous line to the spot where you clicked. Repeat this move-and-click procedure to add more sides. To complete the polygon, click the start of the first side to enclose the shape.

◆ **Fill with Color**   This tool looks like a can of paint being poured, and that's more or less what it does. That is, it fills an enclosed shape with a specified color. To use it, just click anywhere inside the shape (make sure it's completely closed!) and Paint fills it up with the current foreground color.

◆ **Airbrush**   This tool resembles (and works like) a can of spray paint, so I'm not sure why it's called an Airbrush. No matter, it's loads of fun to use because as you drag the mouse, Paint "sprays" the current foreground color. (Drag the mouse quickly to get a light spray; drag the mouse slowly to get a heavy spray.)

◆ **Text**   If your left brain is feeling thoroughly ignored by now, you can toss it a bone by using the Text tool to add text to your drawing. The first step is to drag the mouse inside the drawing area to create a box to hold your text. When you release the mouse button, Paint places a cursor inside the box, so you can just start typing. Paint also displays the Text toolbar (see Figure 7.5). To change the font of the text, select the typeface, size, and other font options. Note, too, that this tool offers two styles: opaque (the text is the foreground color and the text box is filled with the background color) and transparent (the text is the foreground color and the text box background is transparent).

Look Out!

Be careful when typing your text with the Text tool because after you enter the text and then click outside the box to finish up, the text becomes uneditable. If you try to click inside the box to make changes, Paint ignores the existing text and starts a new text box. If you make a mistake, erase the text and start over or use **Undo.**

Figure 7.5

A Paint file demonstrating the opaque and transparent text styles.

Paint's Nondrawing Tools

The Paint Tool Box also offers a few other nondrawing tools to enhance your creative powers:

◆ **Pick Color** You use this tool to select an existing color from the currently open image. This is handy, for example, if the image has a color that doesn't appear in the Color Box. You select the color by clicking (for the foreground color) or right-clicking (for the background color) an example of the color within the image.

◆ **Eraser** This not-to-be-wielded-lightly tool enables you to erase parts of your image. The tool styles offer various widths, and dragging the mouse in the drawing area wipes out everything in the mouse pointer's path. Also refer to the section "Erasing Paint Mistakes" later in this chapter for more tips.

Windows Wisdom

If you prefer to erase only a particularly ill-chosen color and replace it with something else, use the Color Eraser tool. First, set the foreground color to the color you want to wipe out, and set the background color to the color you want to use in its stead. Now select the Eraser tool and then right-drag the mouse inside the drawing area.

◆ **Magnifier**   You use this tool to zoom in on your drawing and get a closer look at things, which is handy for doing detail work. When you select this tool, use the tool styles box to choose a magnification: 1x (normal size), 2x, 6x, or 8x. The latter gets you so close that you can see the individual pixels, which are the individual pinpoints of light that make up a Paint drawing (and, for that matter, everything you see on your screen). Then click the section of the drawing that you want to magnify. Figure 7.6 shows this tool in action.

The thumbnail window

Select a magnification option

Figure 7.6

The Magnifier tool in action.

◆ **Select**   This tool lets you select a rectangular chunk—called a *cutout*—of the drawing, which you can then copy or cut out (hence the name). As you might expect, you use the Select tool much like you do the Rectangle tool. That is, you move the mouse pointer to the corner of the area you want to select, and then drag the mouse until the box encloses the area.

Jargon Jar

A **cutout** is rectangular section of the drawing that you can select and then manipulate on its own.

♦ **Free-Form Select**   This tool is similar to Select, but it lets you mark an area using a free-form line. Click the tool, move the pointer into the drawing area, and then drag the mouse pointer around the area you want to select.

Erasing Paint Mistakes

While you're on the steep part of the Paint learning curve, you'll end up with lots of botched lines and mutinous shapes that you won't want in your final drawing. Here's how to get rid of these things (see also the Eraser tool, discussed in the previous section):

♦ Most of the Paint tools operate by holding down a mouse button and then dragging the mouse. If you make a mess during the drawing, you can start again by clicking the other mouse button *before* you release the button you're drawing with.

♦ If you've already completed the shape, select **Edit, Undo** (pressing **Ctrl+Z** will also get you there). Note that Paint allows you to undo the last three things you did.

♦ If the drawing is a complete write-off, you can start over by selecting **Image, Clear Image** (or by pressing **Ctrl+Shift+N**).

The Least You Need to Know

♦ If you're working only on your computer, the best formats to use are bitmap for drawings and TIF for photos. If you're going to e-mail pictures or publish them on the web, use GIF for drawing and JPEG for photos.

♦ In the My Pictures folder, use the View menu's Thumbnails command to view the images as thumbnails, and use the Filmstrip command to view your images sequentially, sort of like a filmstrip.

♦ To convert an image, display the picture in the Image Preview window, click **Copy To,** and then use the Save as type list to choose the new format.

♦ To grab a screen shot, press **Print Screen** to capture an image of the full screen, or **Alt+Print Screen** to capture an image of just the active window.

♦ The basic Paint method is to click a tool, select a style (if applicable), choose the foreground and background colors, and then draw the shape. Most Paint tools operate by clicking and dragging within the drawing area.

♦ To erase mistakes from a Paint drawing, use the Eraser tool to erase everything and the Color Eraser (right-drag the Eraser) to replace the foreground color with the background color.

Chapter 8

Graphics Gadgetry: Working with Scanners and Digital Cameras

In This Chapter

- Telling Windows XP about your scanner or digital camera
- Making sure your scanner or camera works properly
- Getting images from the scanner or camera to your computer
- Working directly with the photos stored in a digital camera

It used to be that the only way to get an image onto your computer was either to create it yourself or to grab a prefab pic from a clip art collection or photo library. If you lacked artistic flair, or if you couldn't find a suitable image, you were out of luck.

Now, however, getting images into digital form is easier than ever, thanks to two graphics gadgets that have become more affordable. A *document scanner* acts much like a photocopier in that it creates an image of a flat surface, such as a photograph or a sheet of paper. The difference is that the scanner saves the image to a graphics file on your hard disk instead of on paper. A *digital camera* acts much like a regular camera in that it captures and stores an image of the outside world. The difference is that the digital camera stores the image internally in its memory instead of on exposed film. It's then possible to connect the digital camera to your computer and save the image as a graphics file on your hard disk.

The big news is that Windows XP understands both types of doohickeys and often identifies them by a single generic name: *imaging devices* (since both produce image files). Windows XP comes with support for a variety of scanners and cameras, so getting your digital images from out here to in there has never been easier, as you'll see in this chapter.

Installing a Scanner or Digital Camera

Windows XP offers a number of options for installing scanners and digital cameras. Make sure the device is turned on and connected to your computer and then try the following:

◆ **Rely on Plug and Play** Most of today's crop of scanners and cameras are Plug-and-Play compatible. This means that as soon as you turn on and connect the device to your computer, Windows XP should recognize it and set it up for you automatically. Do you have one or more USB ports on your computer? If so, then if you're looking to buy a new scanner or digital camera, you'll save yourself a lot of grief if you make sure that the device supports USB. The advantages to this are twofold: First, it means that Windows XP will almost certainly recognize and install the device as soon as you plug it in to the computer; second, it will take far less time to transfer images from the device to your computer.

◆ **Use the Scanners and Cameras icon** If Windows XP doesn't recognize your scanner or camera, it may just need a bit of convincing. To do that, select **Start, Control Panel,** click **Printers and Other Hardware,** and then click **Scanners and Cameras.** When the Scanners and Cameras window shows up, click **Add an imaging device** to get the Scanner and Camera Installation Wizard on the job. Click **Next** to see a list of scanner and digital camera manufacturers and models. Find your camera or scanner in this list, click **Next,** and follow the instructions on the screen.

Look Out! _____
Only someone logged on as an administrator can add imaging devices using the Scanners and Cameras method.

◆ **Install the device software** Any scanner or digital camera worth its salt will come with software for setting up the device. If the first two options don't work, try installing the software.

When your scanner or camera is installed, you'll see an icon for it in the Scanners and Cameras window, as shown in Figure 8.1. (Remember: To get to this window, select **Start, Control Panel,** click **Printers and Other Hardware,** and then click **Scanners and Cameras.**) Note, however, that if you turn off or disconnect the device, then it no longer appears in this window.

Figure 8.1

The Scanners and Cameras window contains icons for each imaging device installed on your system.

You should also know that Windows XP considers a digital camera to be a type of file storage device. This makes sense because a digital camera uses some kind of memory module or disk to store the digital photos you've taken. The kicker is that because the camera stores files, Windows XP treats it as a folder attached to your computer, so it appears in My Computer, as shown in Figure 8.2. Later in this chapter I'll show you how to use My Computer to get at the images stored in your camera.

Figure 8.2

Windows XP considers a digital camera just another folder, so the camera shows up in My Computer.

Before you use your scanner or camera, it's a good idea to test it to make sure Windows XP can communicate with it.

1. With the device still connected and turned on, click it in the Scanners and Cameras window to highlight it.

2. In the WebView panel's **Imaging Tasks** section, click **View device properties.**

3. This displays a dialog box that's specific to the device. In all cases, however, the General tab has a button named **Test Scanner** or **Test Camera** (or even **Test Scanner or Camera**). Whatever the name, click the button.

If all is well, you'll see a dialog box named Test Successful that tells you the device completed the diagnostic test. If you see the Test Failed dialog box, instead, make sure the scanner is connected and turned on and then try again.

Getting Images from Your Scanner or Camera

The whole point of a scanner or digital camera is to transfer an image of something from the device to your computer hard drive. From there you can edit the image, e-mail it to a friend or colleague, publish it to the World Wide Web, or simply store it for safekeeping. This section shows you how to make a hard (disk) copy of an image.

Using the Scanner and Camera Wizard with Newer Scanners

If you have a newer scanner or camera, Windows XP installs its own Scanner and Camera Wizard to give you a step-by-step method for capturing images. Let's see how it works. First, launch the Scanner and Camera Wizard using one of the following methods:

◆ Connect the device to your computer. After you've installed your scanner or camera, the next time you connect it the Scanner and Camera Wizard will come out to play automatically.

◆ If your device is a scanner and it has some kind of "scan" button, press that button.

◆ In the Scanners and Cameras window, click the device icon and then click **Get pictures** in the WebView panel's Imaging Tasks section.

◆ Give the wizard a poke in the ribs by selecting **Start, All Programs, Accessories, Scanner and Camera Wizard.** If you have more than one imaging device, you'll see the Select Device dialog box. Click the device you want to use and then click **OK.**

When the initial wizard window appears, click **Next** to get the wizard to connect to the scanner. What happens from here depends on whether you're using a scanner or a digital camera.

How the Wizard Deals with a Scanner

For a scanner, you'll see the Choose Scanning Preferences dialog box shown in Figure 8.3.

Figure 8.3

If you're working with a scanner, the wizard displays this dialog box.

The **Picture type** section offers four options:

◆ **Color picture**   Choose this option if the document you're scanning is a color photograph or drawing.

◆ **Grayscale picture**   Choose this option if your document is a picture that renders colors using different shades of gray.

◆ **Black-and-white picture or text**   Choose this option if your document uses only black and white (for example, if it's a page of text).

◆ **Custom**   This option doesn't seem to do much of anything, so you may as well ignore it.

If you know what you're doing, click the **Custom Settings** button to adjust properties such as the brightness, contrast, and *resolution* of the scanned image.

Jargon Jar

The **resolution** determines the overall quality of the scanned image. The higher the resolution, the higher the quality and (on the downside) the bigger the resulting file. Resolution is measured in dots per inch (DPI).

If you want to see what your image will look like before committing yourself to the scan, click the **Preview** button.

How the Wizard Deals with a Digital Camera

For a digital camera, you'll see the Choose Pictures to Copy dialog box shown in Figure 8.4. This dialog box offers up a thumbnail image for each digital photo stored in the camera, and each thumbnail sports a check box in the upper-right corner:

♦ Leave the check box activated for each image you want to copy to your hard disk.

♦ Deactivate the check box for each image that you don't want to copy.

Note, too, that you can rotate an image and see information about an image (such as its size) by highlighting it and then clicking the icons pointed out in Figure 8.4.

Figure 8.4

If you're working with a digital camera, the wizard displays this dialog box.

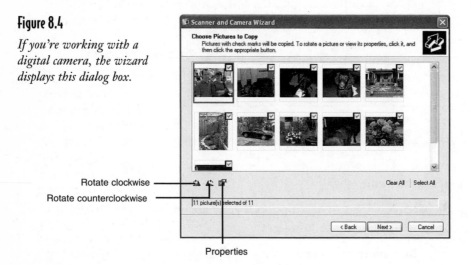

Rotate clockwise

Rotate counterclockwise

Properties

If you have a webcam or other desktop video camera that supports still images, the Scanner and Camera Wizard will display a dialog box named Take and Select Pictures to Copy. This dialog box shows the live video feed in the **Preview** box. When the feed displays the image you want, click the **Take Picture** icon to store the still image in the **Pictures** box. Repeat as necessary and then click **Next.**

Completing the Scan

With either type of device, when you've made your selections, click **Next** to get to the Picture Name and Destination dialog box. Here you'll see two or three of the following controls:

◆ **Type a name for this group of pictures**   Use this text box to enter a name for the saved pictures. This name acts as a kind of prefix for the image file names. For example, if you enter "Vacation," your pictures will be saved with the names Vacation 001, Vacation 002, and so on.

◆ **Select a file format** (scanners only)   Use this list to choose the file format for the scanned image: BMP, JPEG, TIF, or PNG.

◆ **This group of pictures will be saved in the following folder**   Use this list to choose the folder where you want the images stored. The default is My Pictures\ *Name*, where *Name* is the title of the new folder you entered into the text box. Note that you can also pick out an existing folder by clicking the **Browse** button.

When you click **Next,** the wizard gets together with the scanner or camera and arranges to have the image (or images) copied to the folder you specified. When that's done, you come face-to-face with the Uploading Pictures dialog box, which wants to know if you'd like to publish the picture on a website or have them printed online (see Chapter 7). If you don't want to bother with any of this, make sure the **No thanks** option is activated and then click **Next.**

> **Windows Wisdom**
>
> Windows XP gives you another way to scan pictures: In Paint, select the **File, From Scanner or Camera** command, click the image you want in the dialog box, and click **Get Picture**. Note that any decent graphics program also comes with support for scanning stuff. So if you have a better program than Paint, check to see if you can use it to scan pictures.

In the final wizard dialog box, you see a link that displays the name of the folder you used to store the image. If you want to see the image in its new hard disk home, click the link. Don't forget to also click **Finish** to unload the wizard.

How the Wizard Deals with a CompactFlash Disk

Many digital cameras store images using a special kind of memory doohickey called a CompactFlash card. They're handy little devils because after you transfer your images to your computer, you can wipe out the card and start all over again. Although you usually get at the card's images by connecting the camera directly to your computer as described in the previous section, some cameras come with separate units into which you insert the CompactFlash card and then connect the unit to the computer.

Windows XP treats these card holders as disk drives, and they show up in My Computer as either a CompactFlash Drive or as a Removable Disk. You're then free to insert a CompactFlash card and browse its images directly, as described in the next section. In some cases, however, inserting the CompactFlash card prompts Windows XP into displaying the dialog box shown in Figure 8.5. Windows wants to know just what the heck you'd like to do with the images on the card, so click the action you prefer. If you want to make this the default action, activate the **Always do the selected action** check box. Click **OK** to make it so.

Figure 8.5

When you insert a CompactFlash card, Windows XP may toss this dialog box your way.

Browsing Digital Camera Images

One of Windows XP's nicer features is the capability to parley directly with a digital camera using My Computer (or Windows Explorer). This is possible because, as I mentioned earlier, Windows XP treats whatever the camera uses to store the digital photos as an honest-to-goodness folder. This means you can open the folder and get your hands dirty by working with the images yourself.

To do this, Windows XP gives you a few different ways to proceed (all of which assume that your camera is plugged in and ready for action):

♦ In My Computer, double-click the camera icon in the **Scanners and Cameras** section (see Figure 8.2 earlier in this chapter).

♦ If you're displaying My Computer's Folders Explorer bar, click the camera in the **Folders** list.

♦ When you start the Scanner and Camera Wizard, the first dialog box has a link that says **advanced users only.** Click that link.

In each case, Windows XP connects to the camera, grabs the waiting images (this may take awhile), and displays them thumbnail-style, as shown in Figure 8.6. To copy an image from the camera to your hard disk, you have two choices:

Figure 8.6

Windows XP is happy to show your camera's digital photos in a folder window.

♦ Click the picture you want to copy and then click the WebView panel's **Copy this item** link (it's in the **Folder Tasks** section). In the Copy Items dialog box that pops up, select the folder you want to use and then click **Copy.**

♦ Click **Folders** to display the Folder bar and then drag the picture from the camera to the folder you want to use for storage (such as My Pictures).

Note, too, that you can also clear out the camera's photos by clicking **Delete all pictures on camera** in the WebView panel's Camera Tasks section.

The Least You Need to Know

♦ For the easiest installation, go with a scanner or camera that supports Plug and Play, particularly one that connects via a USB cable (provided your computer has a USB port).

♦ To see your installed imaging devices, open the Scanners and Cameras window by selecting **Start, Control Panel,** clicking **Printers and Other Hardware,** and then clicking **Scanners and Cameras.**

◆ To make sure Windows XP and your device are getting along, open the Scanners and Cameras window, click the device's icon, click **View device properties,** and then click the button named **Test Scanner** or **Test Camera** (or even **Test Scanner or Camera**).

◆ To get pictures from a scanner or camera, you usually just need to connect the device to launch the Scanner and Camera Wizard. You can also get to this wizard by pressing the device's "scan" button, clicking **Get pictures** in the Scanners and Cameras window, or by selecting **Start, All Programs, Accessories, Scanner and Camera Wizard.**

◆ To access your digital camera's stored images via My Computer, double-click the camera's icon. Alternatively, start the Scanner and Camera Wizard and, in the initial dialog box, click **advanced users only.**

Sights and Sounds: Music and Other Multimedia

In This Chapter

- ◆ Understanding multimedia files and hardware
- ◆ Playing multimedia files
- ◆ Listening to audio CDs and watching DVD movies
- ◆ Copying music tracks to and from a CD

The graphics you gawked at in the last two chapters represent only a selection of Windows XP's visual treats. There are actually quite a few more goodies that fall into the "sights for sore eyes" category, and even a few that could be called "sounds for sore ears." In this chapter, you see that Windows XP turns your lowly computer into a multimedia powerhouse capable of showing videos, playing audio CDs, making realistic burping noises, watching slick DVD movies, and even creating your own sound recordings.

Notes About Multimedia Files

Most of the multimedia your eyes will see and ears will hear resides in files on your hard disk, on a CD-ROM or DVD disc, or on the Internet. Just to keep us all thoroughly confused, the world's multimedia mavens have invented dozens of different file formats, each of which has its own incomprehensible two- or three-letter acronym. To help you make some sense of all this, I've grouped all the various formats into a mere five categories for easier consumption:

◆ **Sound files** Files that contain sounds or music only. The two main types are audio files and *MIDI* sequence files. You'll deal with audio files mostly, and you'll also hear them referred to using their specific formats, including WAV, AU, AIFF, WMA (Windows Media Audio), and MP3. (The latter is a format that's used to play songs with near- or full-CD quality. MP3 is an extremely popular and growing format on the Internet.)

Jargon Jar

MIDI stands for **Musical Instrument Digital Interface**. It's a sound file that plays music generated by electronic synthesizers.

◆ **Animation files** Files that contain animated movies or shorts, and they might include sound. The three most popular formats are video files (also called AVI files), MPEG files, and QuickTime files.

◆ **Movie files** Files that contain live action movies or shorts, and they usually have a soundtrack. These files use the same formats as animation files.

◆ **Audio CD tracks** Files that Windows XP uses to represent individual tracks on an audio CD; however, you rarely deal with them that way yourself. Instead, you can have Windows XP play some or all of a CD's tracks from your CD-ROM or DVD-ROM drive. You can even talk Windows XP into copying audio CD tracks to your hard drive or to a portable player.

◆ **DVD movies** Files that contain high-quality versions of feature films, documentaries, and other big-screen entertainment. Again, you never have to deal with these files directly.

How can you recognize these files in My Computer? If you're dealing with sound or music files or audio CD tracks that have been copied to your computer (more on this later), then Windows XP displays the files with the icon shown in Figure 9.1. For animation or movie files, you see the first frame of the flick, again as pointed out in Figure 9.1. (Note, however, that you only see the first frame if My Computer is in Thumbnails view, which you get by activating the **View, Thumbnails** command.)

Hacking Windows

My Computer's Details view (activate the **View, Details** command) normally shows four columns only: Name, Size, Type, and Date Modified. However, Windows XP has a number of other columns you can display, such as the dimensions of an image or the bit rate at which a music file was ripped. Select **View, Choose Details** to open the Choose Details dialog box, activate the check boxes of the columns you want to use, and then click **OK.** Alternatively, right-click a column heading and click the detail you want to see.

These are music or sound files

Figure 9.1

How Windows XP displays media files.

These are animation or movie files

Notes About Multimedia Hardware

More than most other computer features, multimedia is strongly tied to specialized hardware. In many (but not all) cases, your multimedia will be multimediocre if your computer isn't loaded down with the requisite devices. To help you get your computer multimedia-ready, this section takes a quick look at the hardware side of things.

Audio Hardware

If you're sick of carrying on a one-way conversation with your computer, you can get into the sound thing by using a *sound card.* This is an internal circuit board that's standard equipment on almost all new PCs. How can you tell if your system has a sound card? The easiest way is just to listen: If Windows XP plays a snippet of music at startup, then you've got sound.

Audio CD Hardware

If you want to listen to the soothing sounds of the Beastie Boys or Rage Against the Machine on your machine, you could just plop the appropriate CD into a nearby stereo. However, it may also be possible to play the CD directly from your computer. All you need is a sound card, some speakers, and either a CD drive or a DVD drive.

DVD Hardware

In the currency of computing power, the bells and whistles that comprise the Windows DVD experience don't come cheaply. Pushing around all those pixels and belting out all those notes puts quite a strain on a machine. So, as you can imagine, specialized hardware for DVD is a must. Unfortunately, how Windows XP reacts to DVD hardware is weird and confusing.

Let's start with the easy part: the basic requirements. The basic needs are a DVD drive and a sound card/speakers combo. Not too bad, so far. Where things get twisted is in the add-on—called a *decoder*—that your system requires to process the video and audio torrent that the DVD drive sends its way. There are two kinds of these decoders:

> **Jargon Jar**
>
> If Windows XP doesn't recognize your hardware **decoder,** you may need to get updated **device driver** files from the manufacturer. A device driver is a little program that lets a device talk to Windows XP—and vice versa. The latest driver will either be on a disk that comes with the decoder or on the manufacturer's website.

- **Hardware decoder** This is a device—usually a circuit board—that attaches to your computer. This is the kind Windows XP prefers. In fact, the DVD Player only plays DVD movies if your system has a hardware decoder *and* if it's a decoder that Windows XP recognizes (that is, it has a *device driver* for it).

- **Software decoder** This is a program that performs the translation from DVD to video and audio output. This requires a reasonably powerful computer: at least a Pentium II machine running at 266 MHz or better. If your machine qualifies, your DVD drive should have a disc that includes a setup program for installing the decoder.

Making Multimedia Whoopee with Media Player

You saw earlier that Windows supports all kinds of multimedia formats. In previous versions of Windows, the bad news was that to play those formats you had to master a passel of player programs. In Windows XP, the good news is that you now need to wrestle with only a single program: Media Player. This clever chunk of software is a true one-stop multimedia shop that's capable of playing sound files, music files, audio CDs, animations, movie files, and even DVDs. It can even copy audio CD tracks to your computer, burn music files to a CD, tune in to Internet radio stations, and more.

To try Media Player, you have a bunch of ways to proceed:

◆ Select **Start, Windows Media Player.** If you don't see the Windows Media Player icon in the main Start menu, you can convince it to come out to play by selecting **Start, All Programs, Windows Media Player.**

◆ Insert an audio CD in your CD drive, or insert a DVD disc in your DVD drive. (Note that most DVD drives are also happy to play audio CDs for you.) If Windows displays a dialog box asking you what you want it to do with the CD, click **Play Audio CD,** activate the **Always do the selected action** check box, and then click **OK.**

◆ If you have a CompactFlash drive, insert a CompactFlash card. If Windows XP asks what you want to do with this disk, highlight **Play the music files.** If you don't want to be pestered with this dialog box each time, activate the **Always do the selected action** check box. Click **OK** to proceed.

◆ Use My Computer to find a media file and then double-click the file. Remember that My Documents has a subfolder named My Music, which is the default folder that Windows XP uses when you save music files.

◆ Download media from the Internet. In most cases, Media Player will launch right away and start playing the sound or movie or whatever. (This is called *streaming* the media.) Sometimes, however, you may have to wait for the entire file to download before Media Player will spring into action.

Figure 9.2 shows the Media Player window that shows up.

Figure 9.2

This is the window you see when you launch Media Player.

As you can see, the Media Player window with its wavy lines and roundish buttons is quite a bit different from what you're probably used to seeing. The first thing I'll point out is that if you don't see the menu bar in your version of Media Player, you can get it out of hiding by clicking **Show/hide menu bar** (pointed out in Figure 9.2) or by pressing **Ctrl+M**.

The second thing I'll point out is the taskbar that runs down the left side of the window. The idea here is that when you click an item in the taskbar, the Media Player switches to a different part of the program. You'll use this feature quite a bit, so let's take a second to run through each item so you know what you'll be getting yourself into:

◆ **Now Playing** This section shows information about the currently playing media (see Figure 9.2). For an audio CD, the left side of the window shows a *visualization* (a psychedelic pattern that moves in time with the music) and the right side shows the *playlist*, the list of tracks on the disc. For a DVD, the left side shows the movie and the right side shows the various chapters that comprise the movie. You can jump directly to a track or chapter by double-clicking it.

◆ **Media Guide**   This section displays the WindowsMedia.com web page, assuming your computer is connected to the Internet. This page gives you access to all kind of media marvels, including songs, videos, movie trailers, news clips, live feeds, and more.

◆ **Copy from CD**   This section enables you to copy one or more tracks from an audio CD to your computer's hard disk. See the "Hard Disk Rock: Copying Tracks from a CD" section later in this chapter.

> **Windows Wisdom**
>
> The first time you enter the Media Library section, you may see a dialog box that asks if you want Media Player to search your computer—click **Yes**. This will add all your computer's media files to the library for easy access—a very convenient thing. If you don't see this dialog box, select the **Tools, Search for Media Files** command (or press **F3**).

◆ **Media Library**   This section organizes the media that you've played and that's on your computer into various categories. It also enables you to create your own playlists of songs. See the "Becoming a Program Director: Creating a Custom Playlist" section later in this chapter.

◆ **Radio Tuner**   This section enables you to listen to radio stations that broadcast over the Internet. I tell you how it works later in this chapter in the "Web Waves: Listening to Internet Radio" section.

◆ **Copy to CD or Device**   This section enables you to copy music from your computer to a recordable CD or to a device that can play digital music (such as a portable MP3 player). The scoop on this is in the "Rollin' Your Own Music: Copying Tracks to a CD or Device" section.

◆ **Skin Chooser**   This section offers a number of wild and wacky looks for when you put Media Player into *skin mode*. This means that the program shrinks to a smaller version of itself that features just the basic buttons for playback.

To choose a new skin, highlight it and then click **Apply Skin.** To switch to skin mode, select **View, Skin Mode** or press **Ctrl+2**. (Press **Ctrl+1** to return to full mode.)

Giving Media Player Some Media to Play

I mentioned earlier that Media Player will launch and start playing automatically if you double-click or download a media file or insert an audio CD or DVD disc. If you opened Media Player directly or if you want to get it to play something else, then you need to learn how to load media from within the program.

To open a media file, you have two possibilities:

- ◆ **Open a file on your computer** Select the **File, Open** command (or press **Ctrl+O**), use the Open dialog box to highlight the file, and then click **Open.**

- ◆ **Open a file from the Internet** Select **File, Open URL** (or press **Ctrl+U**), use the Open text box to enter the Internet address of the file, and then click **OK.**

If it's an audio CD that you want to start, first click **Copy from CD** in the taskbar.

Let's Make Some Noise: Playing Media

To control the playback of your media, the Media Player program offers the following buttons:

- ◆ **Play/Pause** Starts the media file; pauses the file while it's playing. Alternatives: Select **Play, Play/Pause** or press **Ctrl+P.**

- ◆ **Stop** Stops the media file and returns to the beginning of the file (or to the beginning of the current audio CD track). Alternatives: Select **Play, Stop** or press **Ctrl+S.**

- ◆ **Rewind** Rewinds continuously through a media file (such as a streaming video file). Click **Play/Pause** to continue playing. Alternatives: Select **Play, Rewind** or press **Ctrl+Shift+B.**

- ◆ **Previous** Returns you to the beginning of the file or track. Alternatives: Select **Play, Previous** or press **Ctrl+B.**

- ◆ **Seek** Drag this slider left to rewind or right to fast-forward.

- ◆ **Next** Sends you to the next file or track. Alternatives: Select **Play, Next** or press **Ctrl+F.**

- ◆ **Mute** Turns off the sound playback. Alternatives: Select **Play, Volume, Mute** or press **F8.**

- ◆ **Volume** Controls the playback volume. Drag the slider to the left to reduce the volume, or to the right to increase the volume. Alternatives: Select **Play, Volume, Up** or press **F10** to increase the volume; select **Play, Volume, Down** or press **F9** to decrease the volume.

- ◆ **Fast Forward** Fast-forwards continuously through a media file (such as a streaming video file). Click **Play/Pause** to continue playing. Alternatives: Select **Play, Fast Forward,** or press **Ctrl+Shift+F.**

- **Turn shuffle on/off**   Toggles shuffle mode on and off. Shuffle mode means that an audio CD's tracks play in random order. Alternatives: Select **Play, Shuffle** or press **Ctrl+H.**

And here are a few juicy tidbits you might want to keep in mind:

- To get a DVD up and running, either select it from the media list (refer to Figure 9.2) or select **Play, DVD or CD Audio.** (If you have multiple drives in your system, select the DVD drive from the menu that appears.)

- If you want to control the volume of the other sounds that Windows XP makes (such as its opening theme music), first select **Start, Control Panel.** Click **Sounds, Speech, and Audio Devices** and then click **Adjust the system volume.** In the dialog box that appears, use the **Device volume** slider to raise or lower Windows' voice.

> **Windows Wisdom**
>
> Some audio CDs do double-duty as data CDs and come with programs you can run. In some cases, the program will run automatically when you insert the CD. So be forewarned that after you insert an audio CD, you may see something other than (or in addition to) Media Player on the screen.

- If you want a media file to play over and over, activate the **Play, Repeat** command (or press **Ctrl+T**).

Messing with Media Player's Audio CD Features

If you like to listen to music while you use your computer, the typical MIDI file isn't likely to set your toes a-tapping. No, if it's *real* music you're after, you need to convince Media Player to crank up an audio CD. Audio CDs use the same dimensions as CD-ROM discs, so any audio CD will fit snugly inside your CD drive (or your DVD drive, if you have one). From there, you use Media Player to play the CD's tracks.

Let's run through a few notes to bear in mind when playing audio CDs in Media Player. First, Media Player can access information about a CD over the Internet:

- If your computer is connected to the Internet when you insert the disc, Media Player will automatically reach out and grab various bits of data about the CD: its title, the name of the performer or group, the name and length of each track, and more.

◆ If you connect to the Internet after the disc is already playing, you can get the disc info by clicking **Copy from CD** in the taskbar and then clicking **Get Names.** When Media Player shows the disc data, check it out to make sure it's the right CD. If it is, click **Confirm** to save the data. If you want to make changes to the information, click **Edit,** make your changes in the text boxes that appear, and then click **Finish.** In most cases you need to eject and then re-insert the disc for the changes to take effect.

◆ If Media Player doesn't recognize your disc at all, it will start up a wizard that will ask you for information about the disc and then attempt to locate the disc info on the Internet. If the wizard finds the data, great: Just follow the wizard to the end. Otherwise, click **Not Found** and then enter the disc data by hand.

As an added and slightly surprising bonus, the list of tracks that appears in both the Now Playing section and the Copy from CD section is customizable:

◆ If Media Player can't get the name of a track, or if you want to change the existing name, right-click the track and then click **Edit.** Type in the new name and then press **Enter.**

◆ If you have a track that you particularly dislike, you can ask Media Player to bypass it during playback by right-clicking the track and then clicking **Disable Select Tracks.**

◆ To change the order in which Media Player spins the tracks, right-click any track and then click either **Move Up** or **Move Down.** You can also change the order of the tracks by using your mouse to track them up and down in the playlist.

Hard Disk Rock: Copying Tracks from a CD

Media Player's audio CD playback is flexible, for sure, but playing audio CDs suffers from two important drawbacks:

◆ Shuffling discs in and out of the drive can be a hassle.

◆ There isn't any way to mix tunes from two or more CDs into a single playlist, even if your system has multiple CD and/or DVD drives.

To solve these dilemmas, the Windows XP version of Media Player enables you to copy individual tracks from one or more CDs and store them on your computer's hard disk. From there, you can create a custom playlist that combines the tracks in any order you like.

Before I show you how you go about copying tracks from an audio CD, let's take a second to set a few options related to track copying. In the Media Player window, select the **Tools, Options** command to display the Options dialog box and then select the **Copy Music** tab.

Here's what you can do in this tab:

♦ **Change the location of the copied tracks**   The default location is your My Music folder. Note that Media Player creates a new subfolder for the artist and then uses that to create another subfolder for the CD. Your best bet is to leave this as is, but if you want to change the location, click the **Change** button.

♦ **Set the file name format for the tracks**   By default, Media Player stores the tracks using file names of the form *nn Song Name*, where *nn* is the two-digit track number and *Song Name* is the title of the song. To change that, click **Advanced** (or click **File Name** in Media Play 9) to open the File Name Options dialog box. Activate the check box beside each item you want to include in the file name (such as the Artist name and the Album name).

♦ **Changing the file format**   The default format for the copied tracks is Windows Media Audio. If your computer supports other formats (such as MP3), you'll be able to use the **File format** list to select a different format. If you want to use MP3 but you can't select it in the list, click the **MP3 Information** button (or the **Learn more about MP3 formats** link in Media Player 9) to get data from Microsoft on how to enable the MP3 format.

♦ **Changing the audio quality**   The quality of the copied files is proportional to the acreage they consume on your hard disk. That is, the higher the quality, the fatter the file. Use the **Copy music at this quality** slider (it's called **Audio quality** in Media Player 9) to choose which quality level you want. Each level is measured in kilobits per second (Kbps), where there are 8 bits in a byte and 1,024 bytes in a kilobyte (KB). To help you decide, here's a summary of each quality level for the WMA format and how much disk space it will usurp in kilobytes per minute and megabytes (MB; 1,025 kilobytes) per hour:

Kbps	KB/Minute	MB/Hour
48	360	21
64	480	28
96	720	42
128	960	56
160	1,200	70
192	1,440	84

Click **OK** when you've made your choices.

To do the actual copying, follow these steps:

1. Insert the audio CD from which you want to copy.

2. Display the **Copy from CD** section.

3. For each track that you want to copy, activate the check box to the left of the track number.

4. Click **Copy Music.** Media Player starts the copy process, which you can monitor by watching the **Copy Status** column (see Figure 9.3).

Click here to toggle every check box on or off

Figure 9.3

Use the Copy from CD section to copy audio CD tracks to your hard disk.

Becoming a Program Director: Creating a Custom Playlist

Once you've copied a mess of CD tracks to your hard disk, you're free to combine these tracks and play them in any order. If you just want to play an individual track, here's the easiest way to go about it:

1. Display the **Media Library** section.

2. Open the **Audio** branch.

3. Open one of the sub-branches: Album, Artist, or Genre.

4. Click the album, artist, or genre that contains the track you want (see Figure 9.4).

5. Double-click the track.

Figure 9.4

To play an individual track from the Media Library, find the track you want and then double-click it.

Rather than playing single tracks using this method, you might prefer to combine multiple tracks into a *playlist*. You can then select the playlist and Media Player will play all the tunes for you automatically.

The first thing you need to do is create a new playlist:

1. Click **New Playlist** to display the New Playlist dialog box.

2. Type a descriptive name in the **Enter the new playlist name** text box.

3. Click **OK.** Media Player creates the playlist and displays it in the Media Library's My Playlists branch.

Windows Wisdom

The techniques in this section apply equally to MP3 files and other music files that you download from the Internet.

With that done, use the following techniques to work with the playlist:

◆ **Adding a song to the playlist**   Find the file in the Audio branch and highlight it. Click **Add to Playlist** and then click the name of the playlist you want to use.

◆ **Removing a song from the playlist**   Open the **My Playlists** branch and highlight the playlist. Right-click the song and then click **Delete from Playlist.**

◆ **Changing the playlist order**   Open the **My Playlists** branch and highlight the playlist. Then use your mouse to drag the songs up or down in the list.

Windows Wisdom

You can create a quick playlist from the My Music folder by opening it and clicking the WebView panel's **Play all** link. For a more specific list, create a new subfolder and then copy or move all the music files that you want in your playlist to that folder. Open the folder and click the **Play all** link.

◆ **Playing a playlist**   Open the **My Playlists** branch, highlight the playlist, and then click the **Play** button.

◆ **Renaming a playlist**   Open the **My Playlists** branch, right-click the playlist, and then click **Rename.** Type in the new name and then press **Enter.**

◆ **Deleting a playlist**   Open the **My Playlists** branch, right-click the playlist, and then click **Delete.**

Rollin' Your Own Music: Copying Tracks to a CD or Device

Listening to music while working on your computer is loads of fun, but I certainly hope you don't spend every waking minute in front of your PC. When it's time to get away, why not take some of your digital music with you? Sure you can. Windows XP's version of Media Player can perform the neat trick of copying music files from your computer to a CD-R disc or to a portable digital music player. Here's how it works:

1. Select the **Copy to CD or Device** section.

2. The Music to Copy list holds the music selections from your Media Library. Select the item (playlist, genre, album, or artist) that contains the music you want to copy.

Look Out!

Remember that once Media Player finishes writing to a CD-R disc, it "closes" the disc, which means that you can never write anything else to the disc. Therefore, make sure you have enough music available to fill up the CD-R (about 70 minutes) so as not to waste space on the disc.

3. Activate the check boxes beside the tracks that you want to copy. Make sure that the total number of megabytes (or minutes, if you're recording to a CD-R disc) that you select isn't greater than the total number of megabytes (or minutes) available on the recording device (see Figure 9.5).

4. Use the **Music on Device** list to select the drive or device that you want to use to store the tracks.

5. Click **Copy to Music.**

Make sure this total …   … doesn't exceed this total

Figure 9.5

In the Media Library, open the Audio branches until you get to the song you want to play or work with.

Web Waves: Listening to Internet Radio

Hundreds of radio stations are sending their signals over the Net, and Media Player can tune in to many of them. First, click **Radio Tuner** in the taskbar. The **PRESETS** list shows some stations defined by Media Player. To hear a station, highlight it and then click **Play.**

Media Player also enables you to create a custom list. To add your own stations, first select **My Presets** in the **PRESETS** list. Now move over to the **STATION FINDER** side of the window and use the **Find By** list to choose how you want to search for a station (such as by format or location). Use the controls that appear to enter your search criteria and run the search. Click the station you want and then click the **<<<** button to put the station in your presets list.

Assigning Sounds to Things Windows XP Does

As you work with Windows XP, you'll hear various beeps and boops in response to certain events, such as when some dialog boxes appear and when a new e-mail message arrives. Although you might think all these sounds are set in stone, it turns out that you can control not only which sounds play in response to which events, but whether Windows XP plays *any* sounds at all.

To change the sound that plays for a Windows event, follow these steps:

1. Select **Start, Control Panel,** click **Sounds, Speech, and Audio Devices** and then click **Change the sound scheme.** You eventually end up at the Speech and Audio Devices Properties dialog box.

Windows Wisdom

Not sure what a particular sound sounds like? No problem: Just click the **Play** button (the right-pointing arrow), and Windows XP will give you a preview of the sound.

2. Use the **Program events** list to highlight the event you want to work with. (If an event has a volume icon beside it, it means a sound is associated with that event.)

3. Use the **Sounds** list to select the sound you want played when the event occurs. If you'd prefer blissful silence, select **(None).** If the sound you want doesn't appear in the list, click **Browse** to pick out the sound file using a dialog box.

In addition to changing the sounds for individual events, you can also work with entire *sound schemes* that control many events at once. Windows XP offers two methods for dealing with sound schemes:

◆ **To select a predefined sound scheme**   Use the **Sound scheme** list. If you want to put a gag on Windows XP, select the **No Sounds** scheme.

◆ **To create your own custom sound scheme**   Begin by associating sounds to the various events you want to hear. After that's done, click **Save As,** enter a catchy name for the new scheme, and then click **OK.**

When you've completed your sound labors, click **OK** to confirm everything.

The Least You Need to Know

◆ Multimedia files come in five generic flavors: sound files (such as wave, WMA, and MP3), animation files, movie files, audio CD tracks, and DVD movies.

◆ The Media Player program can handle almost any kind of multimedia file. To use it, launch the Start menu's **Windows Media Player** icon or double-click a file.

◆ In most cases, your audio CDs and DVDs will start playing automatically after you insert the disc.

◆ Before copying audio CD tracks to your computer, your first task should be to choose the quality setting you want. To do this, select **Tools, Options** and use the **Copy Music** tab's **Copy music at this quality** slider.

10

Avoiding Fistfights While Sharing Your Computer

In This Chapter

◆ Creating accounts for each person who uses your computer

◆ Understanding the differences between administrators and limited accounts

◆ Setting up accounts with passwords and custom pictures

◆ Sharing and hiding your documents

Do you share your computer with other people either at work or at home? Then you've probably run smack dab into one undeniable fact: People are individuals with minds of their own! One person prefers Windows in a black-and-purple color scheme; another person just loves the far out "Vortec space" wallpaper; yet another person prefers to have a zillion shortcuts on the Windows desktop; and, of course, *everybody* uses a different mix of applications and creates their own documents. How can you possibly satisfy all these diverse tastes and prevent people from coming to blows?

Well, it's a lot easier than you might think. Windows XP enables you to set up a different *user account* for each person who uses the computer.

These accounts keep your stuff separate from everyone else's stuff, which includes not only documents and programs, but also the desktop and Start menu configuration, Internet Explorer favorites, and more. This means that each person can customize Windows XP to their heart's content without foisting their tastes on anyone else. This chapter shows you how to set up, maintain, and use Windows XP's user accounts.

Understanding Windows XP's New User Accounts

Previous versions of the "consumer" line of Windows (Windows Me, Windows 98, and so on) tried various methods for letting people share a computer. There was one problem, however: Those methods didn't work very well! In Windows XP, Microsoft is giving it another shot with something called *user accounts* and the good news is that this time it looks like they finally got it right.

> **Jargon Jar**
>
> The **user accounts** feature is part of Windows XP Home, and you also get it if you use Windows XP Pro either on its own or on a small, noncorporate network. If you use Windows XP Pro on a corporate network (technically, a network where your computer is part of a **domain**), then setting up users is part of the network user setup.

In a sense, a user account gives each person their own version of Windows XP that they can muck around with as they see fit. This includes the following:

- All the customization stuff covered in Part 5 of the book. This means that each user can set up his or her own colors, wallpaper, and screen saver, customize a toolbar, and change the icons that appear on the Start menu.

- Favorite websites defined in Internet Explorer.

- E-mail and newsgroup accounts set up in Outlook Express.

Not only that, but Windows XP also supports a new doohickey called *fast user switching*. What this means is that different users can switch in and out of Windows while leaving their programs running. For example, suppose little Alphonse is blowing away some aliens and Dad needs to check his e-mail. In the old days, Alphonse would have to shut down his game so that Dad could log on and run his e-mail program. In Windows XP, Alphonse can leave his game running while Dad switches to his account and does his e-mail duties. Alphonse can then switch back right away and resume doing nasty things to strange creatures.

The last thing you need to know before getting started is that Windows XP offers two different user account types:

♦ **Computer administrator**   This type of account has full access to the computer. The administrator can install any type of program or device, make changes that affect the entire system, access the documents created by all users, and add, change, and delete user accounts.

♦ **Limited**   This type of account has access to only some of the computer's features. It can view its own files, view those files that have been set up to be shared with other users, perform their own customizations, and change their password.

The idea here is that you set up only the most trusted or competent users (such as yourself, of course, and maybe, just *maybe*, your spouse) as administrators and you set up everyone else (such as the kids) as limited users.

Creating a New Account

When you or some suitably savvy geek set up Windows XP on your computer, the installation program asked for the name of one or more users. At the very least, a computer administrator account will have been created for the person who has overall responsibility for the machine, and a "Guest" account will have been created for temporary users of the machine.

If there were other accounts created, you'll see the Windows XP Welcome screen each time you start the computer (refer to Figure 1.1). If you don't see that screen, then only the one account was created. In any case, if you're the administrator, then you're free to add more accounts as you see fit.

Here are the steps to follow:

1. Select **Start, Control Panel** to open the Control Panel window and then click **User Accounts.** Windows XP sends the User Accounts window over to you.

2. Click **Create a new account.** This launches a wizard to guide you through the process.

3. In the first wizard window, use the **Type a name for the new account** text box to enter a name for the user and then click **Next.**

4. Choose an account type—**Computer administrator** or **Limited**—and then click **Create Account.**

Changing an Existing Account

If you need to make changes to a user account, what you can do depends on your account type:

- ◆ **If you're an administrator**   You can change anything about any account, including the user's name, password, picture, and account type. You can also delete any account.

- ◆ **If you're a limited user**   You can only change your own account and there are only three tasks you can perform: creating or changing a password, changing your picture, and setting up a .NET passport.

In either case, you get started by selecting **Start, Control Panel** to open the Control Panel window and then clicking **User Accounts** to return to the User Accounts window. If you're an administrator, click the icon for the user you want to work with. The next few sections run through the instructions for all the available tasks.

Changing the User's Name

If a user doesn't like the name you supplied, or if they've changed their name or joined a cult, it's not a problem to supply them with a new name that's more to their liking. If you're one of the poobah administrators, here's what you do to change the user's name:

1. Click **Change user name.**

2. In the **Type a new name for** *User* text box (where *User* is the user's current name), enter the new name for the user.

3. Click **Change Name.**

Creating an Account Password

After you go to all this trouble to set up separate user accounts, you'll likely be shocked and appalled to discover a dismaying fact: Any other user can log on to your account just by selecting it in the Welcome screen. To get around this, you can protect your things with a password.

Here are the steps to cruise through to set a password for the selected account:

1. Click **Create a password.**

2. Use the **Type a new password** text box to enter the password for the user. (Note that you see a bunch of dots instead of the actual characters you type. This is a security feature to prevent someone from spying the password.)

3. Use the **Type the new password again to confirm** text box to enter the password once again.

4. Use the **Type a word or phrase to use as a password hint** text box to enter a password. This word or phrase is accessible in the Welcome screen and is visible to all and sundry. Therefore, make the hint as vague as possible while still being useful to you if you forget your password.

5. Click **Create password.**

> **CAUTION**
>
> **Look Out!**
>
> If you store sensitive data on your computer (or just don't want someone to snoop), then you should think carefully about the password you choose. That is, don't use an obvious word (such as your name), use words that are at least five characters long (the longer the better), and mix uppercase and lowercase letters and toss in a number or two.

Once you've created a password, the user account window sprouts two new tasks:

◆ **Change the password** (or **Change my password,** if it's your own account) Click this link to change the password. Note that you need to enter the old password before Windows XP sets the new one.

◆ **Remove the password** (or **Remove my password,** if it's your own account) Click this link to stop using a password. (Again, you need to enter your existing password first.)

Changing the User's Picture

User accounts isn't the most exciting topic in the computing world, so it's a welcome relief that Windows XP includes a feature that lets you have a bit of fun: You can assign a picture to each user. This picture is visible in the Welcome screen and on the top of the Start menu when the user is logged on. Windows XP supplies a random picture when you create an account, but here's how you change it to something else:

1. Click **Change the picture** (or **Change my picture** if this is your account). Windows XP displays a selection of pictures, as shown in Figure 10.1.

2. Click the picture you want and then click **Change Picture.** If you have your own picture, click **Browse for more pictures,** use the Open dialog box to find the image you want, and then click **Open.**

Figure 10.1

Use this window to select a picture for the user's account.

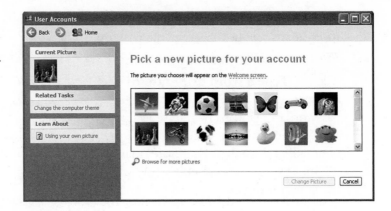

Changing the Account Type

If you want to promote a trusted user to administrator status, or if you want to demote some miscreant to limited status, it's not hard:

1. Click **Change the account type.**

2. Activate either **Computer administrator** or **Limited.**

3. Click **Change Account Type.**

Setting Up Your Account with a .NET Passport

In 2000, Microsoft announced what is by far its most ambitious project yet: Microsoft. NET. The idea behind .NET is both big and bold: to enable you to access your documents, e-mail messages, web favorites, and other digital essentials no matter where you are and no matter what device you have in front of you. As this book went to press, the Microsoft programmers were busy making this vision a reality, so the specifics of .NET weren't available. However, the one thing we do know is that you're going to need a *passport* from Microsoft as your point of entry into this new system.

Look Out!

A **passport** is a .NET feature that gives you access to web sites and other online locations that support Microsoft.NET.

To associate a passport with your account, click your icon in the User Accounts window and then click **Set up my account to use a .NET Passport.** This launches the .NET Passport Wizard. You now follow these steps:

1. The opening wizard window just offers an overview of what a passport is, so click **Next** to move along. You now come to a fork in the wizard's road, and the

path you take depends on whether you have a Microsoft e-mail account (click **Next** when you're done):

- ◆ **Yes, use an existing e-mail account**   Activate this option if you already have an account with Hotmail, MSN, or Passport.com.

- ◆ **No, create a new free e-mail account for my default Windows Passport** Activate this option if you don't have a Microsoft e-mail account. Clicking Next launches Internet Explorer and takes you to the Hotmail site where you can register for an account. Follow the instructions on the page. When you're done, close Internet Explorer, return to the wizard, and click **Next**.

2. Use the **E-mail address or Passport** text box to enter your Microsoft e-mail address and then click **Next.**

3. Now the wizard asks for your **Password.** If you don't want to have to enter this info every time you log on to the Windows Messenger service, be sure to activate the **Sign me in automatically on this computer** check box. Click **Next** to keep on keeping on.

4. In the final wizard dialog box, click **Finish** to put a cap on things.

Deleting an Account

If you no longer need an account, you may as well delete it to reduce clutter in the User Accounts window. Here's how:

1. Click **Delete the account.** Windows XP asks if you want to keep the contents of the account's My Documents folder and desktop.

2. If you want to save these things, click **Keep Files** to store them in a new folder named after the user. Otherwise, click **Delete Files.**

3. Click **Delete Account.**

Logging On to an Account

Once you have two or more user accounts on the go (excluding the Guest account, that is), then each time you crank up Windows XP you'll see the Welcome screen, as shown earlier in the book in Figure 1.1. Click your user icon to log on to Windows. If the account is protected by a password, a text box will appear. In that case, enter the password and press **Enter.** (If you need to see your password hint, click the question mark button.)

Once you're logged on to an account, you can switch to another user by following these steps:

1. Select **Start, Log Off.** The Log Off Windows box appears.

2. Click one of the following buttons:

   ◆ **Switch User** Click this button if you want to leave the current user's windows and programs open and running. (This is the *fast user switching* feature that I mentioned earlier.)

   ◆ **Log Off** Click this button if you prefer to shut down all of the current user's windows and programs.

3. When the Welcome screen reappears, log on as a different user.

Sharing Documents with (and Hiding Them from) Other Users

Although you'll want to keep most of your documents to yourself, it's conceivable that you'll want other users to be able to see and work with some files. For example, you might scan in some family photos that you want everyone to see or you might store some music that you want other folks to hear.

Using the Shared Documents Folder

By far the easiest way to go about this is to take advantage of the special "shared" folders that Windows XP sets up automatically. To get to these folders, select **Start, My Documents** and then click **Shared Documents** in the Other Places section. The Shared Documents folder is the shared equivalent of My Documents, and it also includes two subfolders—Shared Music and Shared Pictures—that are the equivalent of My Music and My Pictures. If you move or copy a document into one of these folders, every user will be able to see and work with the file.

Sharing (or Keeping Private) My Documents

Access to a user's My Documents folder is controlled by the account type:

◆ If you're an administrator, you can access My Documents for any limited user.

◆ If you're a limited user, you can't access any other user's My Document folder.

However, it's possible to change this behavior. To see how, follow these steps:

1. Select **Start, My Computer.**

2. Click the toolbar's **Folders** button.

3. In the Folders bar, open the drive where Windows XP is installed (this is usually drive C), then open the **Documents and Settings** folder. The subfolders you see are where the user documents and computer settings are stored:

   ◆ The **All Users** subfolder is where the Shared Documents folder exists, along with the stuff everyone sees on the Start menu.

   ◆ There's also a subfolder for each user.

4. Right-click your subfolder and then click **Sharing and Security.** (If you're an administrator, you can do this to any of the user subfolders.) Windows XP launches the Properties dialog box for the folder with the Sharing tab displayed, as shown in Figure 10.2.

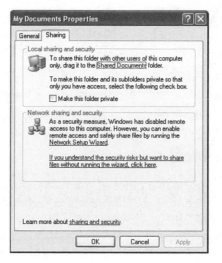

Figure 10.2

Use the Sharing tab to make a folder private or share it with others.

5. You have two choices:

   ◆ If you're a limited user and you don't want an administrator to be able to access your documents, activate the **Make this folder private** check box. If your account doesn't have a password, Windows XP asks if you want to create one. If you do, click **Yes** and then create a password as described earlier.

   ◆ If you're an administrator and you want limited users to be able to access your documents, deactivate the **Make this folder private** check box.

6. Click **OK.**

Making a Program Available Only to Specific Users

By default, if an administrator installs a program, it usually shows up on the Start menu's **All Programs** submenu and anyone can run it from there. That's usually a reasonable setup, but there may be times when you want to hide a program from one or more users. To do that, you need to manipulate the various Start menu icons by hand.

Here are the basic steps to follow:

1. Select **Start, My Computer.**

2. Click the toolbar's **Folders** button.

3. In the **Folders** bar, open the drive where Windows XP is installed (usually drive C), then open the **Documents and Settings** folder.

4. Open **All Users** and then **Start Menu,** then click **Programs.** You should now see a folder icon for the program you're dealing with. Right-click that folder's icon and then click **Cut.**

Cross-Reference

To manipulate the various Start menu icons by hand, see Chapter 21 (the section titled "A Smart Start: Reconstructing the Start Menu").

---

5. Open the subfolder of whatever user you want to have access to the program, then open **Start Menu** and click **Programs.** Select **Edit, Paste** to add the program's folder.

6. Repeat step 5 for any other user that you want to access the program.

The Least You Need to Know

◆ Windows XP supports two types of user: *administrators* who can pretty much do what they want, including install programs and devices, change system settings, access documents for all users, and work with user accounts; and *limited users* who can only view their own files, view shared files, and perform their own Windows customizations.

◆ The User Accounts window is where everything happens; you get there by selecting **Start, Control Panel, User Accounts.**

◆ To create a new user account, click **Create a new account** in the User Accounts window.

◆ To change a user's account doodads, open the User Accounts window and then click the user's icon.

◆ If you have important stuff you want to keep secure, add a password to your account and make sure that the password isn't an obvious word, is at least five characters long, and combines uppercase and lowercase letters and numbers.

◆ To switch to a different user, select **Start, Log Off,** click **Switch User,** and then click the user's icon.

Part 3

Windows XP at Work

Playing around with images and videos and music can be a heckuva lot of fun, but one of these days you've gotta get some work done. (Insert groan of disappointment here.) When the time comes for your nose and the grindstone to get reacquainted, Windows XP will be there for you with some competent business tools. The chapters in Part 3 look at the most commonly used of these tools. Chapter 11 covers Notepad and WordPad; Chapter 12 covers faxing; and Chapter 13 covers the Windows XP notebook features. Don't work too hard!

Prose Programs:
Windows XP's Writing Tools

In This Chapter

◆ Using Notepad for simple text tasks

◆ Using WordPad for full-bore word processing

◆ Techniques for automatically finding and replacing text

◆ Inserting ã, ö, ¢, ©, and other oddball characters

Windows XP comes with just about all the writing tools you'll ever pine for, whether you just need to dash off a quick to-do list or whether you need to compose a professional-looking letter or resumé. This chapter gives you the goods on these writing tools.

Before getting started, you should know that the written documents you deal with come in two flavors: plain and formatted. A plain document contains characters that have no special formatting: just plain, unadorned text. So, unshockingly, these types of documents are called *text files*. In the Windows XP world, you read, edit, and create text files using the Notepad text editor. A formatted document contains characters that have (or can have) formatting such as **bold** or *italics*. These types of documents are called *word processing files*. In Windows XP, you read, edit, and create word processing files using the WordPad word processor.

Notepad is the subject of the first part of this chapter, and I discuss WordPad's eccentricities a bit later (see the section "Using WordPad for Fancier Word Processing Files" later in this chapter). Note also that whether your computer comes stocked with Microsoft Word, Microsoft Works, or some other program, if you write a lot, you'll be better off using the other program rather than WordPad.

Using Notepad for Garden-Variety Text Files

If text files are so plain, why on earth would anyone want to use them? Perhaps you want to send a document to another person and you want to make sure they can open it. Most of the personal computers on the planet can deal with a text file, so that's your safest bet. If you used WordPad, on the other hand, your friend has to have WordPad (or a relatively recent version of Microsoft Word) installed to open the file. Another reason to use a text file is that perhaps you need to create a document that *must* be plain text. For example, if you want to create a web page from scratch, you have to save it as a text file; a word processing file won't work.

Just about anyone using just about any PC can read a text file. This universality means that you'll get a lot of text files coming your way. For example, if you examine the installation disk of most programs, you'll almost always see at least one text file with a name like "Readme" or "Setup." This file usually contains information about the installation process (such as how to prepare for the install and how the install operates), last-minute changes to the manual, and so on.

You can identify these and other text files by the icon they use in My Computer. Figure 11.1 points out a couple of text files. When you see the text file icon, double-click the file to open it in Notepad.

These are WordPad files   These are text files

Figure 11.1

Windows XP shows text files using a special icon.

This icon means Windows XP has no idea what the file is

If you need to create a text file, begin by opening Notepad: **Start, All Programs, Accessories, Notepad.** Figure 11.2 shows the window that materializes on your screen.

Figure 11.2

Notepad: a simple window for a simple type of file.

As you can see, Notepad sports a plain, no-frills look that perfectly matches the plain, no-frills text files you work with. There's nary a bell or whistle in sight, and even the menus contain, for the most part, just a bare-bones collection of commands: New, Open, Save, Cut, Copy, Paste, and so on. Dullsville. That's okay, though, because that's the nature of the Notepad beast. You just fire it up and then read, type, and edit as necessary. However, Notepad is not without its small quirks and one-of-a-kind features. Here's a summary:

> **Windows Wisdom**
>
> If you come across a text file that doesn't have the proper icon, you can talk Notepad into attempting to open the file by highlighting the file and then selecting **File, Open With** to get to the Open With dialog box. Highlight **Notepad** in the list, and then click **OK**. If you see gobbledygook instead of words and phrases, then it wasn't a text file.

- ◆ **Inserting the date and time**   To plop the current date and time into your text file, select the **Edit, Time/Date** command (or press **F5**).

- ◆ **Wrapping text**   When you type in most normal programs and the cursor hits the right edge of the window, the cursor automatically jumps down one line and starts again on the left edge of the window (this feature is known as *word wrap*). But not Notepad, no. It just blithely continues along the same line for exactly 1,024 characters, and only *then* will it wrap onto the next line. Dumb! To avoid this annoyance, activate the **Format, Word Wrap** command.

- ◆ **Opening other files**   I mentioned earlier that some text files don't have the Notepad icon. Unfortunately, if you select Notepad's **File, Open** command, the Open dialog box only shows files with that icon. To see other text files, go to the **Files of type** drop-down list at the bottom of the dialog box and select the **All Files** option.

◆ **Tweaking the page** The **File, Page Setup** command displays the dialog box shown in Figure 11.3. You can use this dialog box to set various page layout and printing options, including the paper size and orientation, the size of each margin, and text that you want printed in each page's Header and Footer. (The **&f** thingy tells Notepad to print the name of the file, and the **&p** combo tells it to print each page number. You can also enter **&d** to print the current date, **&t** to print the current time, and **&l, &c,** or **&r** to align the header or footer text on the left, center, or right, respectively.)

Figure 11.3

Use the Page Setup dialog box to spell out various page layout and printing options for Notepad.

◆ **What's up with the Font command?** Despite what I said about text files not using formatting, Notepad sports a Font command on its Format menu. What gives? I assure you I wasn't lying: That command can and should be ignored because regular text files *don't* use fonts. However, Windows XP does support a special type of text file that can use fonts. So if (and only if) you'll be sending your text file to another Windows XP (or Windows 2000) user, you can select a font (it applies to the entire document). When you go to save the file, make sure you open the **Encoding** list and select **Unicode**.

Using WordPad for Fancier Word Processing Files

Like Dorothy getting whisked from the black-and-white world of Kansas into the Technicolor world of Oz, we turn now to WordPad, Windows XP's word processor. To get this program down the electronic yellow brick road, select **Start, All Programs, Accessories, WordPad.** Figure 11.4 shows the WordPad window. Unlike the Spartan expanse of Notepad, the WordPad window offers a well-appointed interior with lots of word processing amenities.

Toolbar   Format bar

Figure 11.4

The WordPad window gewgaws include a couple of toolbars and a ruler.

Ruler

WordPad and Word Processing Files

Here are a few notes to bear in mind when working with WordPad and its word processing files:

◆ **The WordPad file icon**   Like text files, WordPad files also have their own unique icon, as shown earlier in Figure 11.1. When you see a file with this icon, double-click it to load the file in WordPad.

◆ **What type of document do you want?**   When you select the **File, New** command, WordPad winds up and delivers the New dialog box to you. WordPad is wondering what type of document you want to create. You have three choices:

> **Rich Text Document**   This produces a file in the Rich Text Format (RTF, for short), which accepts all kinds of formatting. It's a standard format in computing circles, so it's readable by many other word processing programs. This is a good choice if you'll be sending the document to someone and you're not sure what program they'll be using.

> **Text Document**   This gets you a plain text file.

> **Unicode Text Document**   This is a relatively obscure type of text file that in all likelihood you'll never have to worry about.

◆ **Opening documents: Are you my file type?**   As you've seen, there are several different types of files that fall under the aegis of WordPad. Unfortunately, when you select the **File, Open** command, the Open dialog box only shows RTF files. If you're trying to open a different type (such as Word or text), you need to drop down the **Files of type** list and select either the type you need (such as **Word for Windows** or **Text Documents**) or **All Documents**.

♦ **Working on two files at once** WordPad's one-track mind means that it can only have one file open at a time. However, there will be plenty of times when you need to work with *two* files at once. For example, you might want to compare text in the two files, or you might want to copy or move text from one file to the other. No problemo! All you have to do is open up a second copy of WordPad and use it to open the second file.

Text-Selection Tricks

Before you can format, cut, or copy text, you first have to select it. I showed you the basic text-selection maneuvers in Chapter 4, but WordPad has a few extra techniques that can make your life a teensy bit easier:

♦ **To select a word** Double-click it.

♦ **To select a line** Click inside the narrow strip of white space to the left of the line (that is, between the line and the WordPad window's left border). In word processing circles, this strip is called the *selection area*.

♦ **To select a paragraph** Double-click the selection area beside the paragraph. (Those with energy to burn can also select a paragraph by *triple*-clicking inside the paragraph.)

♦ **To select the whole document** Hold down **Ctrl** and click anywhere inside the selection area. (You can also choose **Edit, Select All** or press **Ctrl+A**.)

Fancy-Schmancy Formatting I: Fonts

The whole point of using a word processor (as opposed to a text editor, such as our pal Notepad) is to turn dull-as-dishwater text into beautifully formatted prose that other people will be clamoring to read. Happily, WordPad offers quite a few formatting features that can turn even the plainest file into a document with text appeal.

Jargon Jar

A **font** is a style of text in which a unique design and other effects have been applied to all the characters.

In this section, you begin with the most common formatting makeover: the *font*. To begin, you need to decide whether you want to format existing text or text that you're about to type:

♦ **To format existing text** Select the text to which you want to apply the font.

♦ **To format new text** Position the cursor at the spot where the new typing will appear.

With that done, here are the steps to follow to apply the font:

1. Select WordPad's **Format, Font** command. The Font dialog box puts in an appearance.

2. Use the **Font** list to choose a typeface. The *typeface* is what most people think of when they use the word "font." It represents the distinctive design applied to all the characters. See Figure 11.5 for some examples. (Wondering what's up with all those typefaces that have the stylized "O" beside them? Those are *OpenType* typefaces and they generally display better than the other typefaces.)

3. Use the **Font style** list to select a style for the text (see Figure 11.5).

Figure 11.5

Some examples of the various font features.

4. Use the **Size** list to choose the font height you want to use. The various values are measured in *points*, where 72 points equals an inch (again, see Figure 11.5 for an example or two).

5. The **Effects** group is populated with three controls: activate the **Strikeout** check box to get ~~strikeout~~ characters; activate the **Underline** check box to format characters with an underline; and use the **Color** check box to change the color of the text.

6. The **Script** list tells you which language scripts are available for the selected typeface. You use these scripts to create multilingual documents. If you plan on using only English, leave this list set to **Western.**

7. Click **OK** to put the new font into effect.

Note, too, that WordPad offers a few toolbar shortcuts for many of these font tricks. Figure 11.5 points out the relevant lists and buttons and shows a few fonts in action.

Speaking of shortcuts, you'll be pleased to hear that WordPad also offers a small collection of keyboard combos for easier font fiddling. For example, to format text as **Bold,** press **Ctrl+B;** *Italic,* press **Ctrl+I;** and <u>Underline</u>, press **Ctrl+U.**

Installing New Fonts

Windows XP brings a few dozen fonts to the formatting table, which isn't bad. (Many programs install their own fonts, so your system may have more than that depending on what software you have installed.) However, there are plenty of font collections available on the market, and they generally cost only pennies a font. If you purchase one of these collections, you have to install it. To do that, follow these steps:

1. Select **Start, Control Panel,** click **Appearance and Themes,** and then click the **Fonts** link.

2. When the Fonts window appears, select **File, Install New Font** to open the Add Fonts dialog box.

3. Insert the font disc and select the appropriate drive in the **Drives** list.

4. After a few seconds, the available fonts on the disc will appear in the **List of fonts.**

5. Highlight the ones you want to install, and then click **OK.**

Fancy-Schmancy Formatting II: Paragraphs

Few things are as uninviting to read as a document that's nothing but wall-to-wall text. To give your readers a break (literally), divide up your text into separate paragraphs. (Press **Enter** once to start a new paragraph; press **Enter** twice to give yourself a bit of breathing room between each paragraph.)

As a further measure, consider formatting your paragraphs. WordPad enables you to indent entire paragraphs, indent only the first line of a paragraph, and align your paragraphs with the margins. Here's how it works:

1. Place the cursor within the paragraph that you want to format.

2. Either select the **Format, Paragraph** command, or right-click the paragraph and then click **Paragraph.** WordPad coaxes the Paragraph dialog box onto the screen.

3. Use the **Left** text box to set how far (in inches) the text is indented from the left margin.

4. Use the **Right** text box to set how far (in inches) the text is indented from the right margin.

5. Use the **First line** text box to set how far (in inches) the first line of the paragraph is indented from the left margin.

6. Use the **Alignment** list to align the paragraph relative to either the left margin or the right margin, by selecting **Left** or **Right,** respectively. You can also select **Center,** which centers the paragraph evenly between both margins.

7. Click **OK.**

Figure 11.6 demonstrates a few of WordPad's paragraph formatting options.

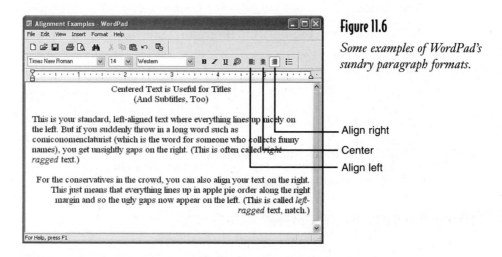

Figure 11.6

Some examples of WordPad's sundry paragraph formats.

Rather than messing around with inches for the various paragraph indents, try WordPad's ruler. The ruler has various markers that set the paragraph indents (see Figure 11.7). Here's a rundown of what they do:

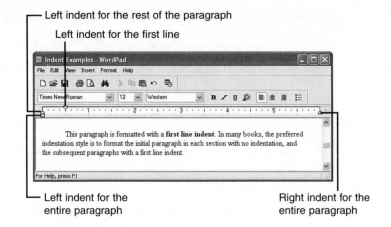

Figure 11.7

WordPad's ruler can make paragraph formatting a breeze.

Left indent for the rest of the paragraph

Left indent for the first line

Left indent for the entire paragraph

Right indent for the entire paragraph

◆ **Left indent for the first line**   Indents the paragraph's first line from the left margin.

◆ **Left indent for the rest of the paragraph**   Indents the rest of the paragraph from the left margin.

◆ **Left indent for the entire paragraph**   Indents the entire paragraph from the left margin.

◆ **Right indent for the entire paragraph**   Indents the entire paragraph from the right margin.

To use these markers to format a paragraph, place the cursor inside the paragraph and then use your mouse to drag the appropriate marker left or right.

Fancy-Schmancy Formatting III: Bullets

When you need to include a list of points or items in your document, it's best to separate those items from the regular text by displaying each one in a separate paragraph. To make these items even easier to read, format them with a *bullet* out front, as shown in Figure 11.8. To use bullets, follow these steps:

Figure 11.8

An example of a bulleted list.

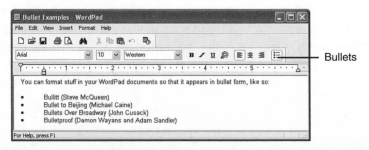

Bullets

1. If you want to turn an existing paragraph into the first item in a bulleted list, first place the cursor anywhere within the paragraph. If you want to convert several paragraphs to bullets, select the paragraphs.

2. Turn on bullets by activating the **Format, Bullet Style** command. (You can also click the **Bullets** toolbar button or right-click the paragraph and then click **Bullet Style.**)

3. To create a new bulleted item, move to the end of the last bulleted item and press **Enter.** WordPad dutifully creates another bullet.

4. Enter the text for the new bullet.

5. Repeat steps 3 and 4 until you've entered all your bulleted items.

6. Press **Enter** twice to tell WordPad to knock off the bulleted style.

Fancy-Schmancy Formatting IV: Tabs

If you place the cursor on a blank line and press **Tab,** you'll notice that the cursor leaps ahead by exactly half an inch. Press **Tab** again, and you get another half-inch jump. These half-inch intervals are known as *tab stops*, and they're great for making columns or tables that line up like a precision drill team.

WordPad goes one better by enabling you to set your own tab stops anywhere you like. The easiest way to do this is via the ruler. To begin, place the cursor inside the paragraph that you want to mess with. Here are the techniques to use:

♦ **To set a tab stop** Move your mouse pointer into the ruler at the spot where you want the tab stop to appear, and then click. WordPad adds what looks like a small "L" to the ruler; that's your tab stop.

♦ **To move a tab stop** Use your mouse to drag the tab stop marker left or right.

♦ **To delete a tab stop** Use your mouse to drag the tab stop marker off the ruler.

Just for the record, there *is* a hard way to set the tabs: Select the **Format, Tabs** command to display the **Tabs** dialog box. In this case, you enter the position (in inches) where you want the tab to appear and then click **Set.** In addition, clicking the **Clear All** button removes all the tabs from the current paragraph or selection.

Finding and Replacing Text

In Chapter 5, I showed you how to use Windows XP's Search feature to find a file needle in a hard disk haystack. However, what if the haystack is a huge, multipage document and the needle is a word or phrase? Not to worry: Windows XP has a solution. It's called the Find feature, and it's part of both Notepad and WordPad.

Here's how it works:

1. In Notepad or WordPad, open the document you want to search, if it isn't open already.

2. Select the **Edit, Find** command (or press **Ctrl+F**). The Find dialog box punches in.

3. Use the **Find what** text box to enter the word or phrase you want to find.

4. (WordPad only) Activate the **Match whole word only** check box to force Find to match only the exact word or phrase you entered in step 3. If you leave this option deactivated, Find looks for text that *includes* the word or phrase. For example, if your search text is *waldo* and this check box is deactivated, Find will match not only the name *Waldo*, but also words such as *Waldorf* and *Oswaldo*.

5. Activate the **Match case** check box to run a *case-sensitive* search. This means that Find matches only those words or phrases that exactly match the uppercase and lowercase letters you used in your search text. For example, if your search text is *Bill* and you activate this check box, Find will match the name *Bill* and will ignore the word *bill*.

6. Click the **Find Next** button to let Find loose. If it finds a match, it highlights the text. If that's not what you wanted, click **Find Next** again to resume the search; otherwise, click **Cancel** to shut down the dialog box. If Find fails to ferret out a match, it will display a dialog box to let you know the bad news.

7. If you end up back in the document and realize that the found text was not the instance you needed after all, you don't have to fire up the Find dialog box all over again. Instead, either select the **Edit, Find Next** command, or press **F3**. Find simply repeats your last search from the current position.

Instead of merely finding some text, a more common editing chore is to find some text and then replace it with something else. For example, you may have written "St." throughout a document and you want to change each instance to "Street." The Replace feature makes these kinds of adjustments a snap:

1. In Notepad or WordPad, open the document you want to work with, if necessary.

2. Select the **Edit, Replace** command. (Alternatively, you can press **Ctrl+H.**) This gets you face-to-face with the Replace dialog box.

3. The Replace dialog box is pretty much the same as the Find dialog box, except that it has an extra **Replace with** text box. You use this text box to enter the word or phrase with which you want to replace whatever's in the **Find what** text box.

Look Out!

The Replace All feature can save you oodles of time, but use it with care. For example, you might think it's safe to replace all instances of "St." with "Street," but the sentence "He went last." might end up as "He went lastreet." (This is a good example of when the Match case option would come in handy.)

4. Enter the other searching options, as needed.

5. You now have two choices:

   ◆ If you want to replace only selected matches, click **Find Next**. Again, Find highlights the text if it zeroes in on a match. To replace the highlighted text with what's in the Replace with box, click **Replace.** Repeat this until you've finished all the replacements.

   ◆ If you prefer to replace every instance of the Find what text with the Replace with text, click **Replace All.**

Using Character Map for Foreign Characters and Other Symbols

If you need to use a symbol such as © or £ in a document, or if you want to spell a word such as resumé with the requisite accent, don't go hunting around your keyboard because you won't find what you need. Instead, spread open the Character Map program and use it to copy all the strange and exotic symbols and characters you require. Here's how it works:

1. Select **Start, All Programs, Accessories, System Tools, Character Map.** This opens the Character Map window shown in Figure 11.9.

2. Use the **Font** list to pick out a typeface to work with. (Hint: For foreign characters and some common symbols, select any regular typeface; for other symbols, try the Webdings, Wingdings, or Symbol typefaces.)

3. Select the symbol you want by clicking it and then clicking **Select** (you can also double-click the symbol). The symbol appears in the Characters to copy box.

4. Click the **Copy** button to copy the character.

5. Return to WordPad or Notepad, position the cursor where you want the character to appear, and select the **Edit, Paste** command (or press **Ctrl+V**).

When you click a symbol to highlight it, you may see a **Keystroke** listed in the lower-right corner of the window (see Figure 11.9). This means that you can bypass Character Map and enter the symbol directly by pressing the keystroke in your application. Note, however, that you must enter the numbers using your keyboard's numeric keypad.

Figure 11.9

Use Character Map to get foreign characters, currency signs, zodiac signs, and lots more silly symbols.

Clicking a symbol gives this magnified view.

If the symbol has a keyboard shortcut, it appears here.

The Least You Need to Know

◆ Use Notepad (**Start, All Programs, Accessories, Notepad**) for plain text files, and use WordPad (**Start, All Programs, Accessories, WordPad**) for formatted word processing files.

◆ To avoid frustration in Notepad, always activate the **Format, Word Wrap** command to ensure that text wraps inside the Notepad window.

◆ Don't forget to use WordPad's ruler when setting indents and tabs. It's much easier to drag the indent markers or click and drag tab stops than to do everything via the dialog boxes.

◆ Use the Character Map program (**Start, All Programs, Accessories, System Tools, Character Map**) whenever you need foreign characters or symbols that aren't on your keyboard.

Fax-It-Yourself: Using the Windows XP Faxing Features

In This Chapter

- ◆ Getting Windows XP ready for faxing
- ◆ Sending a fax message
- ◆ Creating custom fax cover pages
- ◆ Receiving incoming faxes
- ◆ Annotating received faxes

Nowadays, faxing is just another humdrum part of the workaday world, and any business worth its salt has a fax machine on standby. Increasingly, however, dedicated fax machines are giving way to *fax/modems*—modems that have the capability to send and receive faxes in addition to their regular communications duties. Not only does this make faxing affordable for small businesses and individuals, but it also adds a new level of convenience to the whole fax experience.

You can send faxes right from your computer without having to print the document. Because faxes sent via computer aren't scanned (as they are with a fax machine), the document that the recipient gets is sharper and easier to read. And, you can use your printer to get a hard copy of a fax on regular paper, thus avoiding fax paper (which, besides being inherently slimy, has an annoying tendency to curl; fortunately, most newer fax machines can handle regular paper).

If you want to enjoy the fax fast lane from the comfort of your computer, look no further than the fax service from Windows XP. This chapter shows you how to install and configure the fax service, and how to use it to send and receive faxes.

Setting Up Windows XP to Do the Faxing Thing

Windows XP isn't fax-ready right out of the box. To convince XP that, yes, you *really* want to send and receive faxes, you need to set up and configure the fax service.

The first step is to install the fax service:

1. Select **Start, Control Panel** to open the Control Panel window.

2. Click **Printers and Other Hardware.**

3. Click **Printers and Faxes.** The Printers and Faxes window shows up.

> **CAUTION**
>
> **Look Out!**
>
> Only a user who is set up as an administrator can install the fax service in Windows XP.

4. Click **Set up faxing.** The Windows Components Wizard kicks in.

5. If you see the Insert Disk dialog box at this point, insert your Windows XP CD, wait 5 or 10 seconds, and then click **OK.**

The wizard then takes quite a while to install the fax service. When the wizard has completed its labors, it drops you off back at the Printers and Faxes window where a new **Fax** icon appears, as shown in Figure 12.1.

Figure 12.1

After you set up the fax service, a new Fax icon appears in the Printers and Faxes window.

With that out of the way, wipe the digital dirt from your hand and get ready for the next step, configuring the fax service. Here it goes:

1. In the Printers and Faxes window, double-click the **Fax** icon. The first time you do this, the Fax Configuration Wizard leaps onto the desktop.

2. The first wizard dialog box is as useful as a screen door in a submarine, so click **Next.** The wizard displays the Sender Information dialog box.

3. Use this dialog box to enter your name, fax number, address, and so on. Remember that this information will be added automatically to your fax cover pages, so only enter data that you want your fax recipients to eyeball. When you're done, click **Next.** You now see the Select Device for Sending or Receiving Faxes dialog box.

4. This dialog box has the following controls (click **Next** when you've made your choices):

   ♦ **Please select the fax device**   This is a list of the fax modems installed on your computer. If you have more than one, use the list to choose the one you want to perform the faxing chores.

   ♦ **Enable Send**   Leave this check box activated if you want to be able to send faxes from your computer.

   ♦ **Enable Receive**   Activate this check box if you want to be able to receive faxes on your computer. When this check box is activated, the following two controls come into play:

       Manual answer   Activate this option to answer incoming calls manually (as described later in this chapter).

       Automatically answer after *X* rings   Activate this option to have the service answer incoming calls automatically.

5. The wizard now prompts you for your *Transmitting Subscriber Identification*, or *TSID.* Enter the text (such as your name or your company name) and click **Next.**

6. If you elected to receive faxes, the wizard asks you for your Called Subscriber Identification, or CSID. This identifies your computer to the fax sender. This isn't as important as the TSID, so enter whatever you like and click **Next.**

Jargon Jar

Windows XP assigns a name to your fax machine. This is known in the trade as the **TSID—Transmitting Subscriber Identification** (or sometimes Transmitting Station Identifier). When the other person receives your fax, your TSID is displayed at the top of each page. If the other person is receiving on a computer, the TSID appears in the "TSID" line (or some similar field, depending on the program they're using). Unfortunately, the default TSID in Windows XP is "Fax," which redefines the word "uninspiring." To fix this, edit the TSID as described in step 5. (For example, it's common to change it to your company name, your department name, or your own name.)

Windows Wisdom

The Fax Console is also the place to go to change any of the fax configuration malarkey that you went through earlier. For example, to change your name, fax number, TSID, or other vital fax stats, select the **Tools, Sender Information** command. If you want to run through the entire Fax Configuration Wizard again, select the **Tools, Configure Fax** command.

7. If you'll be receiving faxes, the wizard now wonders what you want to do with incoming faxes (click **Next** when you're done):

 ◆ **Print it on** Activate this check box to have Windows XP automatically print any received fax. Use the list that becomes activated to choose the printer you want to use.

 ◆ **Store a copy in a folder** Activate this check box to store a second copy of each fax in the folder that you specify. The original copy of the fax is saved in the Fax Console, which you learn about in the next section.

8. Click **Finish.**

Checking Out the Fax Console

When the wizard exits the stage and the smoke clears, you end up with the Fax Console window on-screen, as shown in Figure 12.2. The Fax Console is where you'll do your fax work in Windows XP. It includes four "folders" that store fax-related things:

 ◆ **Incoming** This folder displays information about the fax that is currently being received. For example, during fax reception the **Status** column displays **In progress** and the **Extended Status** column displays **Answered** and then **Receiving.**

◆ **Inbox**   This folder stores the incoming faxes that were received successfully. Note that the TSID column shows the name or phone number of the sender.

◆ **Outbox**   This folder stores data about the fax that is currently being sent. For example, during the send the Status column displays In progress, and the Extended Status column displays Transmitting.

◆ **Sent Items**   This folder stores a copy of the faxes that were sent successfully.

Figure 12.2

The Fax Console is your home base for Windows XP faxing.

To get the Fax Console perched on your desktop again in the future, Windows XP gives you two methods:

◆ From the Printers and Faxes window, double-click the **Fax** icon.

◆ Select **Start, All Programs, Accessories, Communications, Fax, Fax Console.**

Using "Fax" as a Verb: Sending a Fax

To fax something to a friend or colleague (or, heck, even a total stranger), Windows XP gives you two ways to proceed:

◆ You can fax a simple note by sending just a cover page.

◆ You can fax a more complex document by sending it to Windows XP fax "printer."

Cross-Reference
For more information on dialing rules and locations, see Chapter 14, particularly the section titled "Locations, Locations, Locations: Setting Up Dialing Rules."

Let's start with the simple cover page route. This is handled by the Send Fax Wizard, which you can call in to work by using any of the following methods:

◆ From the Printers and Faxes window, click the WebView panel's **Send a fax** link. (Alternatively, select the **File, Send Fax** command.)

♦ In the Fax Console, select the **File, Send a Fax** command.

♦ Select **Start, All Programs, Accessories, Communications, Fax, Send a Fax.**

Here's what happens after the Send Fax Wizard arrives on the scene:

1. The initial dialog box isn't much use, so just click **Next** to get on with it. The Send Fax Wizard displays the Recipient Information dialog box, shown in Figure 12.3.

Figure 12.3

The Send Fax Wizard takes you through the steps necessary to send a simple cover page fax.

2. Fill in the following fields:

♦ **To**   Enter the name of the fax recipient.

♦ **Location**   If you're calling long distance and you need to start the dialing with a number other than 1, activate the **Use dialing rules** check box and then use the **Location** list to select the country code for the fax recipient's phone number.

♦ **Fax number**   Use these two text boxes to enter the area code (if necessary) and phone number for the fax recipient. (Note that you can't enter the area code unless you activate the **Use dialing rules** check box.)

♦ If you need to add details such as the recipient's company name, address, and phone number, click **Address Book,** click **New Contact,** and then use the tabs in the Properties dialog box to fill in all the information about the recipient. (Be sure to fill in the **Fax** field in either the **Business** tab or the **Home** tab.) Click **OK** when you're done. When you return to the Address Book, make sure the contact name is highlighted, click **To,** and then click **OK.**

3. Click **Add.** (This isn't necessary if you're sending the fax to a single recipient or if you inserted the recipient via the Address Book.)

4. If you want to send the fax to several people, repeat steps 2 and 3 as necessary.

5. When you're ready to move on, click **Next.** The Preparing the Cover Page dialog box muscles its way onto the screen.

6. Fill in the following fields (click **Next** when you're done):

    ◆ **Cover page template**   Select the cover page you want to use. (See the "Covering Your Fax: Creating a Fax Cover Page" section later in this chapter to find out about these predefined cover pages.)

    ◆ **Subject line**   Enter the subject of the fax.

    ◆ **Note**   Enter your message.

7. The wizard now pesters you for the time you want the fax sent (click **Next** when you're done):

    ◆ **Now**   Sends the fax ASAP.

    ◆ **When discount rates apply**   Sends the fax between 8 P.M. and 7 A.M.

    ◆ **Specific time in the next 24 hours**   Sends the fax at the specified time. (This is a spin box with a time value. To change the value, click the hour, minute, or seconds and then either type the value you want or click the arrows.)

8. In the final wizard dialog box, click **Preview Fax** to check out the fax in the Windows Picture and Fax Viewer.

9. When you're ready to ship the fax, click **Finish.** The Fax Monitor window replaces the wizard so that you can see what's happening with the fax.

Simple notes on a cover page are fine, but if you want to go beyond this, you have to take a different tack. Specifically, you have to use WordPad or some other program to create a document, and you then fax that document to the recipient. Here's how it works:

1. Create the document that you want to ship.

2. Select the program's **File, Print** command to get to the Print dialog box.

> **Cross-Reference**
>
> To learn about the editing buttons in the Windows Picture and Fax Viewer, see the "Annotating a Fax" section later in this chapter. To learn about the other buttons, see the section in Chapter 7 titled "A Closer Look: Previewing a Picture."

3. Select **Fax** as the printer (see Figure 12.4) and then click **Print.** Your old friend, the Send Fax Wizard, reappears.

Figure 12.4

To fax from a program, select Fax as the printer.

4. Follow the previously outlined steps to set the fax options. (Note that with this method you don't have to bother with a cover page. If you'd still like to include one, when you get to the Preparing the Cover Page dialog box, activate the **Select a cover page template ...** check box.)

Covering Your Fax: Creating a Fax Cover Page

You saw earlier that the Send Fax Wizard offers four prefab cover pages that you can use:

◆ **Confident** This cover page includes the word "confidential" on it, so it's useful for faxes that you want only the recipient to see.

◆ **Fyi** This cover page includes the phrase "FOR YOUR INFORMATION" on it, so use it for faxes that don't require a response.

◆ **Generic** This cover page has no extra text on it, so use it for basic faxes.

◆ **Urgent** This cover page includes the word "urgent" on it, so it's good for faxes that you want read and responded to as soon as possible.

If you're not exactly thrilled with these default pages, you can create your own pages from scratch.

To edit and create fax cover pages, Windows XP offers the Fax Cover Page Editor. To launch this program, select **Start, All Programs, Accessories, Communications, Fax, Fax Cover Page Editor.** (If the program displays a tip screen at startup, click **OK** to get it out of the way.) Figure 12.5 shows the Cover Page Editor with a cover page already on the go.

Text button   Drawing toolbar   Style toolbar

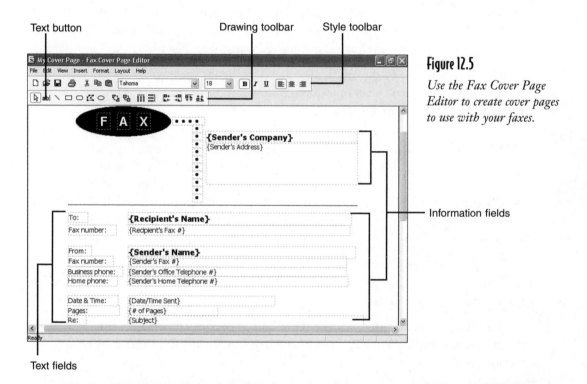

Figure 12.5

Use the Fax Cover Page Editor to create cover pages to use with your faxes.

Information fields

Text fields

You work with the Fax Cover Page Editor by inserting information, text, and graphics fields. *Information fields* hold data. For example, the **{Sender's Company}** field (these fields always show up surrounded by braces) tells Windows XP to insert the name of the sender's company each time you use this cover page when you send a fax. With the Fax Cover Page Editor, you can insert fields for recipient, sender, and message data:

- **Recipient fields** These are fields related to the recipient of the fax. Select **Insert, Recipient** and then select either **Name** or **Fax Number.**

- **Sender fields** These are the fields you fill in during the Send Fax Wizard (particularly if you use the Address Book method). Select **Insert, Sender** to get a submenu with a whack of choices, including **Name, Fax Number,** and **Company.**

- **Message fields** These are fields related to the fax message. Select **Insert, Message,** and then select one of the following: **Note, Subject, Date/Time Sent,** or **Number of Pages.**

Windows Wisdom

To select a field, give it a click. If you need to select multiple fields, hold down **Ctrl** and click each field.

When you select a field command, the editor plops the field onto the cover page. You then use your mouse to drag the field to the position on the page that you want. You also can format a field by using the buttons on the Style toolbar or by selecting the **Format, Font** or **Format, Align Text** commands.

Text fields are basically just text boxes. They're used to provide captions for the information fields or to jazz up the cover page with titles, subtitles, and headings. Here are some techniques you can use with text fields:

- **To insert a text field:** Click the **Text** button on the Drawing toolbar. Now drag the mouse inside the cover page to create a box for the field and then type in your text.

- **To change the text in an existing field:** Double-click the field and then edit the text.

- **To format a text field:** Use the Style toolbar or the **Format** menu commands.

Graphics fields hold images that you can use for logos, separators, or just to add some style to the cover page. The Cover Page Editor's Drawing toolbar sports several buttons for drawing objects. All these tools work the same way as the corresponding tools in Paint. To refresh your skills with the Paint drawing tools, head back to Chapter 7.

The Cover Page Editor also contains quite a few options for mucking around with the layout of the fields. Here's a rundown of the buttons and commands that are available.

Click This	To Do This
	Move the selected field in front of any fields that overlap it. You also can select **Layout, Bring to Front,** or press **Ctrl+F.**
	Move the selected field behind any fields that overlap it. Alternatively, select **Layout, Send to Back,** or tap **Ctrl+B.**
	Space the selected fields evenly across the page. The other way to go about it is to select **Layout, Space Evenly, Across.**
	Space the selected fields evenly down the page. For some variety, select **Layout, Space Evenly, Down.**
	Align the selected fields along their left edges. The other way to go is to select **Layout, Align Objects, Left.**
	Align the selected fields along their right edges. You also can choose the **Layout, Align Objects, Right** command.
	Align the selected fields along their top edges. Selecting **Layout, Align Objects, Top** also works.
	Align the selected fields along their bottom edges. As you've probably guessed by now, you can also select **Layout, Align Objects, Bottom.**

When you're finished with a cover page, save it in the **Personal Cover Pages** folder. Select **File, Save As** and, in the Save As dialog box, open **My Documents,** then **Fax,** then **Personal Cover Pages.**

"Incoming!" Receiving a Fax

The ability to broadcast a fax to the far corners of the planet right from your computer is handy, to say the least. However, my favorite part of computer-based faxing is the opposite chore: receiving incoming faxes. Why? Let me count the ways:

◆ **No more slimy, curly, fax paper**   When you receive a fax on your computer, it's stored as a file which you can keep electronically or later print on *real* paper.

◆ **No more wasted paper**   If a junk fax comes in, you can delete it from existence without having to ever print it.

◆ **Easier storage**   Because received faxes are digital files, you don't need to print them and then file them. Instead, you can use the Fax Console's folders to store them for safekeeping.

◆ **Easier annotation**   As you'll see a bit later, Windows XP comes with a program that lets you "write" on a received fax.

When a fax call comes in, what happens next depends on whether you set up the fax service to answer calls automatically or manually. If it's the latter, you hear a ringing tone and the taskbar's notification area pops up a message that says **The line is ringing.** Click that message to receive the fax. (If you happen to have the Fax Monitor open already, click the **Answer now** button.)

When the fax service answers the call, the Fax Monitor dialog box elbows its way to the fore and shows you the progress of receiving the fax (see Figure 12.6). When it's done, you see a **New fax received** message in the notification area. Click that message to open the Fax Console window where you'll see the new fax in the Inbox folder.

Figure 12.6

The Fax Monitor appears when the fax service answers the incoming call.

Getting the fax service to answer incoming calls is great if you have a dedicated fax line, but what if you share voice and fax calls on the *same* line? In this case, the first thing you need to do is make sure that the fax service is set up so that you can handle incoming calls manually. Then, the next time the phone rings, pick up the telephone handset. If you hear a series of tones, then you know it's a fax, so click the taskbar's **The line is ringing** message and then hang up the handset. (Don't replace the handset before clicking the message or you'll disconnect the call.)

From the Fax Console window, you can perform the following chores:

◆ **Read the fax** Double-click the fax in the Fax Console's Inbox folder (or highlight the fax and select **File, View**). This launches the Windows Picture and Fax Viewer, which displays your fax (see Figure 12.7) and enables you to annotate it (see the next section).

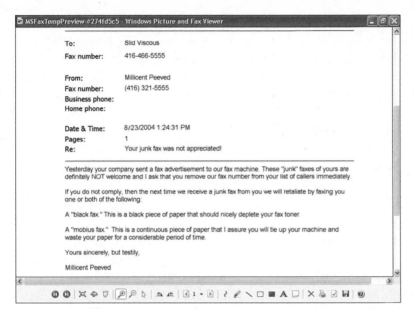

Figure 12.7
Double-click the received fax in the Fax Console to display the fax in the Windows Picture and Fax Viewer window.

◆ **Print the fax**   Highlight the fax and then select **File, Print.**

◆ **Save the fax as an image of a file**   Highlight the fax and then select **File, Save As.** Use the Save As dialog box to choose a name and location for the file and then click **Save.** Note that the fax is saved as a TIF image.

◆ **E-mail the fax as an attachment**   Highlight the fax and then select **File, Mail To.** Use the New Message window to set up the e-mail message and then click **Send.**

◆ **Delete the fax**   Highlight the fax and then select **File, Delete** (or just press the **Delete** key).

> **Cross-Reference**
>
> See Chapter 18 for the Windows XP e-mail details.

Annotating a Fax

The Fax Viewer program lets you edit the fax by adding highlights, lines, snarky comments, "sticky notes," or other annotations. This section shows you how it's done.

I told you about most of the buttons along the bottom of the window back in Chapter 7. Here's a rundown of the rest of the buttons, all of which deal with annotating the fax:

Button	Button Name	What It Does
	New Freehand Annotation	Draws a freehand line on the fax.
	New Highlight Annotation	Draws a yellow highlight on the fax.
	New Straight Line Annotation	Draws a straight line on the fax.
	New Frame Annotation	Draws a border-only rectangle on the fax.
	New Solid Rectangle Annotation	Draws a filled rectangle on the fax.
	New Text Annotation	Draws a text box on the fax. You can then type a note in the text box.
	New Attached Note Annotation	Draws a "sticky note" on the fax. You can then add text to the note.

These buttons work just like those in the Paint toolbox (see Chapter 7). That is, you click the button, move the mouse pointer to the position inside the fax where you want to start, hold down the left mouse button, and then drag the mouse to draw the object.

The Least You Need to Know

- To fax a simple note on a cover page, launch the Send Fax Wizard directly by selecting the Fax Console's **File, Send a Fax** command, or by selecting **Start, All Programs, Accessories, Communications, Fax, Send a Fax.**

- To fax a document from a program, select **File, Print,** choose the **Fax** "printer," and then click **Print.**

- To answer a call manually, click the taskbar's **The line is ringing** message.

- To view a received fax, click the taskbar's **New fax received** message and then double-click the fax in the Fax Console's Inbox folder.

Chapter 3

A Movable Feast: Windows XP and Your Notebook Computer

In This Chapter

◆ Using power management to extend the life of your notebook's battery

◆ Keeping files in sync when sharing them between your notebook and another computer

◆ Proper procedures for inserting and removing PC Card devices

◆ Using a direct cable connection to get your notebook to exchange pleasantries with a second machine

If you have a notebook computer, then you know full well that these machines are fundamentally different from their desktop cousins, and that the difference goes well beyond mere luggability. There are batteries to monitor, weird "PC Card" wafers to slide in and out, and files to exchange with desktop machines.

The Windows XP programmers must have had to wrestle with notebooks a time or two themselves, because they've put together a passel of portable perks. Windows XP offers power management for sensitive notebook batteries and support for those PC Card thingies. It also can help you synchronize files between a notebook and another machine, and even enables you to set up a direct cable connection between them. I discuss all of these capabilities in this chapter.

Better Battery Life Through Power Management

When using batteries to run your notebook computer on an airplane or some other no-power-plug-in-sight location, a worried mind becomes your natural state. That's because the battery can last only so long, so you have a limited amount of time to

Jargon Jar

Power management refers to those Windows XP features that enable you to monitor and manage the power consumption of devices, particularly notebook computer batteries and your hard disk and monitor.

work or play before your electronic world goes dark. Windows XP can help relieve some of that worry thanks to its *power management* features. For example, one of these features enables the system to shut down idle components (such as the hard disk and monitor) to prevent them from gobbling up battery power unnecessarily. Another feature lets you keep an eye peeled on how much power is left in the battery. This section takes you on a tour of these and other Windows XP power-management knickknacks.

Using the Power Icon to Monitor Battery Life

The first stop on our tour is the taskbar. When you're running under battery power, you'll see the power icon shown in Figure 13.1. This icon gives you several visual clues about the state of the battery. When the battery is fully charged, the icon is blue from top to bottom; as the battery gradually loses its steam, the level of blue in the icon falls. For example, when there is 50 percent of battery life remaining, the icon shows as half blue and half gray. If you move your mouse pointer over the icon, a small banner shows up with the percentage of power remaining.

Figure 13.1

The power icon tells you how much juice is left in your battery.

The power icon

Displaying the Power Options

If your notebook is running on AC power, Windows XP doesn't display the power icon. If you'd prefer to see the icon full-time, you have to first display Windows XP's Power Options dialog box:

1. Select **Start, Control Panel** to open the Control Panel folder.

2. Click **Printers and Other Hardware.**

3. Click the WebView panel's **Power Options** link. Windows XP opens the Power Options Properties dialog box.

From here, display the **Advanced** tab, activate the **Always show icon on the taskbar** check box, and then click **Apply.** (Don't click **OK** just yet because you'll need the Power Options dialog box in the next section.)

A Word of Warning: Setting Battery Alarms

The power icon is useful, but it's too easy to forget to check it when you're hard at work. To help ensure that you don't power down without warning, Windows XP maintains two different "alarms"—called Low and Critical—that can notify you when your battery's goose is almost cooked. To work with these alarms, follow these steps:

1. Display the Power Options dialog box, as described in the previous section. (Click **Start, Control Panel, Printers and Other Hardware, Power Options.**)

2. Display the **Alarms** tab.

3. The **Low Battery Alarm** group gives you three things to play with:

   ◆ Use the check box to toggle the alarm on and off.

   ◆ Use the slider to set the power level percentage at which the alarm goes off.

   ◆ Click the **Alarm Action** button to display the Low Battery Alarm Actions dialog box. From here, you can request that Windows XP **Sound alarm** or **Display message** when the alarm goes off. You can also activate the **When the alarm goes off, the computer will** check box, and then select **Standby, Hibernate,** or **Shut down** in the list. It's also probably a good idea to activate the **Force stand by or shut down even if a program stops responding** check box. Click **OK** when you're done.

   > **Cross-Reference**
   >
   > I discussed the differences between standby, hibernate, and shut down in Chapter 1.

4. Use **Critical battery alarm** group to set up the critical alarm. Note that you have the same choices as in the Low battery alarm group.

5. Click **OK.**

It's been my experience that when battery power gets low, it tends to go south in a hurry. So although you might think the low battery alarm still gives you a few minutes to keep working, don't believe it! Instead, you should immediately save all your work and either get to an AC outlet as soon as possible, or exit Windows XP until a power source comes your way.

Power to the People: Specifying a Power Scheme

As I mentioned earlier, Windows XP cheerfully shuts down some system components in an effort to keep your battery on its feet longer. Follow these steps to control which components get shut down and when:

1. Display the Power Options dialog box, as described earlier, and activate the **Power Schemes** tab.

2. Use the **Power schemes** list to choose one of the Windows XP predefined power schemes (such as **Portable/Laptop**).

3. To adjust the power scheme time intervals, use the following lists in both the **Plugged in** and **Running on batteries** columns:

   Turn off monitor Sets the number of minutes the notebook must be idle before Windows XP shuts off the monitor.

   Turn off hard disks Sets the number of minutes the notebook must be idle before Windows XP stops your hard disk (or disks) from spinning.

   System standby Sets the number of minutes the notebook must be idle before Windows XP puts the notebook into standby mode.

   System hibernates Sets the number of minutes the notebook must be idle before Windows XP puts the notebook into hibernation mode.

4. If you made changes in step 3 and you want to save those changes under a different scheme name, click **Save As,** enter a new name for the scheme, and then click **OK** to return to the Power Options dialog box.

5. Click **Apply** or **OK.**

Configuring Your Notebook's Power Buttons

Most newer notebooks enable you to configure three "power buttons": closing the lid, the on/off button, and the sleep button. When you activate these buttons, they put your system into standby or hibernate mode, or turn it off altogether. On some notebooks, there isn't a separate sleep button. Instead, you tap the on/off button quickly.

Follow these steps to configure these buttons for power management:

1. Display the **Power Options** dialog box, as described earlier.

2. Select the **Advanced** tab.

3. In the **Power buttons** group, use the three lists to set a power management option (**Do nothing, Ask me what to do, Stand by, Hibernate,** or **Shut down**) for closing the lid, pressing the **on/off** (power) button, or pressing the **sleep** button.

4. Click **Apply** or **OK**.

Using a Briefcase to Synchronize Files

Do you have to deal with both a notebook computer *and* a desktop computer? If so, then I'm sure you know all too well the problems that arise when you try to share files between them. For example, if you transport a few files to the notebook and you end up changing a couple of those files, it's crucial to be sure that the desktop machine gets a copy of the updated files.

In other words, you want to be sure that the notebook and the desktop remain *synchronized*. To help you do this, Windows XP offers a feature called Briefcase. To understand how it works, let's examine how you use a real briefcase to do some work at home. You begin by stuffing your briefcase full of the files and documents you want to work with. You then take the briefcase home, take out the papers, work on them, and put them back in the briefcase. Finally, you take the briefcase back to work and then remove the papers.

Windows XP's Briefcase feature works in much the same way, except that you don't work with the original documents. Instead, you work with special copies called *sync copies*. A Briefcase is really a special type of folder. The basic idea is that you place the documents you want to work with inside a Briefcase, and then lug around the Briefcase using a floppy disk, Zip disk, or some other removable disk.

> **CAUTION**
>
> **Look Out!**
>
> The Briefcase keeps careful tabs on its files: both where they came from originally on the desktop computer and where you copy them to on the notebook. Therefore, don't move or rename the files after they're safely stowed on the notebook, or you'll break the synchronization.

You can then copy the documents from the Briefcase to the notebook and work on them. The key thing is that the Briefcase "remembers" where the documents came from originally, and it automatically tracks which ones have changed. You can update the original files with just a couple of mouse clicks.

Before getting started, you need to create a Briefcase. The best place to create the Briefcase is on the removable disk you'll be using to transport the files. Here are the steps to follow to create a Briefcase:

1. Insert the disk you want to use.

2. Use My Computer to display the disk.

3. To create a new Briefcase on the disk, either select **File, New, Briefcase,** or right-click the folder and then click **New, Briefcase.** Windows XP adds an icon named New Briefcase to the disk.

4. Rename the Briefcase (this is optional).

With the Briefcase created, follow these steps to transfer and synchronize documents between a desktop and a notebook computer:

1. Copy the files you want to work with from the desktop computer to the Briefcase. (If you're using drag-and-drop, you don't have to hold down Ctrl because Windows XP will automatically make sync copies of the files that you drop.)

2. Remove the disk and insert it into the notebook.

3. On the notebook, use My Computer to open the removable disk and then open the Briefcase. (The first time you open the Briefcase you'll see a Welcome dialog box. It's a waste of time, so just click **Finish.**) Copy the files from the Briefcase to the notebook computer.

4. Work with the files on the notebook.

5. When you're done, insert the disk into the notebook and open the Briefcase folder. The Briefcase then checks its files with the copies you sent to the notebook. As you can see in Figure 13.2, the Briefcase's **Status** column tells you which files have been changed. (To get the various columns, activate the **View, Details** command.)

6. To update the Briefcase copies of the changed files, either click **Update all items** in the WebView panel or select **Briefcase, Update All.** (You can also click the **Update All** toolbar button.) Briefcase displays a list of the files to be updated.

Update All

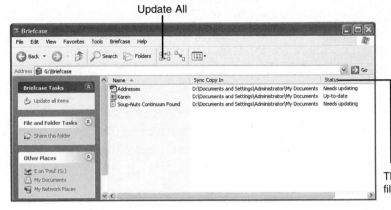

Figure 13.2

The Briefcase folder keeps track of which files you changed on the notebook.

This column tells you which files have been changed

7. Click **Update.** Briefcase grabs copies of the changed files.

8. Close the Briefcase window.

9. Insert the disk into the desktop computer and open the Briefcase folder. This time, the Briefcase compares its files with the originals on the desktop machine. Again, the **Status** column tells you which files have been changed.

10. To update the desktop computer's original copies of the changed files, either click **Update all items** in the WebView panel or select **Briefcase, Update All.** (Again, you can also click the **Update All** toolbar button.) Briefcase displays a list of the files to be updated.

11. Click **Update.** Briefcase copies the changed files to the desktop computer.

Windows Wisdom

PC Cards were originally known as PCMCIA cards, where PCMCIA stood for Personal Computer Memory Card International Association. I use PC Card in this section, but just remember that PC Card and PCMCIA are the same thing. In addition, there's a newer type of PC Card device that is known as a CardBus device. Most newer notebooks support both types in the same socket.

Working with Those Little PC Card Doodads

Notebook computers are, by definition, small and lightweight to ensure easy luggability. Their relatively Lilliputian size means that there just isn't enough internal room to "expand" a notebook in the same way that you can a desktop machine. That's good news for non-nerds because it means the notebook engineers had to find some other way to enable users to "add on" to their machines. The result was the PC Card: a

Jargon Jar

Hot swapping sounds like some sort of swinging singles party, but it's really just the capability to insert and remove PC Cards without having to shut down the system.

small, credit card–sized wafer that plugged into a special slot—or *socket*—on the *outside* of the notebook. There are PC Card devices for modems, network adapters, hard disks, and much more. So, now even the digitally maladroit can upgrade their machines with little or no effort.

Windows XP helps by recognizing your notebook's PC Card sockets (most machines have at least two), and by supporting *hot swapping*.

Popping In a PC Card Device

To use a PC Card device, insert it gently and as far as it will go into any free PC Card socket. (You should feel a slight "click" at the end.) Windows XP recognizes that a new device is in the socket and beeps the speaker. One of two things now happens. If you've used the device before, it will be ready for use within a few seconds. Or, if you've never used the device before, you'll see the New Hardware Found message and Windows XP will proceed to install the necessary software to make the device run. You might see the New Hardware Found Wizard, which will take you through the appropriate steps.

After the device is up and at 'em, Windows XP displays a special Safely Remove Hardware icon on the right side of the taskbar, as shown in Figure 13.3. (Note, too, that this icon will also appear if you have certain other devices—such as certain USB devices—plugged into the machine.)

Figure 13.3

When you wedge a PC Card device into your notebook, Windows XP displays this icon in the taskbar.

The Safely Remove Hardware icon

If you want to see a list of all your PC Card devices, right-click the Safely Remove Hardware icon. Windows XP displays the Safely Remove Hardware dialog box shown in Figure 13.4.

Figure 13.4

Right-click the Safely Remove Hardware icon to see a list of all your plugged-in devices.

Yanking Out a PC Card Device

This hot-swapping thing should really be called *tepid swapping* because you can't just grab out a PC Card device by the scruff of the neck and drag it out of the slot. Such willy-nillyness is frowned upon. Instead, you need to tell Windows XP which device you're giving the heave-ho. This gives Windows a chance to shut down the device. Here's the easiest way to go about this:

1. Click the **Safely Remove Hardware** icon. Windows XP displays a list of the devices attached to your system.

2. Click the device you want to remove. Your computer beeps, and Windows XP displays a message telling you it's safe to remove the device.

3. Click the message and then remove the device. (On most notebooks, you do this by pushing a button beside the socket.)

If your computer is turned off, you can just go ahead and spit out the device without any danger. Note, too, that another way to go about this is to display the Safely Remove Hardware dialog box (as described in the previous section), highlight the device you want to spit out, and then click **Stop**.

Setting Up a Direct Connection Between Two Computers

Instead of using floppies to transfer files between your notebook and another machine, connect them with a cable and then perform the transfers along that cable. What kind of cable do you need? Windows XP gets along with two kinds:

- ◆ **A null-modem cable**   This is a special cable that attaches to the serial port in the back of both machines. Null-modem cables are common and are available from any decent computer or electronics store. Note, however, that this is *not* the same as the cable you use with your modem.

- ◆ **A Direct Parallel cable**   This cable attaches to the parallel (or printer) port in the back of the computers. This kind is preferred because it can transmit data quite a bit faster than the null-modem variety. Unfortunately, at the time of writing, these cables were available only directly from the manufacturer (see www.lpt.com).

After you've attached the cable to both machines (they don't need to be turned off while you make the attachments), you're ready to begin the setup. This involves setting up the host and guest computers and configuring both machines so that they can converse with each other. The host computer is the one that will be sharing its resources, while the guest computer is the one that will be accessing those shared resources.

The next three sections take you through the necessary steps.

Step 1: Configure the Host Computer

Here's how to configure the host machine:

1. Select **Start, Control Panel** to display the Control Panel window.

2. Click **Network and Internet Connections** to display the Network and Internet Connections window.

3. Click **Network Connections** to get to the Network Connections window.

4. In the WebView panel, click the **New Connection Wizard** link (or select the **File, New Connection** command) to launch the New Connection Wizard.

5. Click **Next.** The wizard asks what kind of connection you want.

6. Activate the **Set up an advanced connection** option, and then click **Next.** The wizard wonders what connection type you want.

7. Activate the **Connect directly to another computer** option and click **Next.** The wizard asks what role you want for the computer.

8. Activate **Host** and click **Next.** The wizard now asks you to choose which communications port you'll be using.

9. Select the port to which your cable is attached and then click **Next.**

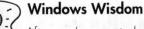

Windows Wisdom _____

After you've created a connection, selecting **Start, Settings, Network and Dial-Up Connections** displays a submenu of the items in the Network and Dial-Up Connections window (including the Make New Connection icon). If you need to access this window in the future, you have to go the long way: **Start, Programs, Accessories, Communications, Network and Dial-Up Connections.**

10. Your next chore is to select which users are allowed to make the connection from the other machine. Activate the check box beside each user you want to have access. If the user isn't listed, click **Add** and enter a **User name, Full name,** and **Password** (twice), and click **OK.** Click **Next** when you're done.

11. In the final wizard dialog box, click **Finish.** The wizard creates the new connection and leaves you in the Network Connections dialog box. You'll see a new icon named **Incoming Connections.**

Step 2: Configure the Guest Computer

To set up the guest computer, follow steps 1 through 7 in the previous section, and then do this:

1. When the wizard asks whether this machine is to be the host or the guest, activate **Guest** and click **Next.** The wizard wonders what the name of the other computer is.

2. Type the name and click **Next.** The wizard asks you to choose a port.

3. Select the port to which your cable is attached and then click **Next.**

Windows Wisdom _____

If you're not sure what the host computer's name is, here's a quick way to find out: On the host computer, click **Start,** right-click the **My Computer** icon, and then click **Properties.** In the System Properties dialog box, display the **Computer Name** tab. The text that appears beside **Full computer name** (without the dot [.] at the end) is the name you want to use in step 2.

4. The wizard next asks whether you want to make this connection available for **Anyone's use** or **My use only.** Make your choice (if in doubt, select the latter) and click **Next.**

5. In the final wizard dialog box, you can put a shortcut to the host on the desktop by activating the **Add a shortcut to this connection to my desktop** check box. To wrap things up, click **Finish.** An icon with the name of the host computer is added to the Network Connections window.

Windows XP will now display the Connect dialog box so that you can connect to the other computer. Continue with the next section and start at step 3.

Step 3: Make the Connection

To establish the connection between the two computers, you need to do the following:

1. On the guest computer, select **Start, Connect To** and then click the name of the connection (the default name is the name of the host computer). Windows XP pastes up a Connect dialog box.

2. Fill in the **User name** and **Password.** These should be the same as one of the users you specified during the host setup. If you want Windows XP to keep an internal sticky note for the password, be sure the **Save this user name and password for the following users** check box is activated, and then choose **Me only** or **Anyone who uses this computer.**

3. Click **Connect.** Windows XP accesses the cable and alerts the host that a guest is knocking on the door. The host authenticates the incoming user and makes the connection. How do you know you're connected? Windows XP offers lots of clues:

   ◆ A connection message appears in the taskbar's notification area.

   ◆ A new icon appears in the notification area on both the host and guest.

   ◆ In the host's Network Connections window, a new icon appears for the guest computer and the Incoming Connections icon includes the text *1 client connected.*

   ◆ In the guest's Network Connections window, the host computer's icon includes the text "Connected."

From here, you use the usual networking techniques to access data on the host.

Direct Connections and the Briefcase

After you have a direct connection established, you might want to use a Briefcase to coordinate the exchange of files. Here's how it works:

1. Be sure that the host folder containing the files you want to work with is either shared directly or resides in a shared folder.

2. Use the guest computer to access the shared folder.

3. Copy the files to the guest computer's Briefcase.

4. Use the guest computer to work on the files directly from the Briefcase folder. (There's no need for a connection at this point.)

5. When you're done, connect again and then open the guest's Briefcase folder.

6. Either click **Update all items** in the WebView panel or select **Briefcase, Update All** to update the host computer's files with the changed files in the guest computer's Briefcase.

Disconnecting from the Host

When you feel you've imposed upon the host computer quite enough, it's time to take your leave. Windows XP gives you the following ways to bid goodnight:

◆ On the host or guest, right-click the **connection** icon in the taskbar's notification area and then click **Disconnect.**

◆ On the host, open the Network Connections window, highlight the **icon for the connected guest,** and then click **Disconnect this connection** in the WebView panel (or select the **File, Disconnect** command).

◆ On the guest, open the Network Connections window, highlight the icon for the direct connection, and then click the WebView panel's **Disconnect this connection** link (or select the **File, Disconnect** command).

The Least You Need to Know

◆ When running your notebook on batteries, be sure you use the power icon to keep a close eye on the battery level.

◆ To maximize battery life, create a power scheme that shuts down the monitor and hard disk within a minute or two of idle time.

◆ The easiest way to use a Briefcase is to move it onto a removable disk and keep it there. You can then add files to the Briefcase, copy those files to the other machine, and use the update feature to keep the files synchronized.

◆ You can insert a PC Card, and Windows XP would recognize it right away (and, if necessary, install the required files). Before removing a PC Card device, tell Windows XP to stop using it.

◆ String a null-modem or Direct Parallel cable between two machines and then set up one as the host and the other as the guest.

Part 4

Windows XP on the Internet

For many years, lots of purse-lipped parents, uptight teachers, and pontificating pundits frowned on computers because they saw them as noninteractive machines that only served to encourage antisocial behavior. Boy, did they ever get that wrong! As proof, you need look no further than the tens of millions of people who are on the Internet, and the hundreds of millions of people who want to be on the Internet. Believe me, these people aren't clamoring to listen to cheesy MIDI music. No, they want to connect. They want to read what other people have written; they want to exchange e-mail epistles; they want to natter in newsgroups; they want to chin-wag in chat rooms. In other words, the opposite has happened: Computers have become interactive machines that encourage socializing. Who'da thunk it? If you want to get in on all this fun, the six chapters here in Part 4 will tell you everything you need to know.

Chapter 14

Getting On the Internet

In This Chapter

◆ Setting up a spanking new Internet account

◆ Specifying the details of an existing account yourself

◆ Getting connected to the Internet

◆ A review of Windows XP Internet tools

◆ Working with dialing rules

The Internet's tentacles have insinuated themselves into every nook and cranny of modern life. Businesses from corner-hugging Mom 'n' Pop shops to continent-straddling corporations are online; web pages are now counted in the billions; and people send far more e-mail messages than postal messages.

It truly is a wired (which, remember, is just "weird" spelled sideways) world, and if you feel like you're the only person left who isn't online, this chapter will help. I'll tell you exactly what you need to make it happen, and then I'll take you through the connection process, step-by-finicky-step.

Modems and Phone Cables

If you're like most people, your telephone and modem will probably share the same line. In this case, you don't have to switch the cable between the phone and the modem all the time. Instead, it's possible to get a permanent, no-hassle setup that'll make everyone happy. The secret is that all modems have two telephone cable jacks in the back:

- **Line jack**   This one is usually labeled "Line" or "Telco," or has a picture of a wall jack.

- **Telephone jack**   This one is usually labeled "Phone" or has a picture of a telephone.

Follow these directions to set things up:

1. Run a phone cable from the wall jack to the modem's line jack.

2. Run a second phone cable from the telephone to the modem's telephone jack.

This setup lets you use the phone whenever you need it—the signal goes right through the modem (when you're not using it, of course)—and lets you use the modem whenever you need it.

What to Look For in an Internet Service Provider

The route to the Internet isn't a direct one. Instead, you can only get there by engaging the services of a middleman or, more accurately, a middle company: an *Internet Service Provider* (*ISP*, for short).

An ISP is a business that has negotiated a deal with the local telephone company or some other behemoth organization to get a direct connection to the Internet's highways and byways. These kinds of connections cost thousands of dollars a month, so they're out of reach for all but the most well-heeled tycoons. The ISP affords it by signing up subscribers and offering them a piece of the ISP's Internet connection. After you have an account with an ISP, the connection process works as follows:

Jargon Jar

An **Internet Service Provider (ISP)** takes your money in exchange for an Internet account, which you need in order to get online.

1. You use your computer's modem to dial up the ISP.

2. The ISP's computer verifies that you're one of their subscribers.

3. The ISP's computer sets up a connection between your computer and the Internet.

4. You go, girl (or boy, as the case may be)!

So before you can do anything on the Internet, you have to set up an account with an ISP and then you need to give Windows the details. Before we get to that, let's take a second to run through a few pointers to bear in mind when deciding which ISP to use:

◆ Most ISPs charge a monthly fee, which typically ranges from $5 to $30. Decide in advance the maximum that you're willing to shell out each month.

◆ When comparing prices, remember that ISP plans usually trade off between price and the number of hours of connection time. For example, the lower the price, the fewer the hours you get.

> **Windows Wisdom**
>
> Most people find that they spend a ton of time on the Internet for the first few months as they discover all the wonders and weirdness that's available. After they get used to everything, their connection time drops dramatically.

◆ It's important to note that most plans charge you by the minute or by the hour if you exceed the number of hours the plan offers. These charges can be exorbitant (a buck or two an hour), so you don't want to get into that. Therefore, you need to give some thought to how much time you plan to spend online. That's hard to do at this stage, I know, but you just need to ballpark it. If in doubt, get a plan with a large number of hours (say, 100 or 150). You can always scale it back later on.

◆ Most major ISPs offer an "unlimited usage" plan. This means you can connect whenever you want for as long as you want, and you just pay a set fee per month (usually around $20). This is a good option to take for a few months until you figure out how often you use the Internet.

◆ All modems made in the past few years support a faster connection speed called 56K (or sometimes V.90). If you have such a modem (if you're not certain, it's probably safe to assume that you do), make sure the ISP you choose also supports 56K (almost all of them do nowadays).

◆ Make sure the ISP offers a local access number to avoid long-distance charges. If that's not an option, make sure they offer access via a toll-free number. (Note: Watch out for extra charges for the use of the toll-free line.) Even better, some nationwide ISPs offer local access in various cities across the land. This is particularly useful if you do a lot of traveling.

Look Out!

You can set up an Internet connection only if your Windows XP account has administrator access. Also, if you'll be connecting via your modem, make sure your phone cable is plugged into your modem.

◆ Make sure the ISP offers a local or toll-free number for technical support.

◆ I recommend dealing with only large ISPs. There are still plenty of fly-by-night operations out there, and they're just not worth the hassle of dropped connections, busy signals, lack of support, going belly-up when you most need them, and so on.

◆ If you can't decide between two or more ISPs, see what extra goodies they offer: space for your own web pages, extra e-mail accounts, Internet software bundles, and so on.

To help you compare major ISPs, the Windows XP Internet Connection Wizard has a feature that can display rates and special offers from the companies that provide Internet access in your area.

Getting Started on Your Road to the Internet

The Windows XP installation program has a section where it offers to set up an Internet connection. This means that there's a good chance your computer is already Net-friendly. To find out, select **Start, Internet.** If Internet Explorer starts and takes you to a web page, your Internet connection is a going concern. If you see the New Connection Wizard instead, then you've got a few hoops that you still need to jump through.

Windows XP offers no fewer than three different routes to Internet connection glory. Whichever avenue you pursue, you start things up either by trying to access the Internet (as just described) or by selecting **Start, Control Panel, Network and Internet Connections, Network Connections, Create a new connection.** The New Connection Wizard fades in and requires the following steps off the bat:

1. Click **Next** in the initial dialog box.

2. Activate the **Connect to the Internet** option and click **Next.**

3. Choose one of the following options and then click **Next:**

   ◆ **Choose from a list of Internet Service Providers**   Choose this option to sign up for a new Internet account through Windows XP. When you click **Next,** the wizard downloads a list of ISPs in your area and gives you information about each one. You choose the one you want and then run through a signup process.

◆ **Set up my connection manually**   If you have an existing Internet account, choose this option to provide the details about it by hand. See the "Setting Up an Existing Account Manually" section that follows.

◆ **Use the CD I got from an ISP**   This is the easiest road of them all. Insert the ISP's CD and then click **Next** until the installation program begins. Then run through the install and let the ISP handle all the hard stuff for you.

Setting Up an Existing Account Manually

If you need to build the connection to your existing account with your bare hands, this section runs through the data you need and takes you through the rest of the New Connection Wizard's steps.

What You Need to Know Before Getting Started

To successfully set up a connection to your Internet account, you need to have the proper bits of information from your ISP. Here are the basic tidbits you need to *log on:*

◆ The phone number you have to dial to connect to the ISP.

◆ The user name (which might also be called your log-on name) and password that you use to log on to the ISP.

Jargon Jar

To **log on** means to provide your ISP with your user name and password, and so gain access to the wonder that is the Internet.

Some ISPs also require some or all of the following advanced settings:

◆ The type of connection the ISP requires. This is usually PPP, but SLIP is also sometimes used. (Don't worry if you don't understand these terms. Believe me, you'll never have to deal with them face-to-face in the real world.)

◆ Whether you need to log on to the ISP manually.

◆ Whether your ISP provides you with a "script" for the log-on procedure. A script is a tiny program that automates the log-on so that you don't have to enter your user name, password, and whatever other tidbits your ISP requires. Most ISP log-ons are automatic anyway, these days, so it's unlikely you'll ever need a script.

◆ Whether your ISP assigns you a permanent *IP address*. If so, you need to know the address.

◆ Whether your ISP provides you with IP addresses for their Domain Name Servers (DNS). If so, you need to know the addresses for the primary and alternate servers.

> **Jargon Jar** _____
>
> An **IP address** is a crazy-looking series of numbers and dots (such as 123.234.56.78) that serves as your computer's address when you're connected to the Internet.

Didn't I tell you this was finicky stuff? Don't worry if you find all this gobbledygook to be completely meaningless. You need to hold it in your brain only for as long as it takes to set up your connection, and then it can be discarded for all time (or at least until you get your next computer and have to start everything from scratch once again; doh!).

What You Need to Do After Getting Started

With all that info at your side, you're now ready to set up the account. Here are the rest of the steps to trudge through:

1. The next wizard dialog box presents you with some options related to how you connect to your ISP (click **Next** when you've made the appropriate choice):

   ◆ **Connect using a dial-up modem**   Choose this option if you use a regular modem to connect.

   ◆ **Connect using a broadband connection that requires a user name and password**   Choose this option if you have a broadband (high-speed) connection using a cable modem or a Digital Subscriber Line (DSL) modem and you also have to enter a user name and password.

   ◆ **Connect using a broadband connection that is always on**   Choose this option if you use a cable modem or a DSL (high-speed) modem but you don't have to enter a user name and password. If you choose this route, the wizard will end because it assumes your connection is already set up. If it's not, click **Back,** activate the **Use the CD I got from an ISP** option, and then follow that path, instead.

2. The wizard asks for the name of your ISP. This is really just the name that XP will assign to your connection, so enter anything you darn well please and click **Next.**

3. If you're configuring a dial-up connection, the wizard now asks you for the phone number of your ISP. Enter the phone number (including the country code and area code, if they're required) and click **Next.**

4. The wizard may now wonder who you want to use this connection. If you want all who use your computer to be able to use the connection, activate **Anyone's use;** if you prefer to keep the connection to yourself, activate **My use only** instead. Click **Next.**

5. In the next wizard dialog box, enter your user name and password. You need to enter the latter twice: In the **Password** text box and in the **Confirm password** text box (in both cases, the password appears only as asterisks, for security).

6. The wizard also foists the following options on you (click **Next** when you're done):

   ◆ **Use this account name and password when anyone connects to the Internet from this computer**   You only see this check box if you activated the **Anyone's use** option in the previous dialog box. If the other users have different user names and passwords with the ISP, deactivate this check box.

   ◆ **Make this the default Internet connection**   Leaving this check box activated tells Windows XP to use this connection whenever you attempt to access an Internet resource (such as a website or your e-mail account).

   ◆ **Turn on Internet Connection Firewall for this connection**   Leave this check box activated to protect your computer from crackers and other Net miscreants.

7. In the final wizard dialog box, click **Finish.**

Windows Wisdom _____

Why on earth does your Internet connection need protection from a fire? Actually, that's just a metaphor: There are no real fires on the Internet. Instead, there are plenty of nefarious types who would like nothing more than to break into your computer system. The problem, you see, is that your computer exposes itself (so to speak) to the Internet while you're connected. (This is particularly true if you have one of those "always on" cable modem or DSL connections.) Crackers (as hackers who have succumbed to the dark side of the Force are usually called) can take advantage of well-known vulnerabilities to look around or even commandeer your machine. To protect yourself, you need to block those vulnerabilities by setting up what's known in the security trade as a *firewall*. To check that your computer is connected, use Internet Explorer to go to grc.com and click the **Shields Up** link (you may have to click **Shields Up** again on the new page that appears).

Configuring Advanced ISP Settings

If your ISP requires you to configure any of the advanced settings that I mentioned earlier, let's see how you do it. Begin by selecting **Start, Connect To, Show all connections.** Click your connection and then click **Change settings of this connection** (or choose the **File, Properties** command). You use the Properties dialog box to put in the advanced settings:

◆ If you need to log on to the ISP manually, display the **Security** tab and activate the **Show terminal window** check box.

◆ If your ISP provides you with a "script" for automating the log-on procedure, display the **Security** tab and activate the **Run script** check box. Then click **Browse** to locate the script file on your computer.

◆ For the type of connection, display the **Networking** tab and then use the **Type of dial-up server I am calling** list to choose either **PPP** or **SLIP.**

◆ If your ISP assigns you a permanent IP address, display the **Networking** tab, highlight **Internet Protocol (TCP/IP)** and then click **Properties.** Activate **Use the following IP address** and then enter your IP address in the **IP address** text box.

◆ If your ISP provides you with IP addresses for its Domain Name Servers (DNS), display the **Networking** tab, highlight **Internet Protocol (TCP/IP),** and then click **Properties.** Activate **Use the following DNS server addresses** and then enter the DNS server addresses in the **Preferred DNS Server** and **Alternate DNS Server** text boxes.

Making the Connection

Now that you have your account details down pat, it's time to put that account to good use by connecting to the Internet. There are two ways to go about this:

◆ Crank up any of the Internet programs. For example, you can launch the Internet Explorer web browser.

◆ Select **Start, Connect To,** and then click the Internet connection you created.

At this point, Windows XP might mumble something about **The Web Page You Requested Is Not Available Offline.** Say "Well, duh!" and click **Connect.** This gets you to a Connect dialog box that's similar to the one shown in Figure 14.1.

Figure 14.1

This dialog box is the launch pad for your Internet forays.

This dialog box offers the following toys:

◆ **User name**   This is the user name you use to log on to your ISP.

◆ **Password**   This is the password you use to log on to your ISP.

◆ **Save this user name and password for the following users**   When this check box is activated, Windows XP is kind enough to enter your password automatically. If you're worried about somebody else monkeying around with your account, you'll sleep better at night if you activate the **Me only** option.

◆ **Dial**   Click this button to get the connection process going.

◆ **Cancel**   Click this button if you change your mind about connecting.

◆ **Properties**   Click this button to adjust your connection settings.

Adjust the data as necessary and, when you're ready, click **Dial**. Windows XP taps your modem on the shoulder and passes it the phone number, and the connection process begins in the usually noisy modem fashion. If your ISP requires you to log on manually, a screen will appear and the ISP's prompts (such as **User name** and **Password**) will appear. Type in whatever information you're asked for (press **Enter** after you've entered each item).

Windows Wisdom

Many ISPs provide you with two or more phone numbers so that you can try other numbers if the main number is busy or down. To add the other numbers, click **Properties** in the Connect dialog box and then click **Alternates**. In the Alternate Phone Numbers dialog box, click **Add**, enter the **Phone number**, and then click **OK**.

After a few more seconds of navel-gazing, Windows XP finally lets you know that you're now up and online by adding a connection icon to the notification area and displaying a message that you're connected. If you need to track how long you've been online, click the connection icon. The dialog box that shows up tells you how long you've been connected.

Hacking Windows

If the bansheelike wailing that your modem goes through when making the connection drives you (or your neighbors) nuts, you can turn it down or turn it off altogether. Select **Start, Control Panel, Printers and Other Hardware, Phone and Modem Options,** and then select the **Modems** tab. If you have more than one modem, click the one you use to connect to the Internet. Click **Properties** and then select the **Modem** tab. Click and drag the **Speaker volume** slider to the left to turn down the modem. Dragging the slider all the way to the left will turn off the noise.

Severing the Connection

When you've stood just about all you can stand of the Internet's wiles, you can log off by right-clicking the **connection** icon in the taskbar's notification area, and then clicking **Disconnect** (see Figure 14.2).

Figure 14.2

Right-click the connection icon to disconnect from the Internet.

This icon appears while you're connected to the Internet

Locations, Locations, Locations: Setting Up Dialing Rules

Do you get your Internet fix using a modem and a dial-up connection? If so, then you probably always use your modem from the same place (such as at the office or at home). In that case, it's fine that Windows XP just dials the modem the same way every time. However, what if your location changes and you need to deal with different dialing options? (I'm assuming here that you're using a notebook computer that can come along for the ride.) Here are some examples:

♦ You travel to another area code, so the call becomes long distance.

♦ You're out of town on business and you need to place all calls through a long-distance provider or a calling card.

♦ You want to connect from some remote location that requires you to first dial 9 to get an outside line.

♦ You bring your computer home and have to disable call waiting before making the connection.

For all these and many similar situations, Windows XP lets you set up separate *locations* in which you change one or more *dialing rules*. This section shows you how to create and work with these locations and rules.

To get things going, follow these steps:

1. Select **Start, Control Panel, Printers and Other Hardware, Phone and Modem Options.**

2. Make sure the **Dialing Rules** tab is displayed.

3. The locations you create will be listed in the **Locations** list. You should see an existing location—called **New Location**—that was set up during the Windows XP installation. Click **New** to drag the New Location dialog box in by the scruff of the neck.

The **General** tab contains the basic options for the new location:

♦ **Location name**   Enter a name for the new location (such as "Calls from the Coast" or "Call Waiting's Outta There!").

♦ **Country/region**   Use this list to specify the country you'll be in when you're dialing.

♦ **Area code**   Use this text box to specify the area code you'll be in when you're dialing.

♦ **To access an outside line for local calls, dial**   Use this text box to type in the number (or numbers) that must be dialed to get an outside line for local calls (such as 9).

Windows Wisdom

Your modem spends much of its time converting computer data into tones that can be sent across phone lines. Call waiting also uses tones to signal an incoming call. If the modem hears those tones, it will probably get *very* confused and you could lose your connection.

◆ **To access an outside line for long-distance calls, dial**   Use this text box to type in the number (or numbers) that must be dialed to get an outside line for long-distance calls (such as 8).

◆ **Use this carrier code to make long-distance calls**   Use this text box to type in the number (or numbers) that must be dialed to access your long-distance provider.

◆ **Use this carrier code to make international calls**   Use this text box to type in the number (or numbers) that must be dialed to access your international call provider.

◆ **To disable call waiting, dial**   Activate this check box to disable call waiting before initiating the call. Note, too, that you also have to use the list to specify the proper code that the phone system requires to disable call waiting. (If you're not sure about the proper code, ask your phone company. If the code they give you isn't in the list, type it in by hand.)

◆ **Dial using**   Activate the appropriate option for your phone dialing: **Tone** or **Pulse**.

Area Code Rules, Dude!

Area codes are getting increasingly confusing. There are two main things that are causing the weirdness:

◆ **Calling the same area code**   In this situation, you don't usually have to bother with the area code. However, some phone systems insist that you include the area code even if the other number is in the same area code. In some cases, these are long-distance calls, so you even have to dial a 1 (or some other country or region code) to start the call.

◆ **Calling a different area code**   This situation normally requires that you dial a 1 (or whatever), followed by the area code, followed by the number. However, in some larger cities, the phone company has actually run out of numbers in the main area code, so they've created a whole new area code for the city. These aren't usually long-distance calls, however, so even though you have to include the area code, you don't usually have to dial a 1 to get started.

Note that in both cases, the area code may apply only to certain phone number prefixes. (The prefix is the first three digits of the seven-digit number.) If you have to make any calls in these situations, you need to define a new *area code rule* to handle it. Here's how it's done:

1. In the New Location dialog box, display the **Area Code Rules** tab.

2. Click **New** to display the New Area Code Rule dialog box.

3. Use the **Area code** text box to enter the area code you'll be calling.

4. If the rule will apply only to certain phone number prefixes, activate the **Include only the prefixes in the list below** option. Then click **Add,** enter the prefix (or prefixes), and click **OK.**

5. If you need to dial a country code (such as 1) before the area code, activate the **Dial** check box and use the text box to enter the number.

6. To force Windows XP to dial this area code, activate the **Include the area code** check box.

7. Click **OK.**

Using Calling Card Dialing

When you're on the road, you'll often find yourself having to make calls that cost money. For example, if you're in a hotel that charges for calls, you might want the charge to go through your calling card.

For this type of situation, Windows XP lets you specify a calling card to use when making the call. To get started, display the **Calling Card** tab in the New Location dialog box.

Here's the simplest route to take:

1. In the **Card Types** list, highlight the type of calling card you have.

2. Enter your **Account number.**

3. Enter your **Personal ID Number (PIN).**

If your calling card isn't in the list, click **New** to get to the New Calling Card dialog box. Alternatively, if your card is listed, you might need to adjust its settings. In that case, highlight the card and then click **Edit** to get the Edit Calling Card dialog box (which is identical to the New Calling Card dialog box). This dialog box has four tabs, so let's see what each one holds.

The **General** tab is as good a place as any to start. Here you need to enter three things: the **Calling card name** (this will appear in the Card Types list), your **Account number,** and your **Personal Identification Number (PIN).**

You use the **Long Distance** tab to specify the steps that must be followed to make a long-distance call. The first thing to do is specify your card's **Access number for long-distance calls.** After that's done, you define the steps by clicking the buttons below the **Calling card dialing steps** box. There are six buttons for your clicking finger to tickle:

◆ **Access Number**   Click this button to add the long-distance access number to the steps.

◆ **PIN**   Click this button to add your PIN to the steps.

◆ **Wait for Prompt**   Click this button to display a dialog box with various things that the system must wait for before continuing the dialing. You can have the system wait for a dial tone, a completed voice message, or a specified number of seconds.

◆ **Account Number**   Click this button to add your account number to the steps.

◆ **Destination Number**   Click this button to add the number you're calling to the steps. You also get a dialog box in which you can tell Windows XP to also dial the country code and area code.

◆ **Specify Digits**   Click this button to add one or more digits (as well as * and #) to the steps.

The idea is that you click these buttons in the order that they must appear in the card's calling sequence. If you make a mistake, use the **Move Up** and **Move Down** buttons to shuffle things around. If your card requires different sequences for international and local calls, follow the same steps using the **International** and **Local Calls** tabs. When you're done, click **OK** to return to the New Location dialog box. Then click **OK** to return to the Phone And Modem Options dialog box.

Using a Different Location When Connecting to the Internet

To put all this to good use when connecting to the Internet, first select **Start, Connect To** and then click your Internet connection. In the Connect dialog box, click **Properties.** In the **General** tab, activate the **Use dialing rules** check box. You now have two choices:

◆ Enter an **Area code** and/or the **Country/region code.**

◆ Click **Dialing Rules** to get to the Phone and Modem Options dialog box, use the **Locations** list to highlight the location you prefer to use, and then click **OK.**

The Least You Need to Know

◆ If you'll be setting up your connection by hand, your ISP should provide you with the settings and data you need: the access phone number, your user name and password, your IP address, and so on.

◆ Making the leap to the Internet is as easy as starting any Internet program, such as Internet Explorer. When the Connect dialog box wanders in, click **Dial.**

◆ To return to the real world, right-click the connection icon in the taskbar's system tray and then click **Disconnect.**

◆ To have both your phone and your modem available for use, run a phone cable from the wall jack to the modem's line port, and run a second cable from the phone to the modem's telephone jack.

◆ If you're using your modem on a line that has call waiting, be sure you tell Windows XP to turn off call waiting before dialing for data dollars.

Chapter 15

It's a Small Web After All: Using Internet Explorer

In This Chapter

♦ Using Internet Explorer to navigate web pages

♦ Saving web pages to your Favorites list

♦ Working with web pages offline

♦ Searching for the information you need

♦ How to use Netscape instead of Internet Explorer

Whether you're 19 or 90, a world traveler or a channel surfer, I don't think I'm going out on a limb when I say that you've probably never seen anything quite like the World Wide Web. We're talking here about an improbably vast conglomeration of the world's wit, wisdom, and weirdness. Arranged in separate pages of information, the web is home to just about every conceivable topic under the sun. If someone's thought of it, chances are someone else has a web page about it.

The great thing about the web is that it's not just a bunch of corporate marketing hoo-ha (although there's plenty of that, to be sure). No, *anyone* can publish a page, so the web reflects the different interests, idiosyncrasies, and eccentricities of the general population.

The web may sound like just some giant encyclopedia, but it boasts something that you won't find in any encyclopedia printed on mere paper: interaction. For example, almost every web page in existence comes equipped with a few *links*. Links are special sections of the document that, when clicked, immediately whisk you away to some other page on the current site or even to a page on another site (which may be on the other side of town or on the other side of the planet). You can also use the web to play games, post messages, buy things, sell things, grab files and programs, and much more.

If the web has a downside, it's that it's *too* big (there's no "index," per se, so finding the info you need can be hard) and that it's *too* easy to publish a page (with no editors in sight, there's no guarantee that the info you find is accurate or even true). Still, there are ways to search for data, and you can usually corroborate something by looking for other pages that have the same data.

Cross-Reference

If you haven't yet signed up with an Internet service provider, it means you've skipped ahead in this book (and I've caught you!). To learn about signing up with an ISP, check out Chapter 14.

So the web is definitely worth a look or three. This chapter helps you get those looks by showing you how to use the Windows XP Internet Explorer program, which is designed to surf (to use the proper web verb) websites. You'll learn all the standard page navigation techniques, and you'll learn all the features that Internet Explorer offers for making your online journeys more efficient and pleasant.

Internet Explorer Nuts and Bolts

The most straightforward way to get Internet Explorer up and surfing is to select **Start, Internet.** If this doesn't launch Internet Explorer for some reason, you can also select **Start, All Programs, Internet Explorer.**

If you connect to the Internet using a modem, you may now see a dialog box telling you that something or other is "not available offline." If so, click **Connect.**

If you don't have a connection established with your Internet service provider, the Dial-Up Connection dialog box shows up at this point. Go ahead and click **Connect** to reunite Windows XP and the Internet.

There's a good chance that you'll now arrive at the MSN.com website, shown in Figure 15.1. (You may end up at a different site if your version of Windows XP comes with custom Internet settings.) Note that this screen changes constantly, so the one you see will almost certainly look different than the one shown in Figure 15.1.

Page title   Address bar

Figure 15.1

When you launch Internet Explorer, you usually end up at the MSN.com website.

Links bar

Point at a link …   … and the address of the linked page appears here

MSN.com is Microsoft's Internet starting point. (This kind of site is known as a *portal* in the web trade.) With its colorful layout, generous graphics, and loads of links, MSN.com is a typical example of the professionally designed pages that the big-time sites offer.

Hacking Windows

If you don't like MSN.com (or whatever you have as Internet Explorer's default start page), it's easy to change it. First, surf to the page that you want to use as the new start page. Then select the **Tools, Internet Options** command to lure the Internet Options dialog box out into the open. In the **General** tab, click **Use Current**. If you decide later on that you prefer Internet Explorer's default home page, click **Use Default**. If you'd rather not see any page at startup, click **Use Blank**.

Before I show you how to use this page to see more of the web, let's take a minute or two and get our bearings by checking out the main features of the Internet Explorer window (most of which I've pointed out in Figure 16.1):

◆ **Page title**   The top line of the screen shows you the title of the current web page.

◆ **Address bar** This area shows you the address of the current page. Web page addresses are strange beasts, indeed. I'll help you figure them out a bit later in this chapter.

◆ **Links bar** This barely visible toolbar has various buttons that each represent a predefined link.

Windows Wisdom

When you light out for another page, Internet Explorer may pause for a while and then display a message that says **This page cannot be displayed.** This often means that the website is kaput or down temporarily. However, I've found that Internet Explorer displays this message for no good reason a lot of the time, and that pressing **F5** to refresh the page will bring the program to its senses.

◆ **Content area** This area below the Address and Links bars takes up the bulk of the Internet Explorer screen. It's where the body of each web page is displayed. You can use the vertical scrollbar to see more of the current page.

◆ **Links** The content area for most web pages also boasts a link or two (or 10). These links come in two flavors: images and text (the latter are usually underlined or in a different color than the rest of the text). When you put the mouse pointer over a link, Internet Explorer does two things (see Figure 15.1): It changes the pointer into a hand with a pointing finger, and it displays, in the status bar, the address of the linked page.

Web Page Navigation Basics

With that brief introduction out of the way, it's time to start wandering the web. This section runs through a few techniques for getting from one page to another.

The most straightforward method is to click any link that strikes your fancy. Click the link, and you're immediately (depending on the speed of your Internet connection) whisked to the other page.

How can I tell what's a link and what isn't?

That, unfortunately, is not as easy as it used to be. Originally, link text appeared underlined and in a different color. That's still the usual case for a link these days, but you can also get nonunderlined links, as well as images that are links. The only real way to be sure is to park your mouse pointer over some likely looking text or an image, and then watch what happens to the pointer. If it changes into the hand with a pointing finger, then you know for sure that you've got a link on your hands.

What if I know the address of the page I want to peruse?

Easy money. Here's what you do:

◆ Click inside the Address bar, delete the existing address, type in the address you want to check out, and then either press **Enter** or click **Go** (it's to the right of the Address bar).

◆ If the address is one that you've visited recently, use the Address bar's drop-down list to select it.

Windows Wisdom

Internet Explorer also assumes that most web addresses are of the form http://www.whatever. com. Therefore, if you simply type the "whatever" part and press **Ctrl+Enter**, Internet Explorer automatically adds the http:// www. prefix and the .com suffix. For example, you can get to my home page (http://www. mcfedries.com) by typing `mcfedries` and pressing **Ctrl+Enter**.

Why the heck are web addresses so, well, weird!

Probably because they were created by geeks who never imagined they'd be used by normal people. Still, they're not so bad after you figure out what's going on. Here's a summary of the various bits and pieces of a typical web address (or *URL*, which is short for Uniform Resource Locator, another geekism):

http://www.mcfedries.com/cigwinxp/index.asp

http://	This strange combination of letters and symbols tells the browser that you're entering a web address. Note that the browser assumes every address is a web address, so you don't need to include this part if you don't want to.
www.mcfedries.com	This is what's known as the domain name of the server computer that hosts the web page (www.mcfedries.com is my web server).
/cigwinxp/	This is the web server directory in which the web page makes its home.
index.asp	This is the web page's file name.

Ugh. Is there any easier way to get somewhere?

If you're not sure where you want to go, the default start page—it's called MSN.com—has lots of choices. For example, click any of the categories on the left (Autos, Careers & Jobs, and so on) to see lots of links related to that topic.

What if I jump to one page and then decide I want to double back to where I was?

That's a pretty common scenario. In fact, you'll often find that you need to leap back several pages, and then leap forward again. Fortunately, Internet Explorer makes this easy thanks to its Back and Forward toolbar buttons. Here's what you can do with them:

◆ Click **Back** to return to the previous page.

◆ Click **Forward** to move ahead to the next page.

◆ To go back several pages at once, drop down the **Back** button's list and click the page you want.

◆ To go forward several pages, drop down the **Forward** button's list and click the page you want.

◆ What if you want to go forward or back to a page but you also want to keep the current page in view? Easy money: Select **File, New, Window** (or press **Ctrl+N**) to open up a copy of the Internet Explorer window. You can then use that copy to leap to whatever page you want.

> **Windows Wisdom**
>
> After you've used Internet Explorer for a while, it will often "suggest" an address after you've typed in a few characters. If you see the address you want in the list that appears, use the down arrow key to highlight the address, and then press **Enter** (or click **Go**).

Techniques for Efficient Web Gallivanting

The paradox of the web is that even though it doesn't really exist anywhere (after all, where is the amorphous never-never land of cyberspace?), it's still one of the biggest earthly things you can imagine. There aren't hundreds of thousands of pages, or even millions of them for that matter. No, there are *billions* of web pages. (Of course, if you ignore all the pages that are devoted to Pamela Anderson Lee, then, yes, there *are* only a few hundred thousand pages.)

To have even a faint hope of managing just a tiny fraction of such an inconceivably vast array of data and bad MIDI music, you need to hone your web browsing skills with a few useful techniques. Fortunately, as you'll see in the next few sections, Internet Explorer has all kinds of features that can help.

Saving Sites for Subsequent Surfs: Managing Your Favorites

One of the most common experiences that folks new to web browsing go through is to stumble upon a really great site, and then not be able to find it again later. They try to retrace their steps, but usually just end up clicking links furiously and winding up in strange Net neighborhoods.

If this has happened to you, the solution is to get Internet Explorer to do all the grunt work of remembering sites for you. This is the job of the Favorites feature, which holds "shortcuts" to web pages and even lets you organize those shortcuts into separate folders.

Here's how you tell Internet Explorer to remember a web page as a favorite:

1. Use Internet Explorer to display the page.

2. Select **Favorites, Add to Favorites** to get the Add Favorite dialog box on-screen. (I'm going to ignore the **Make Available Offline** check box for now. I'll tackle it later on in Chapter 16.)

3. The **Name** text box shows the name of the page, which is what you'll select from a menu later on when you want to view this page again. If you can think of a better name, don't hesitate to edit this text.

Windows Wisdom

You can add the current page to your list of favorites lickety-split by pressing **Ctrl+D**.

4. Most people end up with dozens or even hundreds of favorites, so it's a good idea to organize them into folders. To save this favorite in a folder, click **Create In.** (If you don't want to bother with this, skip to step 7.)

5. The Favorites feature has only one folder at the start: Links, which you shouldn't use for this. Instead, click **New Folder,** enter a name for the new folder in the dialog box that comes up, and then click **OK.**

6. Click the folder in which you want to store your favorite.

7. Click **OK** to finish.

After you have some pages lined up as favorites, you can return to any one of them at any time by pulling down the **Favorites** menu and clicking the page title. (If the favorite is stored in a folder, click that folder to open its submenu, and then click the page.)

If you need to make changes to your favorites, you can do a couple of things right from the Favorites menu. Pull down the menu and then right-click the item you want to work with. In the shortcut menu that slinks in, click **Rename** to change the item's name, or click **Delete** to blow it away. If your list is jumbled, you can put things in alphabetical order by clicking **Sort by Name.**

For more heavy-duty adjustments, select the **Favorites, Organize Favorites** command. Not surprisingly, this pushes the Organize Favorites dialog box into view. You get four buttons to play with:

Windows Wisdom

If you find yourself constantly pulling down the Favorites menu to get at your favorite pages, you might prefer to have the Favorites list displayed full-time. You can do that by clicking the **Favorites** button in the toolbar. Internet Explorer then sets aside a chunk of real estate on the left side of the window to display the Favorites list.

◆ **Create Folder**   Click this button to create a new folder. (Tip: If you click an existing folder and then click this button, Internet Explorer creates a subfolder.) Internet Explorer adds the folder and displays **New Folder** inside a text box. Edit the text and then press **Enter.**

◆ **Move to Folder**   Click this button to move the currently highlighted favorite into another folder. In the Browse for Folder dialog box that saunters by, highlight the destination folder, and then click **OK.**

◆ **Rename**   Click this button to rename the currently highlighted favorite. Edit the name accordingly and then press **Enter.**

◆ **Delete**   Click this button to nuke the currently highlighted favorite. When Windows XP asks whether you're sure about this, click **Yes.**

When you're done, click **Close** to return to Internet Explorer.

Order Out of Chaos: Searching for Sites

Clicking willy-nilly in the hope of finding something interesting can be fun if you've got a few hours to kill. But if you need a specific tidbit of information *now*, then a click click here and click click there just won't cut the research mustard. To save time, you need to knock the web down to a more manageable size, and Internet Explorer's Search feature can help you do just that.

The idea is straightforward: You supply a search "engine" (as they're called) with a word or two that describes the topic you want to find. The search engine then scours the web for pages that contain those words, and presents you with a list of matches. Does it work? Well, it depends on which search engine you use. There are quite a few available, and some are better than others at certain kinds of searches. The biggest problem is that, depending on the topic you're looking for, the search engine might still return hundreds or even thousands of matching sites! You can usually get a more targeted search by adding more search terms and by avoiding common words.

Here's the basic procedure to follow to use the Search feature:

1. Click the **Search** button in the toolbar. Internet Explorer responds by shoe-horning the Search Companion into the left side of the content area.

2. Use the text box to enter the word or phrase you want to find.

3. Click **Search.** Internet Explorer runs the search and then displays the results a few seconds later. As you can see in Figure 15.2, you get a series of links and descriptions. (Generally speaking, the higher the link is in the list, the better the page it points to matches your search text.) Clicking a link displays the page.

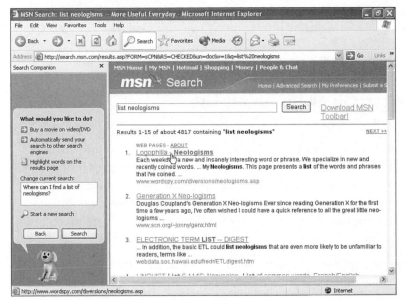

Figure 15.2

After the search is done, Internet Explorer displays a list of links to matching pages.

4. To get to more links, scroll down to the bottom of the Search bar. Here you'll see a **Next >>** link, which displays the next 10 matches.

5. When you've finished searching, click the **Search** toolbar button again to close the Search bar.

Here are a few notes to bear in mind when using the Search bar:

◆ **Putting the pup in the pound**   The animated puppy that accompanies the Search Companion is cute, for sure, but not all that useful. To search without him, click **Change preferences** (if you don't see this option, click **Start a new search**), and then click **Without an animated screen character.** If you're not a dog person, you can change the animated character instead. Click **Change preferences,** click **With a different character,** and then click **Next** until you see the character you prefer; click **OK.**

◆ The Search Companion submits your search text to several search engines. If you have a preferred search site, you can set it as the default engine. To do that, click **Change preferences,** and then click **Change Internet search behavior.** Activate the **With Classic Internet search** option and then click the search engine you want. (Click **OK** to make it so.)

◆ **Address bar searching**   If you don't like the Search Companion usurping a big chunk of the Internet Explorer window, you can also run searches from the Address bar. Just type in a word or phrase, press the **down-arrow** key, and then press **Enter.**

Bread Crumbs in Cyberspace: Using the History List

You've seen so far how Internet Explorer keeps track of the pages you've visited in the current session. You can then use the Back and Forward buttons for to-and-fro surfing. That works well for the sites you've seen in the current Internet Explorer session, but what if you want to go back to a nonfavorite site you saw yesterday or even last week? That might seem like a tall order, but it turns out that Internet Explorer has a tall memory. In fact, the program offers a History feature that remembers pretty much everywhere you've gone for the past 20 days! Here's how it works:

1. Click the **History** button in the toolbar. By this time, you won't be surprised to see a History bar show up on the left side of the window, as shown in Figure 15.3.

2. You now do one of the following:

   ◆ If the date you want to work with was this week, click the day (such as **Monday**).

   ◆ If the date you want is in a previous week, click the week (such as **2 Weeks Ago**) and then click the day.

3. Internet Explorer displays a list of the sites you visited that day. Click the site you want. This gives you a list of the pages you visited on that site.

4. Click the page you want to see. Internet Explorer displays the page in the rest of the content area.

History button

Figure 15.3

Use the History bar to see a list of the places you've seen over the past 20 days.

Click an item
here …

… and the page
loads here

Internet Explorer also offers a couple of methods for dealing with the History bar's links:

◆ **Sorting the list**   Click the History bar's **View** button and then click a sort option (such as **By Most Visited**).

◆ **Searching the list**   If you do a lot of surfing, your History bar will be crammed to the gills with links. To find the one you want, click the History bar's **Search** button, enter a word or phrase in the **Search for** text box, and then click **Search Now.**

When you're done with the History bar, you can hide it by clicking the **History** toolbar button once again.

"What If I Want to Use Netscape?"

Internet Explorer comes free with Windows XP, and it's built right into the fabric of the operating system. However, that doesn't mean you can't use an alternative web browser such as Netscape Navigator. Just download the browser from Netscape (go to home.netscape.com) and then install it.

You should note, however, that Netscape will probably set itself up to be the Windows XP default browser. (Some versions of Netscape are polite enough to ask you whether this is what you want.) This means that if you launch a shortcut to a web page, it's Netscape that displays the page, not Internet Explorer.

Windows Wisdom

If you use both Internet Explorer and Netscape, a big problem you'll run into is that they don't share a common list of favorites—which are called *bookmarks* in the Netscape world. However, Internet Explorer is happy to either export the Favorites look to Netscape's bookmarks list or import the bookmarks as favorites. Select the **File, Import and Export** command.

What do you do if you'd prefer to use Internet Explorer as the default browser? This isn't a problem, but you first have to tell Internet Explorer to check to see whether it's the default. You do this by following these steps:

1. Select **Tools, Internet Options** to open the Internet Options dialog box.

2. Display the **Programs** tab.

3. Make sure the **Internet Explorer should check to see whether it is the default browser** check box is activated.

4. Click **OK**.

Now shut down Internet Explorer and then start it back up again. This time, you'll see a dialog box telling you that Internet Explorer isn't your default browser and asking if you want to make it the default. If you want to restore Internet Explorer's position as the default browser, click **Yes;** otherwise, click **No**.

The Least You Need to Know

◆ To start Internet Explorer, select **Start, Internet.** (Alternatively, select **Start, All Programs, Internet Explorer.**)

◆ To light out for another page, either click a link or type an address in the Address bar and then press **Enter.** Use the toolbar's **Back** button to return to the previous page, and use the **Forward** button to head the other way.

◆ To scour the web for a particular topic, click the **Search** button to get the Search Companion on-screen, enter a word or two, and then click **Search.**

◆ Run the **Favorites, Add Favorites** command (or press **Ctrl+D**) to save a page on the Favorites menu.

◆ To return to any site you visited in the last 20 days, open the History bar by clicking the **History** toolbar button.

Chapter 16

The Savvy Surfer: More Internet Explorer Fun

In This Chapter

- ◆ Working with web pages offline
- ◆ Taking advantage of the Links bar
- ◆ Dealing with file downloads
- ◆ Customizing, converting, and otherwise cajoling Internet Explorer into doing what you want it to do

Like electrons passing in the night, web users never see each other as they surf sites. If they could, however, there might be a mutual flash of recognition between them because most web users seem to fall into one of three categories:

- ◆ **Clickstreamers** Users who spend their online time wandering aimlessly from site to site, hoping for serendipitous finds (a new word: surfendipity!). By the way, *clickstream* is web jargon for the "path" a person takes as he navigates through the web by clicking links.

- ◆ **Nooksurfers** People who keep going to the same sites over and over and rarely check out new sites.

- ◆ **Researchers** People who use the web exclusively for gathering information.

Whatever kind of web user you are, your online time will be vastly more fun and productive if you can play your browser like a virtuoso. To that end, this chapter presents a master class for Internet Explorer. You learn how to read pages while you're offline, how to customize the Links bar, how to work with Internet Explorer's options, and much more.

Offline Surfing: Reading Pages When You're Not Connected

Many web fans have a few pages that they check out regularly because the content is always changing. Let's say you have 12 such pages and it takes you an average of five minutes to read each one. That's an hour of online time you've used up. Wouldn't it be better if Internet Explorer could somehow grab those pages while you weren't around (at night, for example), and then let you read them while you're not connected?

Well, *sure* it would! That's probably why the Windows XP programmers added the Synchronize feature to Internet Explorer. This feature lets you designate web pages to be available offline (that is, when you're not connected to the Internet). Then, when you run the Synchronize command, Internet Explorer absconds with the latest version of those pages and stores them on your hard disk. Internet Explorer also is happy to set up an automatic synchronization that can be scheduled to run any time you like.

To make a page available offline, begin by using either of the following techniques:

◆ **If the page is set up as a favorite**   Pull down the **Favorites** menu to display the shortcut for the page. Then right-click that **shortcut** and click **Make available offline.**

◆ **If the page isn't yet set up as a favorite**   Display the page and then select **Favorites, Add to Favorites** to meet up with the Add Favorite dialog box. Activate the **Make available offline** check box and then click **Customize.**

Whichever route you take, you end up with the Offline Favorite Wizard staring you in the face. Here's how it works:

1. The first wizard dialog box just offers an introduction, so click **Next.** (You can save yourself this step down the road by activating the **In the future, do not show this introduction screen** check box.) You end up at the Offline Favorite Wizard dialog box.

2. This wizard dialog box wonders whether you want any pages that are linked to the favorite to be downloaded, as well. If you don't care about the linked pages, activate **No;** otherwise, activate **Yes** and then use the **Download pages X links deep from this page** spin box to specify how many levels of links you want grabbed. Click **Next** when you're ready to proceed.

3. The wizard asks how you want the page *synchronized:*

   ◆ **Only when I choose Synchronize from the Tools menu**   Select this option if you want to control when the synchronization occurs. If you choose this option, click **Next** and then skip to step 5.

   ◆ **I would like to create a new schedule**   Activate this option if you want Internet Explorer to perform the synchronization automatically on a preset schedule. If you select this option, click **Next** and then continue with step 4.

   Jargon Jar

   Synchronize means to download a copy of a web page so that the version you have stored on your computer is the same as (that is, is synchronized with) the version on the web.

4. If you elected to set up a synchronization schedule, you'll see a dialog box with scheduling options. Here's a rundown of the controls you get to mess with (click **Next** when you're ready to move on):

   ◆ **Every X days**   Specify the number of days between synchronizations.

   ◆ **At**   Specify the time you want the synchronization to happen.

   ◆ **Name**   Enter a name for this synchronization schedule.

   ◆ **If my computer is not connected …**   Activate this check box to have Internet Explorer connect your computer to the Internet to download the page (or pages). Note that this option works only if you don't have to type in any log-on information (such as your user name and password) to connect to your ISP.

5. The final wizard dialog box wants to know whether the web page requires you to log on. If not (most sites don't), activate **No;** if so, activate **Yes** and then fill in your **User name** and **Password** (twice). Click **Finish** to complete the synchronization setup.

6. If you're adding a new favorite, you'll end up back in the Add Favorite dialog box. Select a folder for the favorite (if necessary) and then click **OK.**

At this point, Internet Explorer performs the initial synchronization: It connects to the page and hauls in a copy that it stores on your system.

If you elected to go the manual synchronization route, you can download the pages for offline perusing at any time by selecting the **Tools, Synchronize** command. In the Items to Synchronize dialog box (see Figure 16.1), deactivate the check boxes for any items you don't want to synchronize, and then click **Synchronize.**

Figure 16.1

Deactivate the check box beside any page you don't want synchronized.

Customizing the Handy Links Bar

Internet Explorer's Links bar contains a few prefab sites that you can try out to get your web feet wet. To see the buttons, you have two choices:

♦ Click the **right-pointing double arrow.**

♦ View the entire toolbar by moving the mouse pointer over the **Links** label and then dragging it below the Address bar. (If the bar won't budge, right-click any toolbar and then deactivate the **Lock the Toolbars** command.)

Windows Wisdom _____

Internet Explorer's toolbar is a mishmash of text and nontext buttons. Who's the genius who came up that *that?* The buttons would be much easier to decipher if they all displayed text. Fortunately, that's not a problem. Select **View, Toolbars, Customize** to request the presence of the Customize Toolbar dialog box. Use the **Text options** list to select **Show text labels,** and then click **Close.**

Here's a summary of each link:

♦ **Customize Links**   This link takes you to a page that tells you how to customize the Links bar.

♦ **Free Hotmail**   This button takes you to a page where you can sign up for a free e-mail account with Microsoft's Hotmail service.

♦ **Windows**   This link takes you to the Windows home page.

♦ **Windows Media**   This link takes you to the Windows Media page where you can access music, videos, and other media.

I have two words I use to describe the default Links bar buttons: bo-ring! However, I really like the Links bar itself because, in my never-ending quest to minimize mouse clicks and keystrokes, it offers me one-click access to sites. To get the most out of it, however, I give the default links the heave-ho and replace them with my most frequently accessed sites. Here's a rundown of some of the things you can do to remake the Links bar:

♦ **Sizing the Links bar**   After you drag the Links bar to where it can be seen, you're free to change its size. To give this a whirl, position the mouse pointer over the left edge of the bar and then drag your mouse left or right.

♦ **Changing the button positions**   The positions of the Links bar buttons aren't set in stone. To move any button, use your mouse to drag the button left or right along the Links bar.

♦ **Changing a button's address**   If you right-click a button and then click **Properties,** Internet Explorer displays the Properties dialog box for an Internet shortcut. Use the **URL** text box to edit the button's address.

♦ **Creating a button for the current page**   To add a new Links bar button for the current page, drag the page icon from the Address bar and drop it on the Links bar.

♦ **Creating a button from a hypertext link**   If a page has a hypertext link, you can create a button for that link by dragging the link text into the Links bar.

♦ **Renaming a button**   Right-click the button and then click **Rename** in the menu. In the Rename dialog box that barges in, enter the new name and then click **OK.**

♦ **Deleting a button**   To blow away a button from the Links bar, drag the button and then drop it in the Windows XP Recycle Bin. (You can also right-click the button and then click **Delete.**)

Dealing with Files in Internet Explorer

As you click your way around the web, you find that some links don't take you to other pages but are, instead, tied directly to a file. In this case, Internet Explorer throws the File Download dialog box at you, as shown in Figure 16.2. You need to decide what you want to do with the file:

Figure 16.2

When you click a link to a file, Internet Explorer uses this dialog box to find out how you want it to handle the file.

◆ **Open**   Click this button to run the file right away after it has been down-loaded. Only go this route if you're absolutely sure that the file is safe to run.

◆ **Save**   Click this button to save the file to a location on your computer's hard disk. In the Save As dialog box that shows up next, choose a location for the file, and then click **Save.**

◆ **Cancel**   Click this button to bypass downloading the file.

Look Out!

You need to be careful about downloading files because they can contain viruses that wreck your system. To be safe, you should only download from reputable sites, or from sites that you trust explicitly. If you plan on living dangerously and downloading files willy-nilly, at least get yourself a good antivirus program such as McAfee (www.mcafee.com) or Norton (www.symantec.com).

If you elected to save the file, you'll eventually see the Download Complete dialog box, which offers three buttons:

◆ **Open**   Click this button to launch the down-loaded file.

◆ **Open Folder**   Click this button to open a window that displays the contents of the folder into which you saved the file. This is a good choice if you want to do something other than launch the file (such as rename it).

◆ **Close**   Click this button to put off dealing with the file until later.

Sometimes web pages contain things that Internet Explorer can't display properly without installing the appropriate component. This happens with things like Java applets and foreign character sets. In this case, Internet Explorer will pester you with an Install On Demand dialog box similar to the one shown in Figure 16.3. You have two choices:

♦ To update Internet Explorer with the required component, click **Download.**

♦ If you don't want to bother with the component, click **Cancel.** (If you never want Internet Explorer to bug you about this component again, be sure to activate the **Never download any of these components** check box before you click **Cancel.**)

Hacking Windows

If you don't ever see the Install On Demand dialog box, this feature may be turned off in your version of Internet Explorer. To activate it, select **Tools, Internet Options,** display the **Advanced** tab, and activate the **Enable Install On Demand (Internet Explorer)** and **Enable Install On Demand (Other)** check boxes.

Figure 16.3

Internet Explorer displays this dialog box if it needs to install a component to render a page properly.

A Few More Useful Internet Explorer Options

It's probably safe to crown Internet Explorer the undisputed heavyweight customization champion of the Windows world. This baby is bursting at the seams with settings, options, dials, and widgets for changing the way the program works. The secret to the prodigious customizability is the Internet Options dialog box. To shove this dialog box into the fray, use any of the following techniques:

♦ In Internet Explorer, select **Tools, Internet Options.**

♦ Select **Start,** right-click the **Internet** icon, and then click **Internet Properties.**

♦ Select **Start, Control Panel, Network and Internet Connections, Internet Options.**

Either way, you end up eyeball to eyeball with the Internet Options dialog box shown in Figure 16.4.

Figure 16.4

Use the Internet Options dialog box to customize Internet Explorer to suit the way you work.

The **General** tab contains a mixed bag of options:

◆ **Home page**   To change the Internet Explorer home page (the page that first appears when you launch the browser), use the **Address** text box to enter the address of the page you prefer to use. (Alternatively, first navigate to the page you want to use, and then click **Use Current** in this group. To revert to Internet Explorer's default home page, click the **Use Default** button. If you prefer that Internet Explorer not load a page at startup, click **Use Blank.**

◆ **Temporary Internet files**   The temporary Internet files folder is a storage area where Internet Explorer keeps the files associated with the sites that you visit. That way, when you revisit a page, Internet Explorer only has to pick up the local files, which means it can display the page contents much more quickly. You can click **Delete Files** to clear this cache, and you can click **Settings** to adjust a few parameters. I recommend leaving these options as is, however. You can also click **Delete Cookies** to wipe out all your cookie files. (If you prefer to delete individual cookies, click **Settings,** click **View Files,** and then look for file names that begin with **cookie:.**)

Look Out! _____

These temporary Internet files sound like the bees knees, but they have a downside. There's a chance that the page may have changed since your last visit, which means the version stored by Internet Explorer is out-of-date. If you want to make sure you're seeing the most recent edition of a page, either select Internet Explorer's **View, Refresh** command or press **F5**.

- **History**   This group controls various options related to the History list I talked about in the previous chapter. Use the **Days to keep pages in history** spin box to set the maximum number of days that Internet Explorer will store an address in its History list. You can also click **Clear History** to remove all URLs from the History folder.

You'll learn about the **Security** and **Privacy** tabs in Chapter 19, so let's skip over to the **Content** tab, which boasts a wide array of settings for dealing with the content you come across on the web. The buttons in the **Content Advisor** group let you control the type of content that appears in the browser:

- **Enable**   Clicking this button displays the Content Advisor dialog box, described next. When you click **OK,** you see the Create Supervisor Password dialog box, which you use to enter a password for the Content Advisor. After you've done this, the name of this button changes to Disable. You can turn off the ratings by clicking this button and entering your password.

- **Settings**   Clicking this button displays the Content Advisor, which you use to set site restrictions for people who don't know the password. The idea is that you select a category (such as Language or Nudity) and then move the slider to set the maximum level that users who don't have a password can view. If a site is rated higher, users must enter the supervisor password to download the site. (Note that these ratings are *not* provided by Microsoft; instead, they come from the Recreational Software Advisory Council, which you can check out at www.rsac.org.)

Windows Wisdom _____

The Internet is bursting with other tools that can help parents restrict the content their children can view. These packages come with names such as CyberSitter—you get the idea. The Yahoo! Service has a list of these software packages at the following address: http://dir.yahoo.com/Business_and_Economy/Shopping_and_Services/ Communication_and_Information_Management/Internet_and_World_Wide_Web/ Software/Blocking_and_Filtering/Titles/.

The **Certificates** group deals with site certificates that act as positive identifications on the web. This is advanced stuff, and it can be safely ignored.

The **Personal information** group gives you a place to store some data about yourself. Here are the options:

◆ **AutoComplete**   This feature enables Internet Explorer to automatically enter some data for you, including form data. Click this button and then activate the check boxes for the features with which you want to use AutoComplete.

◆ **My Profile**   Click this button to enter more data about yourself that a website can grab automatically.

Windows Wisdom _____

If AutoComplete is off, the first time you enter data into a web form and then submit it, Internet Explorer sends in a dialog box asking if you want to turn AutoComplete on. Click **Yes** to activate AutoComplete, or click **No** to leave it be.

If you decide to go the AutoComplete route, *never* use it to automatically enter passwords for sensitive data such as online banking sites, stock trading, health sites, and so on.

The **Connections** tab stores most of the information you supplied when you set up your Internet connection. You can use the controls in this tab to change some of those settings, or you can click **Setup** to run the wizard all over again.

If you select Internet Explorer's **Tools, Mail and News** command, you see a menu of commands that enable you to read and send mail and to view newsgroups. The controls in the **Programs** tab determine which applications Internet Explorer launches when you select these commands. Again, you'll probably want to leave these as they are.

Finally, the **Advanced** tab boasts a huge list of check boxes and option buttons that controls how Internet Explorer interacts with the web. For example, if you're sick of those lame MIDI files that so many webmasters play when you visit their sites, you can turn them off by deactivating the **Play sounds in web pages** check box.

Unfortunately, there are just way too many options to go through here. If you want to get the lowdown on all these settings, check out the following page on my website: www.mcfedries.com/ramblings/IEAdvanced.asp.

The Least You Need to Know

◆ To get Internet Explorer to download a page for leisurely offline reading, select **Favorites, Add Favorites** and activate the **Make available offline** check box.

◆ Right-click a **Links** bar button to rename or delete the button or to change the link address. To add a button to the Links bar, either drag the Address bar icon into the Links bar or drag a link into the Links bar.

◆ To customize Internet Explorer, select the **Tools, Internet Options** command (or launch the Control Panel's **Internet Options** icon) to display the Internet Options dialog box.

Sending and Receiving E-Mail Missives

In This Chapter

- Giving Windows XP your e-mail account particulars
- How to compose and send an e-mail message
- Working with the Windows XP Address Book
- Handling attachments
- How to get and read incoming messages

The world passed a milestone of sorts a few years ago when it was reported that, in North America at least, more e-mail messages are sent each day than postal messages. Now, e-mail message volume is several times that of "snail mail" (as regular mail is derisively called by the wired set), and the number of e-notes shipped out each day is counted in the *billions*.

The really good news is that e-mail has become extremely easy to use because e-mail programs have become much better over the years. An excellent example of this trend is Outlook Express, the Windows XP Internet e-mail program. As you see in this chapter, shipping out messages and reading incoming messages is a painless affair thanks to the admirable e-mail capabilities of Outlook Express.

Firing Up Outlook Express

Windows XP gives you a couple of ways to launch the program:

- Select **Start, E-mail.**

- Select **Start, All Programs, Outlook Express.**

Setting Up Your Internet E-Mail Account

Before Outlook Express loads for the first time, it calls in the Internet Connection Wizard to handle the various steps required to divulge the details of the e-mail account you have with your ISP (Internet Service Provider). Here's a rundown of the information you should have at your fingertips:

Jargon Jar

The acronyms and abbreviations are thick on the ground in this section. You don't have to understand them to send and receive e-mail, but here's what they mean just in case you're interested: **POP3** stands for Post Office Protocol; **IMAP** stands for Internet Message Access Protocol; **HTTP** stands for Hyper-Text Transfer Protocol; and **SMTP** stands for Simple Mail Transfer Protocol.

Jargon Jar

A **mail server** is a computer that your ISP uses to store and send your e-mail messages.

- The user name and password for your e-mail account. (These are almost always the same as your Internet log-on name and password.)

- The type of server the ISP uses for incoming e-mail: *POP3, IMAP,* or *HTTP.*

- The Internet name used by the ISP's incoming *mail server* (this often takes the form mail. *provider*.com, where *provider* is the name of the ISP). Note that your ISP might call this its *POP3 server.*

- The Internet name used by the ISP's outgoing mail server (this is almost always the same as the incoming e-mail server). Some ISPs call this their *SMTP server.*

Here's what happens:

1. The wizard asks for your display name, which is the name other folks see when you send them a message. Enter the name you want to use in the **Display name** text box (most people just use their real name) and click **Next.**

2. Now the wizard pesters you for your e-mail address. Enter your address in the **E-mail address** text box and click **Next.**

3. Next on the wizard's to-do list is gathering info about your ISP's e-mail server. You have three things to fill in (as usual, click **Next** when you're done):

   ◆ **My incoming mail server is a …**   Use this list to specify the type of e-mail server your ISP uses; most are **POP3.**

   ◆ **Incoming mail (POP3, IMAP, or HTTP) server**   Enter the name of the server that your ISP uses for incoming mail.

   ◆ **Outgoing mail (SMTP) server**   Enter the name of the server that your ISP uses for outgoing mail.

4. The next items on the agenda are your account details: your **Account name** (this should already be filled in for you) and your **Password.** If you don't want to be pestered for your password each time you connect, leave the **Remember password** check box activated. Click **Next** after that's finished.

5. Click **Finish.**

The Lay of the Outlook Express Land

By default, Outlook Express is set up to go online and grab your waiting messages when you launch the program. We'll get there eventually, so for now just close the Connect dialog box if it shows up.

At long last, the Outlook Express window shows itself, and it looks much like the one in Figure 17.1.

Figure 17.1

Use Outlook Express to ship and receive Internet e-mail messages.

The Folders bar on the left uses a treelike structure to list the various storage areas that come with Outlook Express. I talk about folders in more detail in Chapter 18. However, here's a quick summary of what the default folders are all about:

◆ **Inbox**   This folder is where Outlook Express stores the e-mail messages that you receive.

◆ **Outbox**   This folder stores messages that you've composed but haven't sent yet.

◆ **Sent Items**   This folder stores a copy of the messages that you've sent.

◆ **Deleted Items**   This folder stores the messages that you delete.

◆ **Drafts**   This folder stores messages that you're in the middle of composing and have saved.

You also see a Contacts list, which gives you quick access to people who are in your address book.

Windows Wisdom

The default Outlook Express startup screen shows a collection of common chores (such as Create a New Mail message). Most people don't find this screen particularly useful, so they just click the **Inbox** folder (which is where all your incoming messages first get stored). If you want Outlook Express to open the Inbox folder automatically at startup, activate the **When Outlook Express starts, go directly to my Inbox** check box.

The Outbox: Sending an E-Mail Message

Let's begin the Outlook Express tour with a look at how to foist your e-prose on unsuspecting colleagues, friends, family, and *Brady Bunch* cast members. This section shows you the basic technique to use, and then gets a bit fancier in discussing the Address Book, attachments, and other Outlook Express sending features.

The Basics: Composing and Sending a Message

Without further ado (not that there's been much ado to this point, mind you), here are the basic steps to follow to fire off an e-mail message to some lucky recipient:

1. Click the **Create Mail** button in the toolbar, or select **Message, New Message**. (Keyboard fans will be pleased to note that pressing **Ctrl+N** also works.) You end up with the New Message window on-screen, as shown in Figure 17.2.

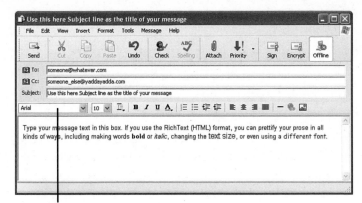

The formatting bar

Figure 17.2

You cobble together an e-mail message in the New Message window.

2. In the **To** text box, type in the e-mail address of the recipient. (It's perfectly acceptable to enter multiple addresses in this text box. Use a semicolon [;] or a comma [,] to separate each address.)

3. The address you put in the To box is the "main" recipient of the message. However, it's common to shoot a copy of the message off to a "secondary" recipient. To do that, enter their e-mail address in the **Cc** text box. (Again, you can enter multiple addresses, if you're so inclined.)

   There's also a *blind courtesy* (or *carbon*) *copy* (Bcc), which delivers a copy of the message to a specified recipient. However, none of the other recipients see that person's address anywhere. To enter a Bcc address, activate the **View, All Headers** command to add a **Bcc** field to the **New Message** window.

4. Use the **Subject** line to enter a subject for the message. (The subject acts as a kind of title for your message. It's the first thing the recipient sees, so it should accurately reflect the content of your message, but it shouldn't be too long. Think *pithy*.)

5. Decide what type of message you want to send. You have two choices, both of which are commands on the Format menu:

   ◆ **Rich Text (HTML)**   Choose this command to include formatting in your message. This enables you to make your message look its best. However, your recipient might have problems if his or her e-mail program doesn't support this formatting. (Just so you know, HTML stands for Hypertext Markup Language. It's a series of codes used to format characters and things, and it's used to create web pages. Don't worry, you don't have to know anything about HTML to use this feature.)

◆ **Plain Text** Choose this command to send out the message without any formatting. This makes life easier for your recipient if he or she doesn't have an e-mail program that supports formatting. If you're not sure what your recipient is using, choose this command.

6. Use the large, empty area below the Subject line to type in the message text (also known as the *message body*).

7. If you chose the Rich Text (HTML) format, after you're inside the message text area, notice that the buttons on the Formatting bar suddenly come alive, as do more of the Format menu commands. Use these buttons and commands to change the font, format paragraphs, add a background image, apply stationery, and more. (*Stationery* is a prefab set of formatting options.)

8. When your message is fit for human consumption, you have two sending choices:

◆ **If you're working online** Click the **Send** toolbar button or select **File, Send Message** (or try **Alt+S** on for size). Outlook Express sends the message, no questions asked.

> **Windows Wisdom**
>
> Outlook Express has a **Spelling** command on the **Tools** menu (as well as a **Spelling** toolbar button). If you can't select it, it's because Outlook Express doesn't actually have its own spell checker. Instead, it rides the spell checking coattails of other programs, such as Microsoft Word. So you can run the Spelling command only if you have a spell-check–equipped program installed.

◆ **If you're working offline** Click the **Send** toolbar button or select **File, Send Later.** In this case, Outlook Express coughs up a dialog box that tells you the message will bunk down in the Outbox folder until you're ready to send it. This is good because it means you can compose a few messages before connecting to the Internet. When you're ready to actually ship the messages, select the **Tools, Send and Receive, Send All** command in Outlook Express. (You also can drop down the **Send/Recv** toolbar button, and then click **Send All.**)

Note that after your message is Net-bound, Outlook Express also is kind enough to save a copy of the message in the Sent Items folder. This is handy because it gives you a record of all the missives you launch into cyberspace.

Easier Addressing: Using the Address Book

If you find yourself with a bunch of recipients to whom you send stuff regularly (and it's a rare e-mailer who doesn't), you soon grow tired of entering their addresses by hand. The solution is to toss those regulars into the Windows XP Address Book. That way, you can fire them into the To or Cc lines with just a few mouse clicks.

Here's how you add someone to the Address Book:

1. In Outlook Express, click the **Addresses** button or select the **Tools, Address Book** command. (Keyboard diehards can get their kicks by pressing **Ctrl+Shift+B.** Note, too, that you also can work on your Address Book when Outlook Express isn't running. In this case, select **Start, All Programs, Accessories, Address Book.**)

2. In the Address Book window that reports for duty, click the **New** toolbar button and then click **New Contact.** (Alternatively, either select **File, New Contact** or click **Ctrl+N.**) The Address Book conjures up the Properties dialog box shown in Figure 17.3.

Figure 17.3

Use this dialog box to spell out the particulars of the new recipient.

3. In the **Name** tab, enter at least the person's **First** and **Last** names.

4. Use the **E-Mail Addresses** text box to enter the recipient's address, and then click **Add.** (If this person has multiple e-mail addresses, repeat this procedure as often as necessary. To set one of these addresses as the default, highlight it and click **Set as Default.**)

5. If you want this person to receive only plain text messages, activate the **Send E-Mail using plain text only** check box.

6. Fill in the fields in the other tabs, if you feel like it.

7. When you're done, click **OK** to add the new recipient.

After you have a contact in your Address Book, Outlook Express gives you a ton of ways to get them a message. Here are my three favorite methods:

♦ In the **New Message** window, start typing the person's name or nickname (a special name you type in when entering a person in your Address Book). If

Outlook Express recognizes the name you're typing, it will fill in the rest of the name for you automatically. When the name is correct, press **Tab** to set it.

◆ In the New Message window, click **To** or **Cc** to get the Select Recipients dialog box. Click the **contact name** and then click **To** (or **Cc** or **Bcc**). (If the person has multiple addresses, Outlook Express assumes you want to use the default address. To use a different address, right-click the **person's name**, click **Action, Send Mail To,** and then click the **address you want to use.**)

◆ The Outlook Express window has a Contacts area that lists everyone in the Address Book. Use this area to double-click the **name of the recipient** you want to use.

> **Windows Wisdom**
>
> If you want to send a message to a particular set of recipients, you can organize them into a *group* and then specify the group name in the To line. To create a group, open the **Address Book**, click the **New** button and then click **New Group**. Enter a **Group Name** and then click **Select Members** to add recipients to the group.

One final note: If you set up the recipient to receive only plain text messages, when you send the message, you see a dialog box asking what format you want to use. In this case, you'd click **Send Plain Text.**

Inserting Attachments and Other Hangers-On

Most of your messages will be text-only creations (perhaps with a bit of formatting tossed in to keep things interesting). However, it's also possible to send entire files along for the ride. Such files are called, naturally enough, *attachments*. They're very common in the business world, and it's useful to know how they work. Here it goes:

1. In the New Message window, either click the **Attach** toolbar button or select **Insert, File Attachment.** The Insert Attachment dialog box rears its head.

> **Jargon Jar**
>
> An **attachment** is a separate file that accompanies an e-mail message.

2. Find the file you want to attach and then highlight it.

3. Click **Attach.** Outlook Express returns you to the New Message window where you see a new **Attach** box that includes the name of the file.

As you can see, adding attachments isn't that hard. However, that doesn't mean you should bolt an attachment or two onto every message you send. Adding attachments can greatly increase the size of your message, so it may take the recipient quite a while to download your message, which won't be appreciated, I can tell you. Some ISP's put an upper limit on the size of a message, so it's also possible that your recipient may never see your note. Use common sense and only attach files when it's absolutely necessary.

The Inbox: Getting and Reading E-Mail Messages

Some people like to think of e-mail as a return to the days of *belles-lettres* and *billets-doux* (these people tend to be a bit pretentious). Yes, it's true that e-mail has people writing again, but this isn't like the letter-writing of old. The major difference is that e-mail's turnaround time is usually much quicker. Instead of waiting weeks or even months to get a return letter, a return e-mail might take as little as a few minutes or a few hours.

So, if you send out a message with a question or comment, chances are you get a reply coming right back at you before too long. Any messages sent to your e-mail address are stored in your account at your ISP. Your job is to use Outlook Express to access your account and grab any waiting messages. This section shows you how to do that and shows you what to do with those messages after they're safely stowed on your computer.

Getting Your Messages

Here are the steps to stride through to get your e-mail messages:

1. Outlook Express offers two different postal routes:

   ◆ **To only receive messages**   Either drop down the **Send/Recv** toolbar button and then click **Receive All,** or select **Tools, Send and Receive, Receive All.**

   ◆ **To send and receive messages**   If you have outgoing messages waiting in your Outbox folder, either drop down the **Send/Recv** toolbar button and then click **Send and Receive All,** or select **Tools, Send and Receive, Send and Receive All.** (Keyboardists can get away with pressing **Ctrl+M.**)

2. Outlook Express connects to the Internet (if necessary), accesses your mail account, absconds with any waiting messages, and then stuffs them into the Outlook Express Inbox folder. If you were working offline previously, disconnect from the Internet if you no longer need the connection.

3. If it's not already displayed, click the **Inbox** folder so you can see what the e-postman delivered.

When you're working online, Outlook Express automatically checks for new messages every 30 minutes. You can change that by selecting **Tools, Options.** In the **General** tab, use the spin box that's part of the **Check for new messages every** X **minute(s)** option to set the checking interval.

Reading Your Messages

Figure 17.4 shows the Inbox folder with a few messages. The first thing to notice is that Outlook Express uses a bold font for all messages that you haven't read yet. You also get info about each message organized with the following half-dozen columns:

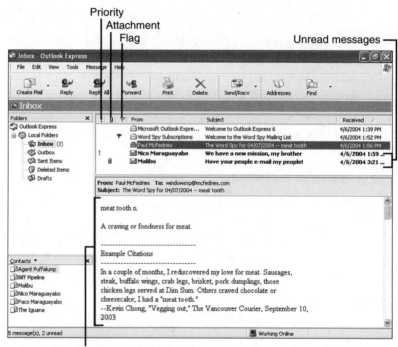

Figure 17.4

After you've pilfered your incoming messages from your ISP, they get stored in your Inbox folder.

◆ **Priority**   This column tells you whether the sender set up the message with a priority ranking. If you see a red exclamation mark, it means the message was sent with high priority (this is the "handle this pronto, buster!" symbol); if you see a blue, downward-pointing arrow, it means the note was sent with low priority (this is the "handle this whenever, man" symbol).

◆ **Attachment**   If you see a paper clip icon in this column, it means the message is accompanied by a file attachment. See the "Attending to Attachments" section later in this chapter.

◆ **Flag** If you want to remind yourself to deal with a message, you can "flag" it for a future follow-up (a sort of digital string-tied-to-the-finger thing). You do this by highlighting the message and then selecting the **Message, Flag Message** command. This adds a flag icon in this column.

◆ **From** This column tells you the name (or occasionally, just the e-mail address) of the person or company that sent you the message.

◆ **Subject** This column shows you the subject line of the message which will, hopefully, give you a brief description of the contents of the message.

◆ **Received** This column tells you the date and time the message was received.

Outlook Express offers two methods for seeing what a message has to say:

◆ Highlight the message in the Inbox folder. Outlook Express displays the text of the note in the Preview pane. After about five seconds, Outlook Express removes the bolding from the message to indicate that it has been read.

◆ Highlight the message in the Inbox folder and then double-click it or select **File, Open.** (For the heck of it, you also can press **Ctrl+O** or just **Enter.**) This method opens the message in its own window.

To read other messages, either repeat these procedures or use any of the following Outlook Express techniques:

◆ **To read the previous message in the list** Select **View, Previous Message.** (**Ctrl+<** works, as well; if you have the message window open, click the **Previous** toolbar button.)

◆ **To read the next message in the list** Select **View, Next, Next Message.** (**Ctrl+>** also does the job; if you have the message window open, click the **Next** toolbar button.)

◆ **To read the next *unread* message** Select **View, Next, Next Unread Message** (or press **Ctrl+U**).

◆ **To read the next unread *conversation*** Select **View, Next, Next Unread Conversation** (or press **Ctrl+Shift+U**).

Jargon Jar

A **conversation** is a series of messages with the same subject line. It's also known as a *thread* in e-mail circles.

If you plan on using the Next Unread Conversation command, you first have to group all the messages from the same conversation. To do that, activate the **View, Current View, Group Messages by Conversation** command.

Attending to Attachments

As I mentioned earlier, if you get a message that has one or more files tied to it, you see a paper clip icon in the Inbox folder's Attachment column. You also see a larger paper clip icon in the upper-right corner of the preview pane. Outlook Express gives you a few ways to handle any attachments in the current message:

♦ **Saving the file**   Select **File, Save Attachments** to convince the Save Attachments dialog box to drop by. If there are multiple files, use the **Attachments To Be Saved** list to highlight the ones you want to save. Use the **Save To** text box to specify where you want the files to be stored (click **Browse** to choose the folder from a dialog box). Then click **Save** to dump the file (or files) onto your hard disk.

> **Cross-Reference**
>
> Although Outlook Express makes it easy to deal with attachments, you should never just blithely open an attached file because you might end up infecting your computer with a virus. To learn more about this and how to protect yourself from virus attachments, see Chapter 19.

♦ **Saving the file from the preview pane**   Click the paper clip icon in the upper-right corner of the preview pane to see a list that includes the file name of the attachment. Click **Save Attachments** and follow the steps I just took you through.

♦ **Opening the file**   If you just want to see what's in the file, you can open it. To do that, click the paper clip icon in the upper-right corner of the preview pane, and then click the file name. This gets you to the Open Attachment Warning dialog box. From here, be sure the **Open it** option is activated, and then click **OK**.

What to Do with a Message After You've Read It

This section gives you a rundown of all the things you can do with a message after you've read it. In each case, you either need to have a message highlighted in the Inbox folder, or you need to have the message open. Here's the list:

♦ **Ship out a reply**   If you think of a witty retort, you can e-mail it back to the sender either by selecting **Message, Reply to Sender,** or by clicking the **Reply** toolbar button. (The keyboard route is **Ctrl+R**.)

♦ **Ship out a reply to every recipient**   If the note was foisted on several people, you might prefer to send your response to everyone who received the original. To do that, either select **Message, Reply to All,** or click the **Reply All** button. (The keyboard shortcut is **Ctrl+Shift+R**.)

◆ **Forward the message to someone else** To have someone else take a gander at a message you received, you can forward it to her either by selecting **Message, Forward,** or by clicking the **Forward** button. (Keyboard dudes and dudettes can press **Ctrl+F.**)

Windows Wisdom

A forwarded message contains the original message text, which is preceded by an "Original Message" header and some of the message particulars (who sent it, when they sent it, and so on). If you want your recipient to see the message exactly as you received it, use the **Message, Forward As Attachment** command instead.

◆ **Move the message to some other folder** If you find your Inbox folder is getting seriously overcrowded, you should think about moving some messages to other folders. The easiest way to go about this is to drag the message from its current folder and drop it on the other folder in the Folders list. If that's too easy, select **Edit, Move to Folder** (or press **Ctrl+Shift+V**). In the Move dialog box that shows up, highlight the destination folder and then click **OK.** (You can create a new folder by clicking the **New Folder** button, entering a name for the folder in the New Folder dialog box, and then clicking **OK.**)

◆ **Delete the message** If you don't think you have cause to read a message again, you might as well delete it to keep the Inbox clutter to a minimum. To delete a message, either select **Edit, Delete,** or click the **Delete** button. (A message also can be vaporized by pressing **Ctrl+D** or by dragging it to the Deleted Items folder.) Note that Outlook Express doesn't get rid of a deleted message completely. Instead, it just dumps it in the Deleted Items folder. If you later realize that you deleted the message accidentally (insert forehead slap here), you can head for **Deleted Items** and then move it back into the Inbox.

The Least You Need to Know

◆ To start Outlook Express, either select **Start, E-mail** or select **Start, All Programs, Outlook Express.**

◆ It's best to launch Outlook Express and go directly to the Inbox folder. To do that, activate the **When Outlook Express starts, go directly to my Inbox folder** check box.

◆ To compose a message, click the **Create Mail** button (or select **Message, New Message**), enter the address and a Subject line, fill in the message body, and then either select **File, Send Message** (if you're online) or **File, Send Later** (if you're offline).

◆ To receive messages, click the **Send/Recv** button and then click **Receive All** (or select **Tools, Send and Receive, Receive All**).

More E-Mail Bonding: Extending Outlook Express

In This Chapter

◆ Basic message folder maintenance

◆ Fonts, stationery, signatures, filtering, and other message techniques

◆ Sharing Outlook Express with others by creating separate e-mail identities

If you are only pecking out your missives and then slamming the Send button, you're missing out on some of the most useful and fun features of Outlook Express. In this chapter, you go beyond the previous chapter's basics and learn many of the program's more interesting features and options. I show you how to manage message folders, work with stationery and signatures, create identities, filter incoming messages, and customize all kinds of Outlook Express options.

Taking Charge of Your Message Folders

Right out of the box, Outlook Express comes with five prefab folders: Inbox (incoming messages), Outbox (messages waiting to be sent), Sent Items (messages that you've sent), Deleted Items (messages that you've blown away), and Drafts (saved messages that you're still working on). Surely that's enough folders for anyone, right?

Maybe not. Even if you're good at deleting the detritus from your Inbox folder, it still won't take long before it becomes bloated with messages and finding the note you need becomes a real needle-in-a-haystack exercise. What you really need is a way to organize your mail. For example, suppose you and your boss exchange a lot of e-mail. Rather than storing all her messages in your Inbox folder, you could create a separate folder just for her messages. You could also create folders for each of the Internet mailing lists you subscribe to, for current projects on the go, or for each of your regular e-mail correspondents. There are, in short, 1,001 uses for folders and this section tells you everything you need to know.

To create a new folder, follow these steps:

1. Select the **File, Folder, New** command to display the Create Folder dialog box. (Attention, keyboardists: Pressing **Ctrl+Shift+E** also gets you where you want to go.) If the Folder command is unavailable, it means you have the Outlook Express "folder" selected in the Folders list. To unlock this command, first click any other folder (such as Local Folders or Inbox).

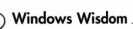

Windows Wisdom

You can save yourself a step or two by heading for the **Folders** list and right-clicking the folder in which you want the new folder to appear. Then click **New Folder,** enter the folder name, and click **OK.**

2. In the **Select the folder ...** list, highlight the folder within which you want the new folder to appear. For example, if you want your new folder to be inside your inbox, click the Inbox folder.

3. Use the **Folder name** text box to enter the name of the new folder.

4. Click **OK.**

Here's a quick look at a few other folder maintenance chores you may need to do from time to time:

♦ **Renaming a folder**   The names of the five predefined Outlook Express folders are written in stone, but it's easy to rename any folder that you created yourself. To do so, highlight the **folder** and then select **File, Folder, Rename.** (Alternatively, press **F2** or click the **folder** twice, with a pause of a couple of seconds between each click.) In the **Rename Folder** dialog box, enter the new name and then click **OK.**

◆ **Compacting a folder** To help minimize the size of the files that Outlook Express uses to store messages, you should *compact* the files regularly. To do this, select **File, Folder** and then select either **Compact** (to compact just the currently highlighted folder) or **Compact All Folders** (to compact the whole shooting match). You don't have to worry about this one too much because Outlook Express keeps an eye peeled on your folders and offers to compact them automatically every once in a while.

Windows Wisdom

You need to compact your folders because when you permanently delete messages, Outlook Express lazily leaves gaps in its files where the messages used to be. Compacting scrunches the files together so that the gaps are eliminated, which makes the files smaller, which saves you disk space. The good news is that this has absolutely no effect on your remaining messages and folders.

◆ **Moving a folder** If you want to move a folder to a different location, the easiest method is to use your mouse to drag the folder and drop it on the new location. (The harder method is to highlight the folder and select **File, Folder, Move.** In the Move dialog box, use the folder tree to highlight the new location for the folder, and then click **OK.**)

◆ **Deleting a folder** To get rid of a folder you no longer need (and all the messages it contains), highlight the folder and then either drag it to the Deleted Items folder or select **File, Folder, Delete.** (If your mouse is tired, the keyboard alternative is to press the **Delete** key.) Outlook Express then wonders if you're sure about this (note that it doesn't do this if you dragged the folder to Deleted Items). Ponder your next move carefully and, if you still want to go ahead, click **Yes** to delete the folder. (Click **No** if you get cold feet and decide not to nuke the folder.) As with messages, folders that you delete are stuffed into the Deleted Items folder. If you made a horrible mistake by deleting the folder, you can get it back by moving it out of Deleted Items.

Some Handy Message Maneuvers

You spend the bulk of your Outlook Express time shipping out messages to far-flung folks, and reading messages that those folks fire back at you. To help you get the most out of these sending and reading tasks, this section looks at the wide range of message options offered by Outlook Express.

Better E-Letters: Setting the Default Message Font

In Chapter 17, you learned about the difference between plain text messages and rich text (HTML) messages. For the latter, you can use the Formatting toolbar to mess with, among other things, the font in which your typed characters appear. The font controls the typeface, the type style (bold or italic, for example), the type size, and the color.

If you have a particular font combo that you're particularly fond of, you can tell Outlook Express to use it automatically. Here's how:

1. Select **Tools, Options** to invite in the Options dialog box.

2. Click the **Compose** tab.

3. In the **Compose Font** group, click the **Font Settings** button that appears beside the **Mail** heading. This lands you smack dab in the middle of the Font dialog box, which looks suspiciously like the WordPad Font dialog box I showed you back in Chapter 11 (see Figure 11.5).

4. Use the various controls to pick the font options you want, and then click **OK** to get back to the Options dialog box.

5. Click **OK** to put the new settings into effect.

Working with Stationery

In the real world, stationery is paper that includes predefined text, colors, and images. Outlook Express lets you set up the electronic equivalent. That is, you can define e-mail stationery that includes a background image and predefined text. This is essentially a web page to which you can also add your own text. Outlook Express gives you three choices:

♦ Use any of the Outlook Express predefined stationery designs on an individual message.

♦ Set up a stationery as the default that gets applied to all your outgoing messages.

♦ Create your own stationery.

Windows Wisdom _____

Keep in mind that your recipients may not have an e-mail program that understands stationery. In fact, some e-mail programs have been known to choke on messages that are festooned with stationery and other nontext frippery. So if a correspondent complains that he or she couldn't read your message, resend it without the stationery.

Let's begin with using one of the built-in stationery patterns on a single message. Outlook Express gives you two ways to do this:

- To start a new message using a specific stationery, select **Message, New Message Using** (you can also click the **downward-pointing arrow** in the **Create Mail** toolbar button). When Outlook Express displays its menu of stationery options (such as Clear Day and Nature), click the one you want to use.

- If you've already started a message, you can choose a stationery by selecting the **Format, Apply Stationery** command, and then picking out the stationery you want from the submenu that appears.

If you find yourself using the same stationery over and over, perhaps it's time to set up that stationery so that Outlook Express applies it automatically whenever you start a new message. Here's what you have to do:

1. In Outlook Express, select **Tools, Options** to request the presence of the Options dialog box.

2. Click the **Compose** tab.

3. In the **Stationery** group, activate the **Mail** check box, and then click the **Select** button to the right of it. Outlook Express reaches into its bag of tricks and pulls out the Select Stationery dialog box.

4. Highlight the **stationery file** you want to use. (If you're not sure, make certain the **Show preview** check box is activated. This displays a preview of the high-lighted stationery in the **Preview** box.)

5. When you've settled on a stationery, click **OK** to return to the Options dialog box.

6. Click **OK.**

Finally, Outlook Express is happy to use a stationery that you create yourself. It even provides a cheerful little wizard to take you through the steps. Here's what happens:

1. In Outlook Express, select **Tools, Options** to request the presence of the Options dialog box.

2. Click the **Compose** tab.

3. In the **Stationery** group, click **Create New.** The Stationery Setup Wizard comes bursting through the door.

4. The initial wizard dialog box just has some not-very-useful introductory material, so click **Next.** The wizard proffers its Background dialog box, shown in Figure 18.1.

Figure 18.1

Use this wizard dialog box to pick out a background picture or color for your stationery.

5. You have two ways to set the stationery background (when you're done, click **Next**):

   ◆ If you want to use a picture as the background, leave the **Picture** check box activated and use the list box below it to select the picture file you want (or click **Browse** to pick out the picture using a dialog box). Use the two **Position** lists to choose where the picture appears in the stationery, and use the **Tile** list to determine whether the picture appears just once (**Do Not Tile**) or is repeated until it covers the stationery.

   ◆ If you prefer (or also want) to use a solid color as the background, activate the **Color** check box and then use the list below it to choose a color that suits your fancy.

Windows Wisdom _____

A few other stationery samples are available on the web. To see them, select **Tools, Options** to get back to the Options dialog box, head for the **Compose** tab, and then click the **Download More** button in the Stationery group.

6. Next up are the stationery fonts. Choose the **Font** (typeface), **Size, Color,** and whether the text is **Bold** and/or **Italic.** Click **Next** to keep things moving.

7. The wizard's to-do list continues with setting the stationery margin widths. The margins determine where in the stationery your typing starts. Use the **Left**

Margin spin box to set the distance from the left edge, and use the **Top Margin** spin box to set the distance from the top edge. Click **Next** to continue.

8. In the last of the wizard's dialog boxes, enter a **Name** for your funky new stationery (such as Funky New Stationery), and click **Finish** to send the wizard home.

After you've completed your stationery creation, you can use it in your messages just like any other stationery.

Setting Up a Signature

In e-mail lingo, a *signature* is a chunk of text that appears at the bottom of all your messages. Most people use their signature to give contact information, and you often see sigs (that's the hip short form) adorned with witty quotations or sayings. Outlook Express even lets you create multiple signatures, so you can tailor them to various audiences.

Here are the steps to plow through to create a signature or two:

1. Select the **Tools, Options** command.

2. In the Options dialog box that climbs into the ring, display the **Signatures** tab.

3. Click **New.** Outlook Express adds a new item to the Signatures list.

4. Use the **Text** box to compose the signature.

5. Annoyingly, Outlook Express gives each signature a boring name such as Signature #1 (see Figure 18.2). A more meaningful name would be nice, so click the signature in the **Signatures** list, click **Rename**, enter a snappier name, and then press **Enter.**

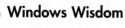 **Windows Wisdom**

The "default signature" is the first signature you create. To set up some other signature as the default, highlight it in the **Signatures** list, and then click **Set As Default**.

6. Repeat steps 3 through 5 to create more signatures, if you so desire.

7. If you want Outlook Express to tack on the default signature to all your messages, activate the **Add signatures to all outgoing messages** check box. If you don't want the signature to show up when you reply to a message or forward a message to someone, leave the **Don't add signatures to Replies and Forwards** check box activated.

8. When you're done, click **OK** to return to Outlook Express.

Figure 18.2

Use the **Signatures** *tab to enter one or more signatures.*

If you elected not to add your signature automatically, it's easy enough to toss it into a message that you're composing. In the **New Message** window, move the cursor to where you want the text to appear, and then select **Insert, Signature.** (If you have multiple signatures defined, a submenu with a list of the sigs slides out. Select the one you want to use.)

Seven Useful Sending Settings

Let's spend a little more time hanging out in the handy Options dialog box. In this section, I'll take you through a few settings related to sending messages. To see these options, select the **Tools, Options** command and then display the **Send** tab.

Here's a once-over of what's available (click **OK** when you're done):

◆ **Save copy of sent messages in the "Sent Items" folder**   Deactivate this check box to tell Outlook Express not to bother putting copies of your messages in Sent Items. I don't recommend doing this because you'll probably refer to previously sent notes on many an occasion.

◆ **Send messages immediately**   When this option is activated and you're work-ing online, Outlook Express transmits your messages as soon as you send them (unless, of course, you select the **Send Later** command). If you want Outlook Express to hold its sending horses, deactivate this check box.

♦ **Automatically put people I reply to in my Address Book**   This option is on by default, which is downright silly because it means that every last person to whom you send a reply will get stuffed into your Address Book. That's dumb, so you may want to consider deactivating this one.

♦ **Automatically complete e-mail addresses when composing**   As I mentioned in the previous chapter, after you have some names in your Address Book, you can start typing a name and Outlook Express will "guess" the rest of the name based on the Address Book entries. If you don't like this feature, deactivate this check box to turn it off.

♦ **Include message in reply**   When this option is activated and you reply to a message, Outlook Express adds the original message to your reply message. This is a good idea because it reminds the recipient of what they said, so you should leave this option on.

♦ **Reply to messages using the format in which they were sent**   When this check box is activated, Outlook Express sets up your replies using the same format that the sender used. For example, if you get a plain text message and you reply to it, the reply will automatically be set up as plain text, as well. Again, I recommend leaving this one on.

♦ **Mail Sending Format**   These options determine the default format that Outlook Express uses for your messages. Select either **HTML** or **Plain Text.**

Sharing Outlook Express with Others: Setting Up Identities

Internet e-mail is such a useful tool that *everyone* wants to get in on the act. That's fine because most ISPs let you set up multiple e-mail accounts, so it's usually not a problem to set up an account for each person in your family or your small office. Sounds good, but what happens if two or more people have to share a single computer? *Nobody* likes having someone else snooping around in their e-mail, so how do you avoid clashes?

There are actually two ways you can go about it:

♦ If you have Windows XP Home, give each person his or her own user account, which includes the ability to set up Outlook Express with just his or her own e-mail account (see Chapter 10).

Cross-Reference

Refer to Chapter 17 to go back through the Internet Connection Wizard's mail account setup duties.

◆ For Windows XP Home or Professional, take advantage of an Outlook Express feature called *identities*. The idea is simple: Each person who uses the computer sets up a distinct identity in Outlook Express. This gives each person his or her own set of folders and settings, and no one sees anyone else's. Each person's identity can be protected with a password to make extra sure that no one pokes around in his or her stuff.

Creating a New Identity

When you set up your Internet e-mail account, Outlook Express created an identity called, boringly, Main Identity. Here are the steps to follow to set up another identity:

1. Select the **File, Identities, Add New Identity** command. Outlook Express whips out the New Identity dialog box.

2. Use the **Type your name** text box to enter a name for the new identity.

3. If you want the identity protected by a password, activate the **Require a password** check box. In the Enter Password dialog box that materializes, type in the password in both the **New Password** and **Confirm New Password** text boxes, and then click **OK** to return to the New Identity dialog box.

4. Click **OK.**

5. When Outlook Express asks whether you want to switch to this new identity now, click **Yes.** Outlook Express shuts down and then restarts. Because no account info has been defined for this identity, the Internet Connection Wizard is called in to take down the details.

6. Run through the wizard to define the Internet e-mail account data for the new identity.

Switching From One Identity to Another

After you've set up two or more identities, Outlook Express will always be "logged in" to one of those identities. How do you know which one? Check out the title bar. As shown in Figure 18.3, the name of the current identity appears to the right of "Outlook Express."

Current identity

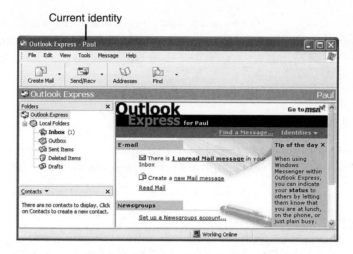

Figure 18.3

The Outlook Express title bar tells you the name of the currently logged-in identity.

To switch to a different identity, follow these steps:

1. Select **File, Switch Identity.** Outlook Express delivers the Switch Identities dialog box.

2. In the list of defined identities, highlight the one you want to use.

3. If the identity is protected by a password, enter it in the **Password** text box.

4. Click **OK.** Outlook Express shuts down and then restarts with the selected identity logged on.

> **Windows Wisdom**
>
> To make changes to your identity, select the **File, Identities, Manage Identities** command. In the Manage Identities dialog box, highlight your identity and click **Properties.**

Logging Off Your Identity

If you exit Outlook Express by selecting the usual **File, Exit** command (or by pressing **Alt+F4** or clicking the window's **Close** button), the current identity remains logged in. Therefore, the next time you crank up Outlook Express, that identity remains the current one.

Chances are that this isn't what you want. After all, it means that if someone else launches Outlook Express, they start off in your identity. To prevent that from happening, be sure to exit Outlook Express by choosing the **File, Exit and Log Off Identity** command.

Having done that, the next time you or anyone else tries to start Outlook Express, the first thing that shows up is the Identity Login dialog box. From there, you choose your identity, enter a password, if necessary, and then click **OK** to get Outlook Express on-screen.

The Least You Need to Know

♦ Make liberal use of folders to organize your messages. You create new folders by selecting the **File, Folder, New** command (or by pressing **Ctrl+Shift+E**).

♦ If you have fonts or stationery that you use all the time, set them up as the default by selecting **Tools, Options** and displaying the **Compose** tab.

♦ If you share your computer with other people, set up separate identities for everyone by selecting the **File, Identities, Add New Identity** command.

♦ To make sure that no one else accidentally logs in to Outlook Express with your identity, always exit by using the **File, Exit and Log Off Identity** command.

Your Net Safety Net

In This Chapter

◆ Guarding against nasty e-mail viruses, spam, and other useless messages

◆ Maintaining e-mail privacy

◆ Understanding Internet Explorer security

◆ Controlling web privacy by controlling cookies

◆ Keeping hackers and other miscreants out of your system

◆ Taking advantage of the Security Center in Windows XP Service Pack 2

The Internet is a more cosmopolitan place now than in its relatively lawless beginnings. However, although the Net is no longer the digital equivalent of the Wild West, we've progressed only to about the level of Al Capone's Chicago of the 1930s. In other words, although most of your Internet dealings will be safe and pleasant, there are plenty of cyberhoodlums and e-gangsters roaming the Net's dark streets and alleyways. You need to exercise some caution to avoid the Internet's version of muggings and extortion.

Fortunately, the situation is not so grim that you can't easily protect yourself. As you'll see in this chapter, avoiding viruses, spam scams, system intruders, and other Internet bad guys is a relatively simple combination of common sense and the prudent tweaking of a few settings.

Working with E-Mail Safely and Securely

E-mail is by far the most popular online activity, but it can also be the most frustrating in terms of security and privacy. E-mail viruses are legion; spam gets worse every day; and messages that should be secret are really about as secure as if they were written on the back of a postcard. Fortunately, it doesn't take much to remedy these and other e-mail problems, as you'll see over the next few sections.

Protecting Yourself Against E-Mail Viruses

Until just a few years ago, the primary method that computer viruses used to propagate themselves was the floppy disk. A user with an infected machine would copy some files to a floppy, and the virus would surreptitiously add itself to the disk. When the recipient inserted the disk, the virus copy would come to life and infect yet another computer.

When the Internet became a big deal, viruses adapted and began propagating either via malicious websites or via infected program files downloaded to users' machines.

Over the past couple of years, however, by far the most productive method for viruses to replicate has been the humble e-mail message. Melissa, I Love You, BadTrans, Sircam, Klez; the list of e-mail viruses and Trojan horses is a long one but they all operate more or less the same way—they arrive as a message attachment, usually from someone you know. When you open the attachment, the virus infects your computer and then, without your knowledge, uses your e-mail client and your address book to ship out messages with more copies of itself attached. The nastier versions will also mess with your computer; they might delete data or corrupt files, for example.

You can avoid getting infected by one of these viruses by implementing a few commonsense procedures:

◆ Never open an attachment that comes from someone you don't know.

◆ Even if you know the sender, if the attachment isn't something you're expecting, assume the sender's system is infected. Write back and confirm that he or she sent the message.

◆ Some viruses come packaged as "scripts"—miniature computer programs—that are hidden within messages that use the Rich Text (HTML) format. This means that the virus can run just by viewing the message! If a message looks suspicious, don't open it, just delete it. (Note that you'll need to turn off the Outlook Express preview pane before deleting the message. Otherwise, when you highlight the message, it will appear in the preview pane and set off the virus. Select **View, Layout,** deactivate the **Show preview pane** check box, and click **OK.**)

◆ Install a top-of-the-line antivirus program, particularly one that checks incoming e-mail. Also, be sure to keep your antivirus program's virus list up-to-date. As you read this, there are probably dozens, maybe even hundreds, of morally challenged scumnerds designing even nastier viruses. Regular updates will help you keep up.

Besides these general procedures, Microsoft Outlook Express also comes with its own set of virus protection features. Here's how to use them:

1. In Outlook Express, select **Tools, Options.**

2. Display the **Security** tab.

3. In the **Virus Protection** section of the dialog box, you have the following options:

   ◆ **Select the Internet Explorer security zone to use**   Later in this chapter you'll learn about the security zone model used by Internet Explorer (see "Caveat Surfer: Internet Explorer and Security"). From the perspective of Outlook Express, you use the security zones to determine whether scripts inside HTML-format messages are allowed to run. If you choose **Internet Zone,** scripts are allowed to run; if you choose **Restricted Sites Zone,** scripts are disabled. This is the default setting, and it's the one I highly recommend.

   ◆ **Warn me when other applications try to send mail as me**   As I mentioned earlier, it's possible for programs and scripts to send e-mail messages without your knowledge. When you activate this check box, Outlook Express displays a warning dialog box similar to the one shown in Figure 19.1 when a program or script attempts to send a message behind-the-scenes. Click **Send** to allow the message; click **Do Not Send** to cancel the message.

Figure 19.1

Outlook Express warns you if a program or script uses Simple MAPI to attempt to send a message.

♦ **Do not allow attachments to be saved or opened that could poten-
tially be a virus** When you activate this check box, Outlook Express
monitors attachments to look for file types that could contain viruses or
destructive code. If it detects such a file, it halts the ability to open or save
that file, and it displays a note at the top of the message to let you know
about the unsafe attachment, as shown in Figure 19.2.

Windows Wisdom _____

The file types that Outlook Express disables are defined by Microsoft Internet
Explorer's built-in *unsafe-file list*. This list includes file types associated with the following extensions: .ad, .ade, .adp, .bas, .bat, .chm, .cmd, .com, .cpl, .crt, .exe, .hlp,
.hta, .inf, .ins, .isp, .js, .jse, .lnk, .mdb, .mde, .msc, .msi, .msp, .mst, .pcd, .pif, .reg,
.scr, .sct, .shb, .shs, .url, .vb, .vbe, .vbs, .vsd, .vss, .vst, .vsw, .wsc, .wsf, .wsh.

4. If you have Internet Explorer Service Pack 1 or Windows XP Service Pack 2
installed, display the Read tab and activate the **Read all messages in plain text**
check box.

5. Click **OK** to put the new settings into effect.

Figure 19.2

*If Outlook Express detects an
unsafe file attachment, it displays a notice at the top
of the message to let you
know that you do not have
access to the file.*

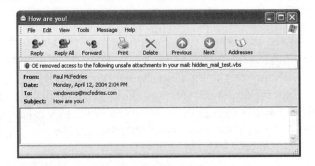

Dealing with the Onslaught: Filtering Messages

It's an unfortunate fact of online life that the e-mail system is the source of many
unwanted messages. Whether it's the scourge of unsolicited commercial e-mail (also
know whimsically as spam), or someone you've had a falling out with, you inevitably
end up getting some messages that you instantly delete.

You can save yourself the bother by setting up Outlook Express to delete these an-
noyances for you. You can also go beyond this by having Outlook Express look for
certain messages and then automatically move them to another folder, send out a
reply, flag the messages, and much more.

Let's begin with the most straightforward case: *blocking* incoming messages from a particular e-mail address. There are two ways to set up the block:

◆ **Block the sender of a message**   If you already have a message from the address that you want to block, highlight the message and then select **Message, Block Sender.** Outlook Express displays a dialog box that tells you the address has been added to the "blocked senders list." It also asks whether you want to expunge any other messages from this address that are in the current folder (click **Yes** if you do).

Jargon Jar

Blocking means that any message that comes in from that address is automatically relegated to the Deleted Items folder, so you never see the message.

◆ **Block a specified e-mail address**   If you don't have an e-mail specimen from the address you want to block, select **Tools, Message Rules, Blocked Senders List.** This displays the Message Rules window with the **Blocked Senders** tab displayed. Click **Add,** enter the **Address** you want to block, and then click **OK.**

If you have a change of heart down the road, you can remove the block by selecting **Tools, Message Rules, Blocked Senders List,** highlighting the address in the **Blocked Senders** tab, and then clicking **Remove.** Click **Yes** when Outlook Express asks you to confirm.

If you need to filter messages based on conditions other than (or in addition to) the e-mail address, or if you want to do something other than just delete a message, then you need to set up *message rules.* These rules tell Outlook Express exactly what to look for (such as specific words in the subject line or message body) and exactly what to do with any messages that meet those conditions (move them to a folder, forward them, and so on).

Jargon Jar

Message rules are specific instructions that tell Outlook Express how to handle certain incoming messages.

Here are the steps to follow to set up a message rule:

1. Select the **Tools, Message Rules, Mail** command. Outlook Express relinquishes the New Mail Rule dialog box.

2. In the **Select the Conditions for your rule** list, activate the check box beside a condition that you want to use to single out an incoming message. Outlook Express adds the condition to the Rule Description box.

3. In most cases, the condition includes some underlined text. For example, if you activate the **Where the Subject line contains specific words** condition, the "contains specific words" portion will be underlined, as shown in Figure 19.3. The idea here is that you click the underlined text to specify the exact condition (in this case, a word or two that specifies which subject lines are to be filtered).

Figure 19.3

Most conditions require you to add specific words or addresses.

4. Repeat steps 2 and 3 to set up other conditions, if necessary.

5. In the **Select the Actions for your rule** list, activate the check box beside an action you want Outlook Express to perform on the selected messages. Again, Outlook Express adds the action to the Rule Description box.

6. Many actions also have the underlined text, so be sure to click the text to enter a specific value.

7. Repeat steps 5 and 6 to set up other actions, if necessary.

8. Use the **Name of the rule** text box to enter a descriptive name for the rule.

9. Click **OK.** Outlook Express displays the Message Rules dialog box with your new rule shown in the **Mail Rules** tab.

If you're creating a rule based on the address of an existing message, you can save yourself a bit of time by highlighting the message and then selecting **Message, Create Rule from Message.** This displays the New Mail Rule dialog box with the **Where the From line contains people** condition activated and filled in with the address of the sender.

Filtering Out Spam

Spam—unsolicited commercial messages—has become a plague upon the earth. Unless you've done a masterful job at keeping your address secret, you probably receive at least a few spam e-mails every day, and it's more likely that you receive a few dozen. The bad news is most experts agree that it's only going to get worse. And why not? Spam is one of the few advertising mediums where the costs are substantially borne by the users, not the advertisers.

The best way to avoid spam is to not get on a spammer's list of addresses in the first place. That's hard to do these days, but there are some steps you can take:

◆ Never use your actual e-mail address in a newsgroup account. The most common method that spammers use to gather addresses is to harvest them from newsgroup posts. One common tactic is to alter your e-mail address by adding text that invalidates the address but is still obvious for other people to figure out:

```
user@myisp.remove_this_to_email_me.com
```

◆ When you sign up for something online, use a fake address if possible. If you need or want to receive e-mail from the company and so must use your real address, make sure you deselect any options that ask if you want to receive promotional offers. Alternatively, enter the address from a free web-based account (such as a Hotmail account), so that any spam you receive will go there instead of to your main address.

◆ Never open suspected spam messages, because doing so can sometimes notify the spammer that you've opened the message, thus confirming that your address is legit. For the same reason, you should never display a spam message in the Outlook Express preview pane. As described earlier, shut off the preview pane before highlighting any spam messages that you want to delete.

◆ Never, I repeat, *never*, respond to spam, even to an address within the spam that claims to be a "removal" address. By responding to the spam all you're doing is proving that your address is legitimate, so you'll just end up getting *more* spam.

There are a host of commercial "spam-killers" on the market, but with a bit of work you should be able to eliminate most spam by using nothing more than the built-in filtering tool available in Outlook Express and described in the previous section.

To filter spam, your rules need to look for incoming messages that meet one or more of the following criteria:

◆ **Specific words in the Subject line**   The sneakier spammers hide their messages behind innocuous Subject lines such as "Here's the information you requested." But most spam comes with fairly obvious Subject lines: "Make

$$$Money Now!!!" or "FREE Business Cards." Instead of creating a rule based on an entire Subject line, you need only to watch for certain key words. Here are a few that I use (I've removed some of the more explicit terms that filter out pornographic spam):

!!!!!!!, $, %, .name, 18+, about your site, adult, adv, advertise, ameritrade, annual reports, are you in debt, back taxes, bargain, be 18, britney, bulk, buy recommendation, cartridges, cash, casino, clients, collect your money, credit card, credit rating, creditor, debts, descrambler, dieting, diploma, don't miss, double your money, dvd movies, earning!, e-mail marketing, emar-keter, erotic, excite game, f r e e, find out anything, flash alert, free cell, free credit, free pda, free phone, free trial, free vacation, free!, freee, get out of debt, giveaway, got debt, guaranteed!, hair loss, hormone, how to make money, increase your sales, incredible opportunity, interest rates, investment goals, is this a picture of you, klez, lemme, life insurance, loans, lose up to, lose weight, lose while you sleep, losing sleep, low on funds, marketing services, maximize your income, merchant, millionaire, mlm, mortgage, new car, new photos from my party, online market, online phar-macy, over 18, over 21, printer cartridge, promote your business, reach millions, reduce your debt, refinance, refinancing, s e x, satellite, saw your site, secure your future, seen on tv, sex, singles, snoring, spec sheet, steroids, stock, stock alert, systemworks, thinning hair, this one's on us, too good to be true, trading alert, trading report, uncover the truth, urgent notice, viagra, web traffic, what are your kids, work at home, work from home, xxx, years younger, you are a winner, you have to see this

♦ **Specific words in the message body** The message body is where the spam-mer makes his or her pitch, so there's rarely any subterfuge here. You can filter on the same terms as you used for the Subject line, but there are also a few tell-tale terms that appear only in spam messages. Here are some that I use:

100% satisfied, adult en, adult web, adults only, cards accepted, check or money order, dear friend, extra income, for free!, for free?, satisfaction guaranteed, money back , money-back guarantee, one-time mail, order now!, order today, removal instructions, special promotion

Jargon Jar _____
To **spoof** an address means to make it appear as though the message came from some other person's address.

♦ **Specific names in the From line** Many spammers *spoof* their From address by using a random address or, more likely, an address plucked from their distribution list. However, some use addresses that have a common theme, such as "sales@" (for example, sales@blah.com).

Here are some common From line names to filter:

@mlm, @public, @savvy, ebargains, free, hello@, link2buy, mail@, profits@, sales@, success, success@

◆ **Specific names in the To line**   The To line of spam messages usually contains either an address from the distribution list or "Undisclosed Recipients." You can't filter on the latter, however, because many legitimate mailings also use that "address." However, there are a few common To line names to watch for:

anyone@, creditcard@, free@, friend, friend@, nobody@, opportunity@, public@, success@, winners@

Maintaining Your Privacy While Reading E-Mail

You wouldn't think that the simple act of reading an e-mail message would have privacy implications, but you'd be surprised. There are actually two scenarios that compromise your privacy: read receipts and web bugs.

If the sender requests a *read receipt* and you either select the message (so that the message text appears in the preview pane) or double-click the message to open it, by default Outlook Express displays the dialog box shown in Figure 19.4. Click **Yes** to send the receipt, or click **No** to skip it.

Jargon Jar

A **read receipt** is an e-mail notification that tells the sender that you've opened the message that he or she sent you.

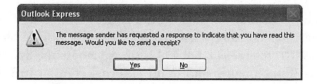

Figure 19.4

You see this dialog box when you open a message for which the sender has requested a read receipt.

Many people like asking for read receipts because they offer "proof of delivery." It has been my experience, however, that getting a read receipt back starts a kind of internal clock that the sender uses to "measure" how long it takes you to respond after reading the message. Because of this annoyance, and because I feel it's nobody's business to know when one reads a message, I always click **No** when asked to send a read receipt. In fact, you can go one better and tell Outlook Express to never send a read receipt:

1. Select the **Tools, Options** command to display the Options dialog box.

2. Display the **Receipts** tab.

3. In the **Returning Read Receipts** section of the dialog box, activate the **Never send a read receipt** option.

Some messages contain an address for a special image known as a *web bug*. When you open the message, Outlook Express uses the address to download the image for display within the message. That sounds harmless enough, but if the message is junk e-mail, then it's likely that the address will also contain either your e-mail address or a code that points to your e-mail address. When the remote server gets a request for this image, it knows not only that you've opened their message but also that your e-mail address is legitimate. You have three ways to combat web bugs:

Jargon Jar

A **web bug** is an image that resides on a remote server and is added to an HTML-formatted e-mail message by referencing an address on the remote server.

♦ Don't open a message that you suspect to be spam, and don't preview the message in the Outlook Express preview pane. In fact, before you can delete the message, you'll need to turn off the preview pane temporarily, as described earlier in this chapter.

♦ Install the Internet Explorer 6 Service Pack 1 or the Windows XP Service Pack 2 (or a later service pack, if one is available by the time you read this). This service pack also updates Outlook Express. In particular, it gives you an easy way to thwart web bugs (although it also thwarts other message formatting, as well). In Outlook Express, select **Tools, Options,** choose the **Read** tab, and then activate the **Read all messages in plain text** check box. This prevents Outlook Express from downloading any web bugs because it displays all messages in plain text.

♦ Install the Windows XP Service Pack 2 (or a later service pack, if one is available). This update includes an option that is specifically designed to squash web bugs. In Outlook Express, select **Tools, Options,** choose the **Security** tab, and then activate the **Block images and other external content in HTML e-mail** check box. This prevents Outlook Express from downloading web bugs and any other items that would otherwise come from some remote server.

Caveat Surfer: Internet Explorer and Security

Tons of people are flocking to the web, and tons of content providers are waiting for them there. Still, many people view the web as an essentially scary and untrustworthy place. There are many reasons for this, but one of the biggest is the security issue. There are two issues, actually:

◆ **Protecting the data that you send to the web**   Many web page forms ask you to supply sensitive data, such as your credit card number. You wouldn't leave credit card receipts lying in the street, but that's more or less what you're doing if you submit a normal web form that has your Visa number on it. The solution here is to only enter sensitive data on web pages that are secure (more on this in a sec).

◆ **Being protected from the data that the web sends to you**   The nature of the web means that all kinds of items—text, graphics, sounds, Java applets (a kind of miniprogram), ActiveX controls (another miniprogram), and more—get deposited on your computer, at least temporarily. How do you know all that stuff is safe? And if you're not sure about something, how do you refuse delivery?

Internet Explorer offers quite a number of features that tackle these issues directly. The Internet Explorer window gives you visual cues that tell you whether a particular document is secure. For example, Figure 19.5 shows Internet Explorer displaying a secure web page. Notice how a lock icon appears in the lower-right corner, and that the address of a secure page uses **https** up front rather than **http.** Both of these features tell you that the web page has a security certificate that passed muster with Internet Explorer.

Figure 19.5

An example of a secure web document.

The lock icon

Internet Explorer also displays security warning dialog boxes. These seemingly paranoid notes are actually quite useful most of the time. They warn you about all kinds of security-related activities:

♦ Entering a secure website

♦ Browsing allegedly secure websites that don't have a valid security certificate

♦ Leaving a secure website (see Figure 19.6)

Figure 19.6

Internet Explorer warns you when you're about to leave a secure page.

♦ Being redirected to a page other than the one you specified

♦ Downloading and running objects, including files, ActiveX controls, Java applets, and scripts

♦ Submitting a form insecurely

> **Windows Wisdom** _____
>
> Many folks want to try out these newfangled e-commerce and online banking sites that everyone's talking about, but they're concerned about security. That's smart, because financial data *must* be as secure as possible. When you investigate these kinds of sites, you often see them yammering on about "128-bit encryption" and similar-sounding gobbledygook. The gist is that any web browser that boasts 128-bit encryption can scramble your financial data to make it virtually uncrackable by nefarious nogoodniks. It used to be that you had to download a special update to get this super-duper security. That's a thing of the past now because the Windows XP version of Internet Explorer comes with 128-bit security built right in.

Note that these dialog boxes contain a check box that enables you to turn the warning off. You can also use the **Security** tab in the Internet Options dialog box (select **Tools, Internet Options** to get there) to toggle these warnings on and off and customize the level of security used by Internet Explorer.

Understanding and Using Security Zones

The way Internet Explorer handles security is to classify web pages according to different security *zones*. Each zone is a collection of web pages that implements a common security level. There are four zones:

- **Internet zone**   This is a catch-all zone that includes all web pages that aren't in any of the other zones. The default security level is medium.

- **Local intranet zone**   This zone covers web pages on your local hard drives and on your local area network (intranet). The default security level is medium-low.

- **Trusted sites zone**   You use this zone to specify websites that you trust. That is, these are sites for which you're certain that any objects you download and run are safe. The default security level is low.

- **Restricted sites zone**   You use this zone to specify websites that you don't trust, and so want to implement the tightest possible security. The default security level is high.

You can add sites to three of Internet Explorer's security zones: Local intranet, Trusted sites, and Restricted sites. Here's how you do it:

1. In the **Security** tab, click the icon of the zone you want to work with.

2. Click the **Sites** button.

3. If you're working with the Local intranet zone, you see a dialog box with three check boxes that determine the sites that are part of the default settings for this zone. Leave these as is and click **Advanced.**

4. To add a site, enter the address in the **Add this website to the zone** text box and then click **Add.**

5. To remove a site from the zone, highlight it in the **websites** list and then click **Remove.**

6. If you want Internet Explorer to make sure each site's web server is using the HTTPS security protocol (a good idea), activate the **Require server verification (https:) for all sites in this zone** check box.

7. Click **OK.**

> **CAUTION**   **Look Out!**
>
> Why not just select the High setting to get the most security? Because this setting blocks certain common website activities such as file downloads and scripting, and without these many sites won't work properly.

Internet Explorer has four predefined security levels: **High** (most secure), **Low** (least secure), **Medium-low,** and **Medium.** You can assign any of these levels within the Security tab by first using the **Zone** list to choose the security zone and then dragging the slider to the security level you want. Note that Internet Explorer displays the types of security each setting provides next to the slider.

Restricting Your Cookie Diet: Internet Explorer's Privacy Features

As you weave your way around the web, you'll occasionally come across sites that offer to "remember" bits of data that you enter. For example, the site shown in Figure 19.7 offers to store the user name and password for a game, which means this data will be entered into the text boxes automatically the next time the person visits the same page. Similarly, if you do any online shopping, your selections get stored in a "shopping cart" that remembers what and how much you ordered. Still other sites (such as MSN.com) enable you to create "customized" pages that display your local news and weather as well as info tidbits of your choosing (such as sports headlines).

Figure 19.7

Some websites have the seemingly miraculous ability to remember things about you.

The source of a website's "memory" is actually a teensy file that gets stored automatically on your computer. This file is called, somewhat bizarrely, a *cookie.* Websites use these cookies to store data (such as the user name and password you use to access the site), shopping cart particulars, customization settings, and much more.

Jargon Jar

The term **cookie** is based on the old programming term *magic cookie*, which the Jargon File (the definitive dictionary of geek speak; see tuxedo.org/jargon/) defines as "something passed between routines or programs that enables the receiver to perform some operation." It's this idea of passing data from one thing to another (in this case, from a page to your computer) that inspired the original cookie creators.

If a site can store a file on my computer, what's to stop them from sending me a virus or some other nasty electronic bug?

That's not possible with cookies because Internet Explorer will only allow the site to store the data in a particular location and in a plain text format that can do no harm to your machine.

Okay, but isn't it dangerous to have user names and passwords and stuff like that sitting around in text files?

Good point, but it's not dangerous because only the site that created the cookie can read it. No other site can access anybody else's cookie, so your data can't get spread around.

So cookies are totally benign creatures and we have nothing to worry about?

Actually, that's not quite true. To understand why, you have to understand about the different cookie types:

- ◆ **Temporary cookie**   This type of cookie lives just as long as you have Internet Explorer running. When you shut down the program, all the temporary cookies are given the heave-ho.

- ◆ **Persistent cookie**   This type of cookie remains on your hard disk even after you exit Internet Explorer. The cookie's length of stay depends on how it's set up, but it can be anything from a few seconds to a few years.

- ◆ **First-party cookie**   This is a cookie that's set by the website that you're viewing.

- ◆ **Third-party cookie**   This is a cookie that's set by a site other than the one you're viewing. Most third-party cookies are created and stored by advertisers who have placed an ad on the site you're viewing.

Given these cookie flavors, there are two types of cookie problems that civil libertarians and other privacy advocates fret about:

♦ A site might store *personally identifiable information*—your name, e-mail address, home address, phone number, and so on—in a persistent first- or third-party cookie and then use that information in some way (such as filling in a form) without your consent.

♦ A site might store information about you in a persistent third-party cookie and then use that cookie to track your online movements and activities. They can do this because they might have (for example) an ad on dozens or hundreds of websites and that ad is the mechanism that enables the site to set and read their cookies. Such sites are supposed to come up with *privacy policies* stating that they won't engage in surreptitious monitoring of users, they won't sell user data, and so on.

To help you handle these scenarios, the Windows XP version of Internet Explorer implements a privacy feature that gives you extra control over whether sites can store cookies on your machine. To check out this feature, select the **Tools, Internet Options** command, and then display the **Privacy** tab.

You set your cookie privacy level by using the slider in the **Settings** group. There are two settings that fall into the all-or-nothing category:

♦ **Accept All Cookies** This setting (it's at the bottom of the slider) tells Internet Explorer to accept any and all cookie comers.

♦ **Block All Cookies** This setting (it's at the top of the slider) tells Internet Explorer to turn back all requests to set and read cookies.

In between there are four settings that offer more detailed control. The following table shows you how each setting affects the three types of privacy issues:

	Third-party cookies with no compact privacy policy	Third-party cookies using personally identifiable information without the type of consent	First-party cookies using personally identifiable information with the type of consent
Low	Restricted	Restricted (implicit)	OK
Medium (the default)	Blocked	Blocked (implicit)	Restricted (implicit)
Medium High	Blocked	Blocked (explicit)	Blocked (implicit)
High	Blocked	Blocked (explicit)	Blocked (explicit)

Here are some notes about the terminology in this table:

◆ *Restricted* means that Internet Explorer doesn't allow the site to set a persistent cookie, just a temporary one.

◆ A *compact* privacy policy is a shortened form of a privacy policy that can be sent along with the cookie and that can be read by the browser.

◆ *Implicit consent* means that on one or more pages leading up to the cookie, you were warned that your personally identifiable information would be used and you agreed that it was okay.

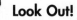 **Look Out!** _____

Blocking all cookies may sound like the easiest way to handle this privacy rigmarole. However, there are a lot of sites out there that rely on cookies to operate properly, so if you shun all cookies you may find that your web surfing isn't as convenient or as smooth as it used to be.

◆ *Explicit consent* means that on the page that reads the cookie, you were warned that your personally identifiable information would be used and you agreed that it was okay.

 Windows Wisdom _____

If you change the privacy setting, you should first delete all your cookies because the new setting won't apply to any cookies already on your computer. To delete your cookies, select **Tools, Internet Options,** display the **General** tab, and then click **Delete Cookies.** (If you prefer to delete individual cookies, click **Settings,** click **View Files,** and then look for file names that begin with "`cookie:`".)

If Internet Explorer comes across a website that tries to set a blocked or restricted type of cookie, two things happen (see Figure 19.8):

◆ A Privacy Report icon appears in the status bar.

◆ The Privacy dialog box appears with a message letting you know what the privacy icon is all about. If you don't want to be bothered by this dialog box each time, be sure to leave the **Don't show this message again** check box activated. Note, too, that you can also click the **Settings** button to bring up the Internet Properties dialog box with the **Privacy** tab displayed.

Figure 19.8

The Privacy Report icon shows up in the Internet Explorer status bar when you visit a site that uses a type of cookie that you've restricted.

The Privacy Report icon

To find out what's going on, double-click the Privacy Report icon to get to a Privacy Report dialog box similar to the one shown in Figure 19.9. This dialog box tells you which sites tried to set the cookies and what action Internet Explorer took (such as **Blocked**).

Figure 19.9

Double-click the Privacy Report icon to see this dialog box.

Keeping Intruders Out of Your System

If you access the Net using a broadband—cable modem or digital subscriber line (DSL)—service, chances are you have an "always on" connection, which means there's a much greater chance that a malicious hacker could find your computer and have his or her way with it. You might think that with millions of people connected to the Internet at any given moment, there would be little chance of a "script kiddie" finding you in the herd. Unfortunately, one of the most common weapons in a black-hat hacker's arsenal is a program that runs through millions of addresses automatically, looking for "live" connections. The problem is compounded by the fact that many cable systems and some DSL systems use addresses in a narrow range, thus making it easier to find "always on" connections.

However, having a cracker locate your system isn't a big deal as long as he or she can't get into your system. There are two ways to prevent this:

◆ Turn off file and printer sharing on your Internet connection.

◆ Turn on the Windows XP Internet Connection Firewall.

Turning Off File and Printer Sharing

File and printer sharing is used to enable network users to see and work with shared files and printers on your computer. Obviously, you don't way to share your system with strangers on the Internet! By default, Windows XP turns off file and printer sharing for Internet connections. To make sure of this, however, follow these steps:

1. Select **Start, Control Panel, Network and Internet Connections, Network Connections**.

2. Click the icon for the connection that gets you on the Internet and then select **File, Properties.**

3. Display the **Networking** tab.

4. Make sure the **File And Printer Sharing For Microsoft Networks** check box is cleared.

Turning On the Internet Connection Firewall

Although disabling file and printer sharing is a must, it's not enough. That's because when a hacker finds your address, he or she has many other avenues with which to access your computer. Specifically, your connection uses many different "ports" for sending and receiving data. For example, web data and commands typically use port 80, e-mail uses ports 25 and 110, file transfer protocol (FTP) uses ports 20 and 21, Domain Name System (DNS) uses port 53, and so on. In all, there are dozens of these ports, and every one is an opening through which a clever cracker can gain access to your computer.

As if that wasn't enough, hackers also can check your system to see if some kind of Trojan horse virus is installed. (Those nasty e-mail virus attachments you learned about earlier in this chapter sometimes install these programs on your machine.) If the hacker finds one, he or she can effectively take control of your machine (turning it into a *zombie computer*) and either wreak havoc on its contents or use your computer to attack other systems.

Again, if you think your computer is too obscure or worthless for someone else to bother with, think again. A typical computer connected to the Internet all day long will get "probed" for vulnerable ports or be installed with Trojan horses at least a few times a day. If you want to see just how vulnerable your computer is, several good sites on the web will test your security:

Jargon Jar

A computer infected by a Trojan Horse virus that enables a hacker to control the machine remotely is called a **zombie computer.**

- ◆ Gibson Research (Shields Up): *grc.com/default.htm*

- ◆ DSL Reports: *www.dslreports.com/secureme_ go*

- ◆ HackerWhacker: *www.hackerwhacker.com*

The good news is that Windows XP includes a *personal firewall* tool called Internet Connection Firewall that can lock down your ports and prevent unauthorized access to your machine. In effect, your computer becomes *invisible* to the Internet (although you can still surf the web and work with e-mail normally). Follow these steps to fire up Internet Connection Firewall:

1. Launch Control Panel's **Network Connections** icon.

2. Right-click the **icon** for the connection that gets you on the Internet and then click **Properties.**

3. Choose the **Advanced tab** and select the **Protect My Computer And Network By Limiting Or Preventing Access To This Computer From The Internet** check box.

4. Click **OK.**

Turning Off the Messenger Service

As a final barrier against unwelcome intrusions, you should also turn off the Windows XP Messenger Service. This service (which is not to be confused with the Windows Messenger instant messaging program) is used by network administrators to broadcast messages to users. However, some advertisers have figured out how to use this service to have ads pop up on your computer. You can block these ads by turning off the service. To do this, follow these steps:

1. Select **Start, Control Panel, Performance and Maintenance, Administrative Tools, Services**. Windows XP displays the Services window.

2. Double-click the **Messenger** service.

3. Click **Stop** to shut down the service.

4. To prevent the service from starting in future Windows XP sessions, use the **Startup type** list to choose **Manual**.

5. Click **OK.**

Blocking Pop-Up Windows

One of the most annoying things on the web are those ubiquitous pop-up windows that infest your screen with advertisements when you visit certain sites. (A variation on the theme is the "pop under," a window that opens "under" your current browser window, so you don't know it's there until you close the window.) Pop-up windows can also be dangerous because some unscrupulous software makers have figured out ways to use them to install software on your computer without your permission. They're nasty things, any way you look at them.

Fortunately, Microsoft has given us a way to stop pop-ups before they start. In the Windows XP Service Pack 2, Internet Explorer comes with a new feature called the Pop-up Blocker that looks for pop-ups and prevents them from opening. Follow these steps to use and configure the Pop-up Blocker:

1. In Internet Explorer, select **Tools, Options** to display the Internet Options dialog box.

2. Display the **Privacy** tab.

3. Activate the **Pop-up blocker** check box.

4. To set options for this feature, click **Settings** to display the Pop-up Blocker Settings dialog box. You have the following options (click **Close** when you're done):

   ◆ **Address of Web site to allow**   Use this option when you have a site that displays pop-ups you want to see. Enter the address and then click **Add**.

   ◆ **Play a sound when a pop-up is blocked**   When this check box is activated, Internet Explorer plays a brief sound each time is blocks a pop-up. If this gets annoying after a while, deactivate this check box.

   ◆ **Block pop-ups opened from links I click**   Some pop-ups are launched when you click a link. To nip these in the bud as well, activate this check box.

   ◆ **Show Information Bar when a pop-up is blocked**   When this check box is activated, Internet Explorer displays a yellow bar below the Address bar each time it blocks a pop-up, just so you know it's working on your behalf.

5. Click **OK.**

With the Pop-Up Blocker on the case, it monitors your surfing and steps in front of any pop-up window that tries to disturb your peace. Figure 19.10 shows the yellow Information bar that appears under the Address bar to let you know when a pop-up was thwarted. If you want to see the pop-up anyway, click the Information bar and then click **Show Blocked Pop-up** in the menu that appears.

Figure 19.10

When the Pop-Up Blocker is active, it displays a yellow information bar each time it blocks a pop-up ad.

Using the Windows XP Service Pack 2 Security Center

If you've installed (or if your new computer comes with) Windows XP Service Pack 2, you can an extra security goodie: the Security Center. This is a simple window that checks your current security settings, makes security recommendations, and gives you access to XP's various security features. It's a one-stop security shop and it's something you should acquaint yourself with.

To get the Security Center to report for duty, use either of the following techniques:

♦ Double-click the **Security Center** icon in the taskbar's information area.

♦ Select **Start, All Programs, Accessories, System Tools, Security Center**.

Figure 19.11 shows the Security Center window that appears.

Figure 19.11

The Security Center, which is new in Windows XP Service Pack 2, gives you easy access to XP's security settings.

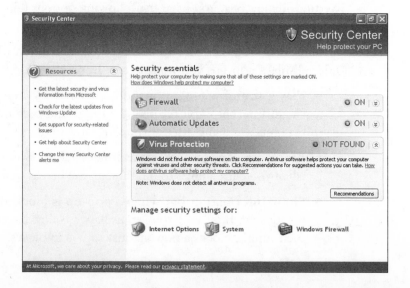

The **Resources** section provides you with links to security-related Internet sites and Security Center settings. The **Security essentials** section shows the status of three security settings:

♦ **Firewall**—This is the XP feature that protects your computer from unauthorized access while its connected to the Internet. It's crucial for your online protection that this feature be turned on. If it's listed as OFF, click **Recommendations** and then click **Enable now**. (Alternatively, click the **Windows Firewall** and then activate the **On** option.)

♦ **Automatic Updates**—This feature automatically downloads and installs security patches that keep XP safe from the latest online threats. Again, it's important to have this feature turned on. If Automatic Updates is OFF, click **System**, display the **Automatic Updates** tab, and then activate the **Automatic** option.

♦ **Virus Protection**—This tells you whether your computer has an antivirus program installed. If Virus Protection is OFF, there is no XP feature that you can tweak because XP doesn't come with its own antivirus program. Instead, you need to purchase and install a third-party antivirus program, such as Norton of MacAfee.

The Least You Need to Know

♦ To guard against e-mail–borne viruses, never open attachments that come from strangers, and double-check with friends before opening attachments they send your way.

♦ To cut down on the spam you receive, don't use your real address in a newsgroup, use a fake address whenever possible when signing up for things online, and never respond to spam or even open suspected spam messages.

♦ Only submit sensitive data (such as your credit card number) to a secure site (that is, one that has a lock icon in the status bar).

♦ Be sure to turn on the Windows XP Internet Connection Firewall if you have a full-time connection to the Internet.

Part **5**

Windows XP at the Shop: Customizing, Maintaining, and Troubleshooting

In these media-saturated times, quoting media guru Marshall McCluhan has become the ultimate badge of the so-hip-it-hurts set. Always happy to jump on a passing bandwagon, I hereby offer this book's token McLuhanism: "The mark of our time is its revulsion against imposed patterns." This shameless name- and quote-dropping is meant not to impress, but to introduce the main theme of Part 5: customizing Windows XP. The out-of-the-shrink-wrap look and feel of Windows XP certainly qualifies as an "imposed pattern," and it was designed by Microsoft to be suitable for what they consider to be a typical user. However, if the notion of being "typical" fills you with fear and loathing, then you've come to the right place because the four chapters coming up will show you how to refurbish Windows XP to suit your tastes and the way you work. This part of the book also proffers a few pointers on keeping Windows running smoothly and on fixing problems that crop up.

Chapter 20

Refurbishing the Desktop

In This Chapter

- ◆ Messing with desktop wallpaper and patterns
- ◆ Redoing the desktop colors and fonts
- ◆ Adding icons and web items to the desktop
- ◆ Monkeying around with the display's screen resolution and colors

For most of its history, the PC has maintained a staid, nay, *dull* exterior. Fortunately, the Nuthin'-But-Beige school has given way in recent years to some almost-stylish machines cavorting in gunmetal gray or shiny black exteriors. And with the Apple iMac available in several different psychedelic shades, it's likely that colorful machines will become the norm before too long.

That's a good thing because lots of people don't like the same old same old. These rugged individualists want to express themselves and that's hard to do with beige. The same goes for the Windows XP desktop. Sure, the standard Windows desktop is pleasant enough, but maybe you prefer a different scene or even a solid color. If so, you'll see in this chapter that Windows XP offers plenty of ways to make your mark with a custom desktop color or background.

Why Customize?

Yo, Geek Boy! Changing the desktop sounds great and everything, but most of the time I can't even see it. Isn't all this just a waste of time?

Hey, who're you calling a geek? It's actually not a waste of time because many of the changes you make to the desktop apply to Windows XP as a whole. For example, you can change the colors of window titles and borders, alter the font used in the taskbar, and change the overall size of the screen area. You'll learn all about these and many more customization options in this chapter.

Every last one of these customizations take place within the friendly confines of the Display Properties dialog box. To get this dialog box on the desktop, use either of the following techniques:

◆ Right-click an empty section of the desktop and then click **Properties** in the shortcut menu.

◆ Select **Start, Control Panel, Appearance and Themes, Display.**

Changing the Desktop Background

It's true that the desktop is usually hidden, particularly if, like me, you prefer to run your programs maximized. Still, there are plenty of times when the desktop is visible, such as at startup and when you close your programs. If that's enough of an excuse for you to tweak the look of the desktop, then you'll enjoy this section where I show you how to change the desktop background or color.

Windows Wisdom

The Windows XP list of approved images isn't the only wallpaper game in town. There's no problem using some other image if that's what you'd prefer. To do this, click the **Browse** button to promote the Browse dialog box, find and highlight the **image file,** and then click **Open.**

Wallpapering the Desktop

Wallpaper is an image or design that replaces the desktop's default solid color background. (Before you ask, no, I'm not sure why Microsoft calls it "wallpaper" when you're supposed to be thinking that your screen is like the top of a desk. It's either a mixed metaphor or the Microsoft offices have a *very* strange interior designer.) You can choose one of the prefab wallpapers that come with Windows XP, or you can easily create your own. Let's start with the simplest case of picking out one of the predefined wallpapers:

1. In the Display Properties dialog box, open the **Desktop** tab.

2. Use the **Background** list to click one of the image names. Keep one eye peeled on the fake monitor above the list. This gives you a preview of what the wallpaper will look like. (Some of the images take a second or two to show up, so patience is required.)

3. Use the **Position** list to select one of the following values:

    ◆ **Center**   Displays a single copy of the image in the center of the screen. This is a good choice for large images.

    ◆ **Tile**   Displays multiple copies of the image repeated so they fill the entire desktop. Choose this option for small images.

    ◆ **Stretch**   Displays a single copy of the image extended on all sides so it fills the entire desktop. This is the one to use if the image almost fills the desktop.

4. Click **OK** to put the wallpaper into effect. (You also can click **Apply** if you'd prefer to leave the Display Properties dialog box open and ready for action—for example, if you want to change the wallpaper again after seeing it full-screen.)

Image Is Nothing: Setting the Desktop to a Solid Color

If you find that using an image as the desktop background makes things too "busy," you can tone everything down a few notches by using a solid color instead. Here's how:

1. In the Display Properties dialog box, make sure the **Desktop** tab is displayed.

2. In the **Background** list, select **(None).**

3. Click the **downward-pointing arrow** on the right side of the Color button. Windows XP spreads out a grid of color boxes, which is known in the trade as a color *palette*.

4. Each of the 20 boxes represents a color. Click the box that represents the color you want to see on the desktop.

You might have noticed that the **Color** palette has a button named **Other.** You can use this option to pick a different color from those in the standard palette, or you can create your own color. When you click the **Other** button, you see the Color dialog box, shown in Figure 20.1.

Color box   Luminance bar

Figure 20.1

Use this dialog box to choose or create a different color.

Color pointer

Luminance pointer

The **Basic colors** area boasts 48 colors. To choose one of them, click its box then click **OK.**

> **Windows Wisdom**
>
> Whenever the **Red, Green,** and **Blue** values are equal, you get a gray-scale color. Lower numbers produce darker grays, and higher numbers produce lighter grays.

To roll your own color, you can use one of two methods. The first method uses the fact that you can create any color in the spectrum by mixing the three primary colors: red, green, and blue. The Color dialog box lets you enter specific numbers between 0 and 255 for each of these colors by using the **Red, Green,** and **Blue** text boxes. A lower number means the color is less intense, and a higher number means the color is more intense.

To give you some idea of how this works, the following table lists eight common colors and their respective red, green, and blue numbers.

Color	Red	Green	Blue
Black	0	0	0
White	255	255	255
Red	255	0	0
Green	0	255	0
Blue	0	0	255
Yellow	255	255	0
Magenta	255	0	255
Cyan	0	255	255

The second method for selecting colors involves setting three attributes—hue, saturation, and luminance:

♦ **Hue**   This number (which is more or less equivalent to the term *color*) measures the position on the color spectrum. Lower numbers indicate a position near the red end, and higher numbers move through the yellow, green, blue, and violet parts of the spectrum. As you increase the hue, the color pointer (refer to Figure 21.1) moves from left to right.

♦ **Sat**   This number is a measure of the purity of a given hue. A saturation setting of 210 indicates that the hue is a pure color. Lower numbers indicate that more gray is mixed with the hue until, at 0, the color becomes part of the gray scale. As you increase the saturation, the color pointer moves toward the top of the color box.

♦ **Lum**   This number is a measure of the brightness of a color. Lower numbers are darker, and higher numbers are brighter. The luminance bar to the right of the color box shows the luminance scale for the selected color. As you increase the luminance, the pointer moves toward the top of the bar.

To create a custom color, you can either enter values in the text boxes, as just described, or you can use the mouse to click inside the color box and luminance bar. The **Color|Solid** box shows the selected color on the left and the nearest solid color on the right (these two colors should be identical on your system). If you think you'll want to reuse the color down the road, click the **Add to Custom Colors** button to place the color in one of the boxes in the **Custom colors** area. When you're done, click **OK**.

> **Windows Wisdom**
>
> Windows XP also enables you to move and sort your desktop icons. Either with your mouse or by right-clicking the **desktop**, click **Arrange Icons By** and then click a sort order: **Name**, **Type**, **Size**, or **Modified** (that is, by date). Felix Unger–types can keep things in apple-pie order all the time by activating the **Auto Arrange** command and the **Align to Grid** command.

Adding Desktop Items

If you used any previous version of Windows, probably the first thing you noticed when you first saw Windows XP was the almost total absence of stuff on the desktop. One measly icon—the Recycle Bin—is all the Windows XP desktop has to show for itself. Gone are the old standbys such as the My Computer icon and the Internet Explorer icon. This was a conscious design choice on Microsoft's part because they'd prefer that you make the Start menu your Windows starting point.

However, if you miss having a satisfyingly cluttered desktop, there's nothing to stop you from tossing as many shortcuts on there as you like. Windows XP can even help out by letting you add *desktop items*, which are icons (program or document shortcuts) and *web items* (web pages or other web knickknacks). The next few sections take you through these desktop shenanigans.

Adding and Customizing Desktop Icons

To get started with desktop items, click the **Customize Desktop** button in the **Desktop** tab of the Display Properties dialog box. In the Desktop Items dialog box that jumps aboard, the **General** tab is where you deal with the Windows XP built-in desktop icons.

There are two sections to try out:

♦ **Desktop icons**   Use the check boxes to add icons such as **My Documents** and **My Computer** to the desktop. If you want to change the icon displayed by Windows XP, highlight it in the list and then click **Change Icon** (see the following section, "Changing an Icon").

♦ **Desktop cleanup**   Windows XP has a feature called the Desktop Cleanup Wizard that can remove desktop icons you haven't used in a while and put them into another folder (called Unused Desktop Shortcuts). This is a good idea, so you should probably leave the **Run Desktop Cleanup Wizard every 60 days** check box activated. Note that you can run the wizard any time you feel like by clicking the **Clean Desktop Now** button.

Changing an Icon

In several places throughout this book (including the previous section), you learn how to customize an object by changing its icon. How you get started depends on the object you're working with. However, in all cases you eventually end up at the Change Icon dialog box shown in Figure 20.2.

Here are some notes about working with this dialog box:

♦ In Windows XP, icons are usually stored in groups within executable files, particularly .exe and .dll files. Files with the .ico extension are pure icon files.

♦ If the icon you want isn't displayed in the Change Icon dialog box, use the **Look for icons in this file** text box to enter the name of an icon file and then press **Tab.** Here are a few suggestions (change C:\windows if your version of Windows XP is installed in a different drive or folder):

C:\windows\system32\shell32.dll

C:\windows\system32\Pifmgr.dll

C:\windows\explorer.exe

♦ If you're not sure about which file to try, click the **Browse** button and choose a file in the dialog box that appears.

♦ Click the icon you want to use, then click **OK.**

Figure 20.2

The Change Icon dialog box lists the icons that are available in an executable or icon file.

Web Items: Your Desktop as a Web Page

The standard desktop backgrounds and colors are fine as far as they go, but they lack that element of interactivity that folks exposed to the World Wide Web have come to expect. If you're one of those folks, then I'm sure you'll get a kick out of the Windows XP web items. This variation on the desktop theme enables you to populate your desktop with stuff normally seen in web pages or even with an entire web page.

To try this out, open the Desktop Items dialog box and display the **Web** tab. The **Web pages** list shows the web items you can display on your desktop. At first, you have only **My Current Home Page,** which is the home page defined in Internet Explorer. If you activate this item's check box, click **OK** and then click **Apply,** the desktop suddenly turns into an actual web page with live links and everything. Note, however, that you can't really "surf" the desktop. If you click a link, Windows XP runs Internet Explorer to fetch the page.

Windows Wisdom

Rather than making do with the Windows XP built-in icons, you might prefer to use your own, either by editing existing icons or by creating icons from scratch. There are a number of decent icon-creation programs available. The ones I like are IconEdit Pro, IconForge, and Icon Easel (all available from www.zdnet.com/downloads).

That's pretty slick, but you also can talk Windows XP into displaying a different web page or other web page content. Here's how:

1. In the **Web** tab, click **New.** Windows XP coughs up the New Desktop Item dialog box.

2. There are two paths you can take from here:

   ◆ **Visit Gallery**   Click this button to launch Internet Explorer and head for Microsoft's Desktop Gallery. This is a Web page that offers quite a few items that you can add to your system. Click the **Add to Active Desktop** button that sits by the item you want. When Internet Explorer asks whether you're sure about all this, click **Yes.**

   ◆ **Location**   Use this text box to enter the address of a web page. This can be the full URL of a page on the web, or the location of an HTML file on your hard disk or your network. (If you're not sure about the location of a nonweb item, click **Browse** to use the Browse dialog box to find it.)

3. Whichever method you use, you eventually end up at the Add item to Active Desktop dialog box. Click **OK.** Windows XP downloads the content and adds the item to the desktop.

4. If you went the Location route, you'll be dropped back in the web tab. Click **OK** or **Apply.**

The nice thing about web items is that they can be moved and sized as required. Here's a review of the techniques to use:

◆ **To move an item**   First move the mouse pointer over the item. This gets you a border around the item. Now click and drag any border.

◆ **To resize an item**   Move the mouse pointer over the top border. After a couple of seconds, you get a larger bar across the top of the item, as shown in Figure 20.3. Click and drag this bar to move the item.

◆ **To maximize an item**   Click the **Cover Desktop** button.

◆ **To maximize an item without affecting the desktop icons**   Click the **Split Desktop with Icons** button.

◆ **To close an item**   Click the **Close** button.

Move the mouse pointer over the top
border to get this bar

Figure 20.3

*Web item doodads can be
moved, resized, and more.*

Cover desktop
Split Desktop with icons
Close

Screen Saver Silliness

In olden times (say, 10 years ago), monitors weren't as good as they are today, and
most of us struggled along using ugly DOS screens. One of the problems people
faced was leaving their monitors on too long and ending up with some DOS hiero-
glyphics burned permanently into the screen (this is usually referred to, not surprisingly, as *burn-in*). To prevent this from happening, some genius came up with the idea
of a *screen saver:* a program that automatically kicks in after the computer is idle for a
few minutes. The screen saver displays some kind of moving pattern on the screen
that helps prevent burn-in. However, with a simple touch of a key or jiggle of a
mouse, the normal screen returns, unharmed and none the worse for wear.

Nowadays, it's pretty tough to burn an image into your screen. Improvements in
monitor quality and the graphical nature of Windows have made such a fate much
more difficult (although not impossible). Curiously, though, screen savers are still
around and are, in fact, flourishing. The reason: Most of them are just plain cool.
Who cares about preventing burn-in when you can watch wild, psychedelic patterns
or your favorite cartoon every few minutes?

There are scads of commercial screen savers
on the market, and Windows XP comes
equipped with some of its own. To try
them out, select the **Screen Saver** tab in
the Display Properties dialog box, drop
down the **Screen saver** list, and select a
screen saver.

You can also choose the following options:

♦ **Wait**   This spin box controls the
amount of time your computer must be
inactive before the screen saver starts
doing its thing. You can enter a number
between 1 and 9,999 minutes.

> **Windows Wisdom**
>
> Most folks use screen savers for
> the fun factor, but they have a
> practical side, as well. For
> example, if you set up the screen
> saver to kick in very soon (say,
> after just one minute), then it's use-
> ful for hiding your screen when
> you're not at your desk. Also, as
> you'll see in this section, you can
> secure your computer by adding
> a password to the screen saver.

◆ **On resume, display Welcome screen** (Windows XP Home) Activate this check box to have Windows XP Home display the Welcome screen when you stop the screen saver. This means you have to log on to Windows again.

◆ **On resume, password protect** (Windows XP Pro) Activate this check box to have Windows XP Professional display the Computer Locked dialog box when you shut off the screen saver. In this case, you have to enter your password to get back to Windows.

◆ **Preview** Click this button to give the screen saver a trial run. To return to the dialog box, move your mouse or press any key.

◆ **Settings** Click this button to set various options for the screen saver (note, however, that some screen savers don't have any options). The Settings dialog box that appears depends on which screen saver you chose. Choose the options you want, and then click **OK** to return to the Display Properties dialog box.

Changing the Desktop Colors and Fonts

It's possible to redo much more of the Windows XP interface (as the geeks like to call the stuff you see on your screen) than just the desktop background. Among many other things, you can change the font, color, and size of icon titles; the color of window title bars, scrollbars, and backgrounds; and the fonts and colors used in dialog boxes. This section shows you how to do it.

It all happens in the **Appearance** tab of the Display Properties dialog box. The easiest way to change things is to select one of the ready-made settings from the following lists:

◆ **Windows and buttons** The styles in this list control the overall look of your windows (including the shape and colors) and the buttons that appear in the windows (including dialog box command buttons and the window buttons: Minimize, Maximize, and Close). If you hanker for the old look of Windows Me, 98, or 2000, choose **Windows Classic** in this list.

> **Windows Wisdom**
>
> If you find you have trouble reading the text on your screen, Windows XP has schemes that can help. Look for scheme names that include either *"large"* or *"extra large"*.

◆ **Color scheme** This list offers one or more general color schemes for whatever style you select in the **Windows and buttons** list.

◆ **Font size** This list contains three relative font sizes: **Normal, Large Fonts,** and **Extra Large Fonts.** This setting applies not only to the window titles, but also to the desktop icon titles, the taskbar text, and the Start menu text.

Each time you select a setting, take a gander at the fake windows above the lists to get a preview of the havoc the new setting will wreak on your system. When you find a combo that's you, click **OK** or **Apply** to put it into effect.

Making Your Own Appearance Scheme

If you're feeling a bit more ambitious, you can create your own appearance scheme by plowing through these steps:

1. Click **Advanced** to meet up with the Advanced Appearance dialog box.

2. Use the **Item** list to choose which element of the screen you want to play with.

3. Use the following techniques to customize the selected element:

    ◆ If it's possible to change the size of the item, the **Size** spin box beside the Item list will be enabled. Use this spin box to adjust the size to taste.

    ◆ If it's possible to change the color of the item, the **Color 1** button will be enabled. Use this color palette control (described earlier in this chapter) to choose the color you want.

    ◆ Some screen elements (such as the Active Title Bar item) can display a color *gradient*, where one color fades into another. In this case, you use the **Color 1** button to pick the first color and the **Color 2** button to pick the second color.

    ◆ If the item has text, use the **Font** list to change the typeface. You also can adjust the font using the **Size** list, the **Color** button, and the **bold** and **italic** buttons.

4. Repeat steps 1 and 2 until you've customized all the items you want, and then click **OK.**

5. Display the **Themes** tab, click **Save As,** enter a name in the **Save As** dialog box, and click **OK** to return to the Display Properties dialog box.

6. Click **OK** or **Apply** to put your new scheme into production use.

Changing Desktop Visual Effects

The final bit of appearance wizardry you can wield is found by clicking the **Appearance** tab's **Effects** button. The Effects dialog box that fades in offers the following check boxes:

◆ **Use the following transition effect for menus and tooltips**   With this check box activated, use the list to choose either **Fade effect** (menus and tooltips fade in and fade out) or **Scroll effect** (menus and tooltips scroll in and scroll out). If either of these effects bugs you for some reason, deactivate this check box to turn them off.

◆ **Use the following method to smooth edges of screen fonts**   Activating this check box tells Windows XP to smooth the jagged edges (*jaggies*, in the vernacular) that appear when you use large fonts. Most screens will look better using the **Standard** method; if you have an LCD screen (such as found on most notebooks) or a high-resolution monitor, choose the **ClearType** method to get exceptionally sharp text.

◆ **Use large icons**   If you crank up this option, Windows XP inflates the size of the desktop and Start menu icons.

◆ **Show shadows under menus**   When this check box is activated, Windows XP renders menus with a subtle shadow underneath them, which gives the menus a slightly 3-D look.

◆ **Show window contents while dragging**   When you move a window, the entire contents of the window remain visible. If your system takes a long time to display the new window position as you move it, your moves will go much faster if you deactivate this check box. If you do this, then you'll see only the outline of a window as you move it.

◆ **Hide underlined letters for keyboard navigation until I press the Alt Key**   When I told you how to use menus in Chapter 1, I told you that you can use the keyboard to pull down a menu by holding down **Alt** and pressing the **underlined letter in the menu** name. Unfortunately, Windows XP shows only the underlined letters after you hold down Alt. If you'd prefer that Windows XP show the underlined letters full-time, deactivate this check box.

Changing the Screen Area and Color Depth

The last bit of desktop decoration I'll put you through in this chapter relates to various display settings. Again, these are options that apply not just to the desktop, but to everything you see on your screen. You'll find these settings in the **Settings** tab of the **Display Properties** dialog box, shown in Figure 20.4.

Figure 20.4

The Settings tab lets you muck around with your display.

Let's begin with the **Display** area. This line shows you two things:

- **The name of your monitor**   This tells you the name or the type of your monitor.

- **The name of your video adapter** This tells you the name or the type of the *video adapter* that resides inside your system.

Jargon Jar

A **video adapter** is an internal circuit board that gets instructions about what to display from the processor, and then tells the monitor what to show on the screen. It's also known as the video card or graphics card.

These two chunks of hardware determine the values you can select in the **Settings** tab's other two groups: Screen resolution and Color quality.

The **Color quality** group consists of a single list. The items in this list specify how many colors Windows XP can use to display stuff. This is called the *color depth*. Here are some notes:

- In general, the more colors you use, the sharper your screen images appear.

- If you're working with graphics, you'll want to use as many colors as possible.

- On the other hand, if you find that your screen display is sluggish, you should consider reducing the number of colors.

The **Screen resolution** slider determines the number of pixels used to display stuff on the screen. I've mentioned pixels before, but it's worth repeating myself here: A *pixel* is an individual pinpoint of light. All the colors you see are the result of thousands of these pixels getting turned on and set to display a specific hue.

Windows Wisdom

The **Color quality** list gives you a general setting (such as **Medium** or **High**) as well as a bit value (such as **16 bit** or **21 bit**). The deal here is that Windows XP uses a specified number of bits (on/off values) for each screen pixel (see my discussion of the Screen resolution setting that follows). The lowest number of bits is 8, and because 2 to the power of 8 is 256, that's the minimum number of colors you can choose. Other typical bit values are 16 (65,536 colors) and 21 (16,777,216 colors). There's also 32-bit color, but that's the same as 21-bit (the extra 8 bits are used by some applications for "masking" existing colors so that they appear transparent).

The lowest screen area value is 800 × 600. This means that Windows XP uses pixels arranged in a grid that has 800 columns and 600 rows. That's nearly half a million pixels for your viewing pleasure! The number of higher screen area values you can pick depends on your monitor and on your video adapter. Here are some notes:

♦ The more pixels you use (that is, the higher you go on the Screen resolution slider), the smaller things will look on the screen.

♦ You might be able to go to a higher screen area value only by using a smaller number of colors. Video adapters have only a certain amount of memory, so you'll often have to trade off one value with the other.

♦ In general, you should tailor the screen area value with the size of your monitor. If you have a standard 14- or 15-inch monitor, try 800 × 600; for 17- or 19-inch monitors, head up to 1,021 × 768; if you're lucky enough to have a 21-inch behemoth, go for 1,600 × 1,200 (if your video adapter will let you).

♦ If you have an older game or other program that has to be run at 640 × 480, it should change the resolution on its own when you start it. If it doesn't, right-click the program's **icon** in the **Start** menu and then click **Properties.** In the **Compatibility** tab, activate the **Run in 640 × 480 screen resolution** check box. Note, too, that you can force a program to run with only 256 colors by activating the **Run in 256 colors** check box.

When you've made your changes, click **OK** or **Apply.** If you choose a different resolution, Windows XP changes the setting and then asks whether you want to keep it. Click **Yes.** If things don't look right for some reason, click **No** to return to your normally scheduled display settings.

Look Out!

If your display goes haywire when Windows XP applies the new settings, it probably means that you tried some combo that was beyond the capabilities of your adapter/monitor team. Your screen likely will be unreadable, but don't panic. Windows XP will automatically reset the display after 15 seconds.

Applying Desktop Themes

Earlier I showed you how to select schemes that govern the look of various objects, including menu bars, window borders, title bars, icons, and more. Windows XP takes this idea a step further with desktop *themes*. A theme is also a collection of customizations, but it covers more ground than a simple scheme. Each theme specifies various settings for not only windows and dialog boxes, but also a screen saver, wallpaper, mouse pointers, sounds, desktop icons, and more.

To choose a desktop theme, follow these steps:

1. In the Display Properties dialog box, display the **Themes** tab.

2. Use the **Theme** drop-down list to choose the theme you want to use. The **Sample** area shows you a preview of the theme. You see not only how the theme will affect the various window objects, but also the wallpaper and desktop icons the theme uses.

3. Click **OK.**

Jargon Jar

A **theme** is a set of related customizations that cover colors, fonts, icons, screen saver, wallpaper, points, and even sounds.

The Least You Need to Know

◆ To open the **Display Properties** dialog box, either right-click the **desktop** and then click **Properties,** or select **Start, Control Panel, Appearance and Themes, Display.**

◆ Most wallpaper images are small, so you need to use the **Tile** option to get the fill effect. For larger images, use either **Center** or **Stretch.**

◆ Unless your computer has lots of video memory, you'll be faced with a trade-off when adjusting the screen resolution and color quality. That is, to get the highest resolution, you may need to use a lower color quality, and vice versa.

◆ Try to use a screen resolution value that matches your monitor. For most monitors, 800×600 is ideal.

◆ To apply a theme that covers colors, desktop settings, pointers, sounds, and more, open the **Display Properties** dialog box and select a theme from the **Themes** tab.

Revamping the Start Menu and Taskbar

In This Chapter

◆ Changing Start menu settings

◆ Adding your own shortcuts to the Start menu

◆ Quick taskbar tweaks

◆ Creating custom taskbar toolbars

You probably deal with the Start menu and taskbar dozens of times a day, so you can save yourself lots of time by using these items as efficiently as you can. That's the focus of this chapter as I show you all kinds of ways to customize the Start menu and taskbar.

A Smart Start: Reconstructing the Start Menu

The Start menu is your royal road to Windows XP riches, as well as to the programs installed on your machine. Because you use this road a lot during the course of a day, you'll probably want to make this road as short and as straight as possible. Fortunately, Windows XP gives you lots of ways to customize the Start menu to do this and to suit the way you work.

Toggling Some Start Menu Settings On and Off

The Windows XP Start menu boasts a number of new settings that you can turn on and off. These settings enable you to, among other things, add the Favorites list as a submenu, display the Control Panel icons as a submenu, and retreat to the "classic" Start menu from older versions of Windows.

To get to these settings, you have a couple of ways to go:

◆ Select **Start, Control Panel, Appearance and Themes, Taskbar and Start Menu.**

◆ Right-click the **Start** button and then click **Properties.**

Either way, the Taskbar and Start Menu Properties dialog box comes off the bench. Now display the **Start Menu** tab. Your first choice involves the Start menu style that you want to use:

◆ **Start Menu**   Choose this option to use the newfangled Start Menu that comes with Windows XP.

◆ **Classic Start Menu**   Choose this option to retreat to the familiar confines of the Start Menu used in Windows Me and Windows 2000.

Personally, I really like the XP incarnation of the Start menu: it's efficient, sensible for the most part, and as you'll see in this section, its not-so-sensible shortcomings are fixable with a couple of tweaks. I digress here in order to justify my decision to cover only the customization settings of the new XP Start menu. Note, however, that if you do decide to revert to the classic menu, many of its customization settings are similar to those I discuss in the rest of this section.

To move on with things, click the **Customize** button that sits next to the **Start menu** option. This gets you a ticket to the **Customize Start Menu** dialog box. The **General** tab serves up three sections:

◆ **Select an icon size for programs**   This inscrutable semisentence is telling you that you use the following option buttons to choose the relative size of the icons that appear in the programs section (the left half) of the Start menu. Choose either **Large icons** (the default) or **Small icons.** (The latter is useful if you up the number of programs Windows XP displays on the Start menu, as described next.)

◆ **Programs**   This section offers a couple of methods to adjust the Start menu's programs section. Recall that this section (excluding the **Internet** and **E-mail** icons at the top) displays icons for the last six programs you fired up. You can use the **Number of programs on Start menu** spin box to set the maximum number of these icons that appear in this section. Enter a number from 0 to 30. If you want to clear out the programs section and get a fresh start, click the **Clear List** button.

◆ **Show on Start menu**   When the **Internet** and **E-mail** check boxes are activated, these items appear at the top of the Start menu's programs section. Note, too, that each one offers a list that enables you to choose which web browser and which e-mail program to associate with these icons.

Hacking Windows

If you want to give an icon a permanent place in the Start menu's programs section, click **Start** to open the Start menu, right-click the **icon,** and then click **Pin to Start menu.** Windows XP moves the icon up into the top part of the menu and displays the icon title in bold. (Note that you can do this with any icon on the **All Programs** menus as well.) If you change your mind about the icon, you can return it to normal by right-clicking it and then clicking **Unpin from Start menu.** If you want to remove a single program icon from the Start menu, click **Start** to open the Start menu, right-click the **icon,** and then click **Remove from This List.**

The **Advanced** tab of the Customize Start Menu dialog box is shown in Figure 21.1.

Figure 21.1

The Advanced tab is bursting with Start menu settings.

For starters, the **Start menu settings** group has a couple of check boxes:

◆ **Open submenus when I pause on them with my mouse**   When this setting is activated, you can open a submenu just by placing your mouse pointer over the menu item. If you deactivate this check box, you can only open a submenu by clicking the menu item.

◆ **Highlight newly installed programs** With this setting lit up, Windows XP monitors the Start menu to see if some program adds its own icons or a submenu to the All Programs menu. If it does, XP displays a notice letting you know and it highlights the new icons or submenu.

What you're dealing with in the **Start menu items** group is a long list of check boxes and options that control the structure and behavior of the icons on the right side of the Start menu (the folders and XP features). The items that deal with folders (Control Panel, My Computer, My Documents, My Music, My Pictures, and, in XP Pro only, System Administrative Tools) offer the same set of three option buttons:

> **Windows Wisdom**
>
> Setting up folders such as Control Panel and My Documents as menus is a faster way to work, but what if you need to see those windows in the future? That's no problem. What you need to do is right-click the **icon** and then click **Open** in the shortcut menu.

◆ **Display as a link** This option means that when you click the folder icon in the Start menu, Windows XP opens the folder in a window.

◆ **Display as a menu** This option means that when you click the folder icon in the Start menu, a submenu slides out to display the contents of the folder.

◆ **Don't display this item** This option means that the folder icon doesn't appear in the Start menu.

(Note that there's also a Network Connections item that offers three similar, but differently worded, options.)

The rest of the list is composed of check boxes. Each one toggles a particular Start menu feature on and off. Here's a quick summary of the features:

◆ **System Administrative Tools** When this check box is activated, Windows XP adds the Administrative Tools menu to the All Programs menu. (These are geeks-only tools, so it's unlikely that you'll want to bother with this one.)

◆ **Enable dragging and dropping** When this setting is activated, it enables you to rearrange Start menu stuff by using your mouse to click and drag the icons here and there. I'll tell you a bit more about this technique later in this chapter; see "Adding Your Own Start Menu Icons."

◆ **Favorites menu** This check box toggles the icon for the Favorites submenu on and off the Start menu.

◆ **Help and Support** This check box toggles the Help and Support icon on and off.

◆ **My Network Places**   This check box toggles the icon for the My Network Places folder on and off.

◆ **Printers and Faxes**   This check box toggles the icon for the Printers and Faxes folder on and off.

◆ **Run command**   This check box toggles the icon for the Run command on and off.

◆ **Scroll Programs**   This setting determines what Windows XP does if the All Programs menu contains so many items that the entire menu can't fit into the height of the screen. When this setting is off, Windows XP displays Programs as a two-column menu. When this setting is on, Windows XP displays Programs as a single menu with up and down arrows on the top and bottom, respectively. You click these arrows to scroll through the menu.

◆ **Search**   This check box toggles the icon for the Search feature on and off.

Finally, the **Recent documents** group has a check box named **List my most recently opened documents.** If you activate this setting, Windows XP adds an icon named **Recent Documents** to the Start menu. This icon opens a submenu that contains a list of the last 15 documents you worked on in any program. If you display this menu and decide later on that you don't want anyone else to see the list of documents, you can scrub it clean by returning to the **Advanced** tab and clicking the **Clear List** button.

> **Cross-Reference**
>
> Remember your Favorites? If you don't, jump back to Chapter 15 and look under "Saving Sites for Subsequent Surfs: Managing Your Favorites."

That's all he wrote for the Customize Start Menu dialog box, so click **OK** to return to the Taskbar and Start Menu Properties dialog box, and then click **OK** to put the new settings into effect.

Adding Your Own Start Menu Icons

Most new users just assume the arrangement of icons on the Start menu is a permanent part of the Windows XP landscape. They're right, to a certain extent. Everything on the main Start menu can only be messed with by using the techniques from the previous section.

What *is* a bit surprising is that the menus that appear when you click **All Programs** are completely open for customization business. You can add icons, move them around, rename them, delete them, and more. I show you how to do all of this in this section.

Let's begin by learning how to add an icon to the Start menu. You usually don't have to worry about this when you install an application. That's because most of today's programs are hip to the Start menu, so they'll add an icon or three during their installation procedure. However, there are two cases when you'll need to add an icon yourself:

◆ If you want easy access to a particular document that you use often.

◆ If you installed an older program that isn't Start-menu savvy.

It's important to bear in mind that the icons you're working with here are *shortcuts* to documents or programs. A shortcut is a teensy file whose sole mission in life is to act as a pointer to some other file. For example, when you launch a shortcut for a document, the shortcut tells Windows XP the location of the *actual* document. XP then finds the document and opens it for you.

Here's how you add an icon to the Start menu:

1. Use My Computer to find the document you want to work with or the file that runs the program you want to add.

2. Click and drag the document or file from My Computer and hover it over the **Start** button. After a second or two, the Start menu pops up.

3. Click and drag the file up into the Start menu.

4. Do one of the following:

◆ If you want to make the icon a part of the Start menu's permanent program icon section (where the Internet and E-mail icons are), click and drag it up into that section and then drop it.

◆ If you want the icon to appear in the All Programs menu, click and drag the file over top of **All Programs,** wait a beat until the menu appears, and then drag the file into the All Programs menu. If you want it to appear in one of the All Programs submenus, drag the file up until you see a line just above the submenu, wait until the submenu appears, drag the file into the submenu, and then drop it inside the submenu.

Windows Wisdom

If you click and drag the document or file from My Computer and then drop it on the **Start** button, Windows XP automatically pins a shortcut to the document or file to the "permanent" part of the Start menu's programs section.

What about the opposite procedure, when you need to get rid of something on the Start menu? I'm glad you asked. What you do is open the Start menu and display the icon you want to remove. Then use your mouse to click and drag the icon off the menu and drop it on the desktop's **Recycle Bin** icon. (Note that you may need to minimize all your running programs in order to see the Recycle Bin icon.)

Windows Wisdom

Remember that the icons you delete are only shortcuts that point to the original program file or document. You're not deleting the originals.

Easy Start Menu Maintenance

To close out your look at customizing the Start menu, here are a few tips and techniques that can make this part of your life even easier:

◆ **Right-click convenience**   You can perform many maintenance chores right from the Start menu itself. Right-click a Start menu icon, and you'll get a menu with all kinds of useful commands, including Cut, Copy, Delete, and Rename. (The actual roster of commands depends on the icon. The largest collection is found with the icon on the All Programs menu.)

◆ **Drag-and-drop rearranging**   You can move things around in the All Programs menu by using your mouse to click and drag the icons directly. You can drop them higher or lower on the same menu or even drop them onto another menu altogether.

◆ **Sorting an out-of-sorts menu**   If you've been dragging icons hither and yon, you might end up with menus that are no longer in alphabetical order. If that offends your inner neat freak, it's easy enough to fix. Just right-click the offending menu and then click **Sort by Name**.

Renovating the Taskbar

Like the Start menu, the taskbar also seems to be a nonmalleable feature of the Windows XP landscape. If that were true, however, then this chapter would end right about here. The fact that you still have a few pages left to slog through tells you that, indeed, the taskbar is readily malleable. Not only that, but most of the taskbar customizations you'll see over the next few sections are practical timesavers and not just mere "Hey, Ma, look what I can do!" tricks.

Unlocking the Taskbar

When Microsoft was testing Windows with new users, they found that people often ended up with inadvertently customized taskbars that they didn't know how to fix. For example, it's actually quite easy to accidentally resize the taskbar while trying to resize a window (as you'll see a bit later). To prevent this kind of faux customization (and the confusion it creates), Windows XP comes with its taskbar locked so that it can't be moved or sized. Here's how to unlock it so that you can manhandle the taskbar on purpose:

1. Right-click an empty section of the taskbar.

2. In the shortcut that appears, look for the **Lock the Taskbar** command. If there's a checkmark beside it, click the command to remove the checkmark and unlock the taskbar.

Taskbar Travels: Moving and Sizing the Taskbar

The taskbar, recumbent on the bottom of the screen, seems quite comfy. However, that position might not be comfy for *you*, depending on the ergonomics of your desk and chair. Similarly, you might have a program where you need to maximize the available vertical screen space, so you might not appreciate having the taskbar usurp space at the bottom of the screen. These are mere molehills that can be easily leapt by moving the taskbar to a new location:

1. Point the mouse at an empty section of the taskbar.

2. Hold down the left mouse button and move the pointer toward the edge of the screen where you'd rather see the taskbar situated. As you approach an edge, the taskbar suddenly snaps into place.

3. When the taskbar is on the edge you want, release the mouse button.

What if you're not so much interested in moving the taskbar as in resizing it? For example, if you're feeling particularly frisky, you might end up with a whack of programs on the go. However, each of those programs claims a bit of taskbar turf. The more programs you have running, the tinier the taskbar buttons become. Eventually, as you can see in Figure 21.2, the text on the buttons becomes all but indecipherable.

Figure 21.2

Who can tell what each of these taskbar buttons represents?

The way you fix that is by expanding the taskbar from its single-row setup to a setup that has two or more rows. Here's how:

1. Move the mouse pointer so that it rests on the top edge of the taskbar. The pointer changes into a vertical two-headed arrow.

2. Click and drag the edge of the taskbar up slightly. After you travel a short distance, a second taskbar row springs into view, as shown in Figure 21.3.

Figure 21.3

To see the button text, stretch the taskbar into this two-row configuration.

3. Keep dragging the taskbar up until the taskbar is the size you want, and then release the mouse button.

If you've moved the taskbar to the left or right side of the screen, dragging the outer edge only increases the width of the taskbar, it doesn't create new rows.

Some Useful Taskbar Options

The next round of taskbar touchups involves a small but useful set of properties, which can be displayed by using either of the following techniques:

◆ Select **Start, Control Panel, Appearance and Themes, Taskbar and Start Menu.**

◆ Right-click an empty section of the taskbar and then click **Properties.**

This reunites you with your old friend the Taskbar and Start Menu Properties dialog box. This time, however, you'll be dealing with the **Taskbar** tab.

The **Taskbar appearance** group controls the look and feel of the taskbar. As you play with the settings in this group, keep an eye on the fake taskbar that appears just above the Lock taskbar check box. This will give you some idea of how the taskbar will change based on the settings you toggle on and off. Here's a summary of the available check boxes:

◆ **Lock the taskbar**   This check box toggles the taskbar lock on and off.

◆ **Auto-hide the taskbar**   If you activate this check box, Windows XP shrinks the taskbar to a teensy blue strip that's barely visible along the bottom of the screen. This gives a maximized window more room to stretch its legs. When you need the taskbar for something, just move the mouse pointer to the bottom of the screen. Lo and behold, the full taskbar slides into view. When you move the mouse above the taskbar, the taskbar sinks back whence it came.

> **Windows Wisdom**
>
> It's still possible to get to the taskbar with the **Keep the taskbar on top of other windows** option turned off. Either minimize the window, or else press **Ctrl+Esc** (or the Windows **logo** key, if you have one), and then press **Esc**.

◆ **Keep the taskbar on top of other windows** When this option is activated, the taskbar remains in view even if you maximize a window. That's usually a good thing. However, if you really need that extra bit of screen room, deactivate this check box. This means that a maximized window takes up the entire screen.

◆ **Group similar taskbar buttons**   As you know, when you run a program, Windows XP adds a button for the program to the taskbar. When this check box is turned on, Windows XP reduces clutter by combining similar taskbar buttons into a single button. For example, if you have two or three instances of Internet Explorer on the go, they'll get grouped into a single button. (Note, however, that this only happens once the taskbar becomes completely filled with buttons.) To get at a particular window, click the button to pop up a list of the windows (see Figure 21.4) and then click the window you want.

Figure 21.4

When Windows XP groups similar taskbar buttons, click the button to get at the grouped windows.

The number of grouped buttons

Click to see the grouped buttons

◆ **Show Quick Launch**   If you activate this check box, Windows XP adds the Quick Launch toolbar beside the Start button, as shown in Figure 21.5. This gives you one-click access to three icons: **Launch Internet Explorer Browser, Show Desktop,** and **Windows Media Player.** The Show Desktop icon minimizes all running programs so that you get a pristine view of the desktop.

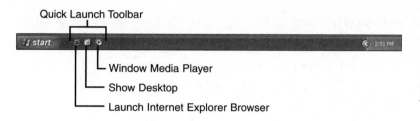

Quick Launch Toolbar

Window Media Player

Show Desktop

Launch Internet Explorer Browser

Figure 21.5

Use the Quick Launch tool-bar for single-click access to some Windows XP features.

The **Notification area** group has just two check boxes:

◆ **Show Clock**   Deactivating this check box hides the clock that normally resides in the notification area.

◆ **Hide inactive icons**   When this check box is activated, Windows XP will hide notification area icons that you haven't used in a while. In their place, you see a left-pointing arrow, as shown in Figure 21.6. Click that arrow to see the hidden icons. To gain some control over this, click **Customize** to meet up with the Customize Notifications dialog box. In the list of notifications, click one to enable a list of options for that icon. You get three choices: **Hide when inactive, Always hide,** and **Always show.**

> ### Hacking Windows
>
> To add your own icons to the Quick Launch toolbar, open My Computer, click and drag the document or program file you want to add, and drop it inside the Quick Launch toolbar. (You can also click and drag an icon from any Start menu and drop it inside the Quick Launch toolbar.)

Click this button to see the hidden icons

Figure 21.6

Windows XP can hide noti-fication area icons that you haven't used in a while.

The Least You Need to Know

◆ The Start menu and taskbar options are available by selecting **Start, Control Panel, Appearance and Themes, Taskbar and Start Menu,** or by right-clicking the **Start** button or an empty stretch of the taskbar and then clicking **Properties.**

◆ To add Start menu stuff, click and drag a document or program file from My Computer, hover the mouse over the **Start** button, and then drop it on the menu you want.

◆ To make direct Start menu modifications, display the Start menu and then right-click any command.

◆ Before embarking on any taskbar modifications, be sure to unlock it first. The quickest route is to right-click an empty part of the taskbar and then deactivate the **Lock the Taskbar** command.

◆ Drag an empty section of the taskbar to move it; click and drag the top edge of the taskbar to size it.

◆ The easiest way to add icons to the Quick Launch toolbar is to click and drag program files and drop them onto the toolbar.

Maintaining Your System in Ten Easy Steps

In This Chapter

◆ Maintain your hard disk by checking for errors, monitoring free space, deleting unnecessary files, and defragmenting files

◆ Set up your system for easier recovery by creating restore points and by backing up your files

◆ Keep your system up-to-date by checking for updates, patches, and security vulnerabilities

◆ Set up a maintenance schedule to keep your system running in peak form without burdening your schedule

We tend to forget that computers are mechanical devices that can fail at any time, or can simply wear out over time. In other words, the data you've stored on your computer is at risk *right now*. Not months or years from now. *Now*. This doesn't mean you should just sit around and wait for your computer to start sucking mud. ("Sucking mud" is a colorful phrase used by programmers to refer to a crashed machine. Legend has it that the phrase comes from the oilfield lament, "Shut 'er down, Ma, she's a-suckin' mud!")

No, what you *should* be doing is a little proactive system maintenance to help prolong your machine's life and to help propel your system to new heights of efficiency and speed. This chapter can help by showing you the Windows XP tools that can get you in what I like to call "ounce of prevention mode" (and to avoid what I call "pound of cure mode" down the road). In particular, I give you a step-by-step plan for maintaining your system and checking for the first signs of problems.

Step 1—Check Your Hard Disk for Errors

You'll see later in this chapter that you should back up your files frequently because all hard disks eventually go to the Great Computer in the Sky. However, it's possible to avoid a premature hard disk death (as well as lost files and otherwise-inexplicable system crashes) by regularly checking your disk for errors. (By "regularly," I mean about once a week or so.) Here's how you do it:

1. Log on to Windows XP with Administrator-level privileges.

2. Shut down any programs that are on the loose.

3. In My Computer, highlight your hard disk and select **File, Properties.** (For the heck of it, you also can try right-clicking the hard disk and then clicking **Properties.**)

4. In the dialog box that clears customs, display the **Tools** tab.

5. Click the **Check Now** button. This gets you an appointment with the Check Disk dialog box.

6. Check Disk offers two checking options:

   ◆ **Automatically fix file system errors** Activate this check box to have Windows XP handle the dirty work of fixing any file problems that it finds. This gives you one less thing to fret about, so activating this option is a good idea.

   ◆ **Scan for and attempt recovery of bad sectors** Activate this option to have Check Disk examine the physical surface of the disk for corruption. This is a good idea because a lot of bad *sectors* means not only that you might not be able to store files reliably, but also that your hard disk might be heading for a crash. Note, however, that this slows down the check considerably, so you should probably use this option only once a month or so.

Jargon Jar

A **sector** is a tiny piece of a disk, and Windows XP uses a disk's sectors as mini–storage bins that hold bits of your files. A "bad" sector is one that has gone wonky for some reason, so it can no longer be used to store anything reliably.

7. Click **Start** to get the Check Disk show on the road.

8. If any errors are found (and you didn't activate the **Automatically Fix File System Errors** option), you'll see a dialog box alerting you to the bad news. Follow the instructions provided.

9. When the check is done, a dialog box lets you know. Click **OK.**

Remember that Check Disk can take quite a while under some circumstances, so only run the program at the end of the day or when you know you won't be needing your computer for a while.

Step 2—Check Free Disk Space

Ever wonder how much free space you have left on your hard disk? It's easy enough to find out:

1. Select **Start, My Computer.**

2. Click your hard disk.

As you can see in Figure 22.1, the information area shows you how much free space you have left to work with.

Make sure this number doesn't get too low

Figure 22.1

Highlight your hard disk in My Computer to see how much disk real estate is left to be developed.

Windows Wisdom

How do you know when your hard disk is getting low on disk space? It depends. If it's the disk where Windows XP is stored, then you should never let that disk get much below 200 megabytes (MB) of free space. If it's some other disk that you use to store programs and files, start getting worried when the free space drops to around 100 MB. If the free space is measured in gigabytes (GB), then don't worry because there are about 1,000 megabytes in every gigabyte, so you have plenty of room.

Step 3—Delete Unnecessary Files

If you find that your hard disk is getting low on free space, you should delete any unneeded files and programs. Windows XP comes with a Disk Cleanup utility that enables you to remove certain types of files quickly and easily. Before discussing this utility, let's look at a few methods you can use to perform a spring cleaning on your hard disk by hand:

♦ **Uninstall programs you don't use** If you have an Internet connection, you know it's easier than ever to download new software for a trial run. Unfortunately, that also means it's easier than ever to clutter your hard disk with unused programs. Use Control Panel's Add Or Remove Programs icon to uninstall these and other rejected applications.

Cross-Reference

To learn how to uninstall a program, in Chapter 6, see the section titled "Giving a Program the Heave-Ho."

Cross-Reference

To learn how to remove a Windows XP component, in Chapter 6, see the section titled "Uninstalling a Windows XP Component."

♦ **Delete downloaded program archives** Speaking of program downloads, your hard disk is probably also littered with Zip files or other downloaded archives. For those programs you use, you should consider moving the archive files to a removable medium for storage. For programs you don't use, consider deleting the archive files.

♦ **Remove Windows XP components that you don't use** If you don't use some Windows XP components such as MSN Explorer, Paint, and some or all of the Windows XP games), use Control Panel's Add Or Remove Programs icon to remove those components from your system.

◆ **Delete application backup files**
Applications often create backup copies
of existing files and name the backups
using either the .bak or .old extension.
Use My Computer's Search utility to
locate these files and delete them.

> **Cross-Reference**
>
> For the details on how to search
> for files, in Chapter 5, see the
> section titled "Finding a File In
> That Mess You Call a Hard Disk."

Once you've completed these tasks, you next should run the Disk Cleanup utility,
which can automatically remove several other types of files, including the following:

◆ **Downloaded Program Files** These are miniprograms used by some World
Wide Web pages and that are downloaded onto your hard disk when you view
such pages. After that, they just sit around doing nothing, so they can be safely
deleted.

◆ **Temporary Internet files** These are copies of web pages that Internet Explorer keeps on hand so that the pages view faster the next time you visit them.
Saying goodbye to these files will slow down some of your surfing slightly, but it
will also rescue lots of disk space.

◆ **Offline web pages** These are web
pages that you've set up as favorites and
for which you've activated the "Make
available offline" feature. This means that
Internet Explorer stores updated copies
of these pages on your computer for offline surfing. Deleting them means that
you'll have to go online to view them.

> **Cross-Reference**
>
> I talked about offline web pages
> in Chapter 16. See the section
> titled "Offline Surfing: Reading
> Pages When You're Not
> Connected."

◆ **Recycle Bin** These are the files that you've deleted recently. Windows XP
stores them in the Recycle Bin for a while just in case you delete a file accidentally. If you're sure you don't need to recover a file, you can clean out the
Recycle Bin and recover the disk space.

◆ **System Restore: Obsolete data stores** These files are created by the System
Restore program (which I discuss later in this chapter) and are used to help you
recover from problems. However, some older files can no longer be used (because,
for example, you reinstalled Windows XP), so they can be safely deleted.

◆ **Setup Log Files** These are files that Windows XP created while it was installing itself on your computer. If your computer is running well, then you won't
ever need to refer to these logs, so you can toss them.

♦ **Temporary files** These are "scratch pad" files that some programs use to doodle on while they're up and running. Most programs are courteous enough to toss out these files, but a program or computer crash could prevent that from happening. You can delete these files at will.

♦ **WebClient/Publisher temporary files** These are copies of existing files that Windows XP stores to improve the performance of the WebClient/Publisher service. It's perfectly okay to delete these copies.

♦ **Temporary offline files** These are copies of network files that Windows XP saves on your hard disk temporarily. It's pretty safe to delete these files.

♦ **Offline files** These are permanent copies of network files that reside on your hard disk. Having these files enables you to work with them even when you're not connected to the network. If you no longer need these files, delete them to clear some room on your hard disk.

♦ **Compress old files** Windows XP can take files that you haven't messed with in awhile (the default is 50 days) and scrunch them down so that they take up less disk space, yet remain accessible to you and your programs.

♦ **Catalog files for the Content Indexer** These are files that have been left behind by the Windows XP Indexing Service. You don't need these files, so you can delete them with abandon.

Note that you may not have all of these types of files on your system, so if you don't see some of them when you run Disk Cleanup, don't sweat it.

Follow these steps to use Disk Cleanup to trash any or all of these kinds of files:

1. Windows XP offers you three different routes to get started:

   ♦ In My Computer, highlight the hard disk and select **File, Properties.** (Alternatively, right-click the hard disk and then click **Properties.**) In the dialog box that beams up, click the **Disk Cleanup** button.

   ♦ Select **Start, Control Panel, Performance and Maintenance, Free up space on your hard disk.**

   ♦ Select **Start, All Programs, Accessories, System Tools, Disk Cleanup.**

2. If you used either of the last two paths and you have multiple hard disks, the Select Drive dialog box will ask you which one you want to work with. Use the **Drives** list to pick out the drive and then click **OK.**

3. Either way, you end up at the Disk Cleanup window shown in Figure 22.2. Activate the check box beside each type of file you want to blow to kingdom come.

Figure 22.2

Use Disk Cleanup to obliterate all kinds of more-or-less useless files from your hard disk.

4. If you activate the **Compress old files** check box, you can determine what "old" means by clicking the **Options** button that appears while **Compress old files** is highlighted. In the Compress Old Files dialog box that puts in an appearance, use the **Compress after X days** spin box to set the age, in days, after which Windows XP will compress your files.

5. Click **OK.** Disk Cleanup asks whether you're sure.

6. Click **Yes.**

Step 4—Defragment Your Hard Disk

With its 3D-ish icons and pastoral desktop, Windows XP surely presents a polished surface to the world. However, when it's just kicking around at home, Windows XP is a bit of a slob. I'm thinking, in particular, about how Windows XP stores files on your hard disk. It's actually remarkably casual about the whole thing, and tosses bits and pieces of each file wherever it can find room. This doesn't matter much at first, but after a while you end up with files that are scattered willy-nilly all over your hard disk. This is a problem because it means that to open a file, Windows XP has to make lots of little, time-consuming trips to the far corners of the hard disk in order to gather up all those disparate chunks.

This is why computers that feel nice and zippy when you first take them out of the box seem to get more sluggish over time. In geek terms, the problem is that the files on your hard disk have become *fragmented.* The solution is to run the Windows XP Disk Defragmenter program, which will rearrange the contents of your hard disk so that each file's hunks are arranged consecutively (or *contiguously,* as the geeks like to say). Don't worry, though: Your documents and programs don't get changed in any way and your disk contents will look exactly the same when you view them in My Computer.

Jargon Jar _____

A hard disk is said to be **fragmented** when pieces of its files are scattered in various places throughout the disk.

Before getting to the Disk Defragmenter details, here's a bit of prep work you need to do:

♦ Log on to Windows XP with Administrator-level privileges.

♦ Shut down all running programs.

♦ Run the Check Disk program to be sure there are no errors on your hard disk. In particular, be sure you activate the **Scan for and attempt recovery of bad sectors** check box.

♦ Run Disk Cleanup and get rid of any files you don't need.

Here's how Disk Defragmenter works:

1. You can get underway by using either of the following techniques:

    ♦ In My Computer, highlight your hard disk and select **File, Properties.** (Or right-click the **hard disk** and then click **Properties.**) In the dialog box that gets piped in, display the **Tools** tab and click the **Defragment Now** button.

    ♦ Select **Start, Control Panel, Performance and Maintenance, Rearrange items on your hard disk to make programs run faster.**

    ♦ Select **Start, All Programs, Accessories, System Tools, Disk Defragmenter.**

2. Figure 22.3 shows the Disk Defragmenter window that results. If you have multiple disk drives, click the one you want to work with.

Figure 22.3

Use Disk Defragmenter to put your hard disk affairs in order.

3. Click the **Analyze** button. This tells Disk Defragmenter to have a gander at the chosen disk and see just how defragmented it is.

4. After a few seconds, you'll see the Analysis Complete dialog box, which will display one of the following messages (note that, in both cases, *volume* is XP-speak for a disk drive):

   ◆ **You do not need to defragment this volume**   This is the "Woo hoo!" message because it means your disk isn't fragmented too much and you can bypass the defragment for now. Click **Close** and exit Disk Defragmenter.

   ◆ **You should defragment this volume**   Disk Defragmenter tends to be a bit reluctant to call for a defragment, so if you see this message, then you *know* that your system needs to be straightened up. In this case, you should click **Defragment** (although you also can click **Close** and start the defragment from the Disk Defragmenter window).

5. If you're back in the Disk Defragmenter window and you want to run the defragment from there, click **Defragment.** Disk Defragmenter reanalyzes the disk and then gets down to work. While this happens, compare the **Estimated disk use before defragmentation** display with the **Estimated disk use after defragmentation** display. Over time, you'll start to see more blue (contiguous files) in the latter and less red (fragmented files).

6. When the job is complete, Disk Defragmenter displays a dialog box to let you know. Click **Close.**

7. If you want to defragment another disk, repeat steps 2 through 6.

8. To exit Disk Defragmenter, select **File, Exit.**

The defragmenting process might take some time, depending on the size of your disk and how severely fragmented it is. Because it's not unusual for a defragment job to take a couple of hours or more, consider running Disk Defragmenter just before you leave the office or go to bed. (Or use the Scheduled Tasks folder—discussed in the next section—to set up Disk Defragmenter to run at night.)

Step 5—Set System Restore Points

One of the most frustrating of Windows experiences is to have your system sailing along without so much as an electronic hiccup, and then to have everything crash or become unstable after installing a program or a chunk of hardware. This all-too-common scenario means that some program component or device driver simply doesn't get along with Windows XP, and that the two are now at loggerheads. Uninstalling the program or device can often help, but that's not a foolproof solution.

To help guard against software or hardware installations that bring down the system, Windows XP has a feature called System Restore. Its job is straightforward, yet clever: To take periodic snapshots—called *restore points* or *checkpoints*—of your system, each of which includes the current Windows XP configuration. The idea is that if a program or device installation causes problems on your system, you use System Restore to revert your system to the most recent restore point before the installation.

System Restore creates checkpoints using the following methods:

♦ Automatically every 24 hours if you keep your computer on full-time. If you turn your machine off periodically, Windows XP creates a restore point every 24 hours that the machine is running.

♦ Automatically before installing an update via the Automatic Updates feature (discussed later in this chapter).

Cross-Reference
I show you how to use System Restore to recover from a problem in Chapter 23. See the section titled "Recovering Using System Restore."

♦ Automatically before installing certain applications. Some newer applications—notably Office 2000—are aware of System Restore and ask it to create a restore point prior to installation.

♦ Automatically when you attempt to install a device driver that is "unsigned" (meaning that it can't be verified that the driver will work properly with Windows XP).

♦ Manually using the System Restore feature.

To create a restore point manually, follow these steps:

1. Use either of the following methods to launch System Restore:

    ♦ Select **Start, Control Panel, Performance and Maintenance, System Restore.**

    ♦ Select Start, All Programs, Accessories, System Tools, System Restore.

2. Activate the **Create a restore point** option and click **Next.**

3. Use the **Restore point description** text box to enter a description for the new restore point and then click **Create.** System Restore creates the restore point and displays the Restore Point Created window.

4. Click **Close.**

Step 6—Back Up Your Files

Other than a few people who insist on living in It-Can't-Happen-to-Me Land, I think most folks get the "why" part of backing up. They just don't get the "how" part. That is, they'd like to run backups, but it's such a time-consuming chore so it just doesn't seem worth the hassle. "Sorry, I'd like to do a backup, but I have to call the IRS to schedule an audit."

If backing up seems like too much of a bother, there are plenty of things you can do to make it easier:

♦ **Forget floppies, if possible**   Backing up to floppy disks ranks just above "root canal" on the Top 10 Most Unpleasant Chores list. The reason, of course, is that a standard 3.5-inch floppy disk holds a mere 1.39 MB of data. If your hard disk contains hundreds of megabytes, you'll have to back up to hundreds of floppy disks, which hurts just to think about.

♦ **Try a tape drive**   Tape drives are the de facto backup standard and come in many different capacities. You can back up hundreds of megabytes or even multiple gigabytes for a relatively low cost.

♦ **Try other backup media**   The big downfall for tape drives is their relatively slow speeds. Fortunately, there are much faster media available. These include CD-R and CD-RW drives or the even more capacious DVD-R, DVD-RW, DVD+R, and DVD+RW drives; removable media such the Zip or Jaz drives; a second hard disk (be sure it's a second disk and not just a single disk that's been divided in two); and a network folder.

◆ **Consider online backups** If your ISP provides you with disk space for a website, use it to back up your most important files. Note, too, that there are also companies that will sell you online disk space for backups.

◆ **Back up your documents first** The only things on your system that are truly irreplaceable are the documents that you've created with the sweat of your own brow. So, if backup space is at a premium, just include your documents in the *backup job*. You can always install your programs again later, if need be.

Jargon Jar

A **backup job** is a file that specifies a few particulars about your backup. These particulars include the files you want backed up, the location where the files will be backed up, and any backup options you specify along the way.

◆ **Organize your documents** If you're going to go the documents-only route, you'll make your life immeasurably easier if you store everything in subfolders that all reside within a single folder (such as My Documents). That way, when you're telling Windows XP which files to back up, you need to only select that folder. Another plus for this approach is that any files you add to this folder will be included automatically the next time you run the backup.

◆ **Back up your downloaded programs** If you've downloaded programs and files from the Internet, it can be a lot of trouble to get new copies of that stuff if your system goes down for the count. So, you should include downloaded files as part of your backup job.

◆ **Take advantage of backup types** After you've decided on all the files that should be part of the backup, don't waste time by backing up every single one of those files each time you do a backup. Instead, it's possible to use backup types to tell Windows XP Pro to back up only those files that have changed. Windows XP Pro supports no fewer than five backup types:

Normal Backs up each and every file, each and every time. (Note that by "each and every file," I mean "each and every file in the backup job.") All files are marked to indicate they've been backed up.

Incremental Backs up only those files that have changed since the most recent Normal or Incremental backup. This is the fastest type because it includes only the minimum number of files. Again, the files are marked to indicate they've been backed up.

Differential Backs up only those files that have changed since the most recent non-Differential backup. That is, the files are *not* marked to indicate they've been backed up. So, if you run this type of backup again, the same files get backed up (plus any others that have changed in the meantime).

Daily Backs up only those files that were modified on the day you run the backup.

Copy Makes copies of the selected files. This type of backup does not mark the files as having been backed up. This means you can use it for quick backups without interfering with your backup strategy (discussed next).

◆ **Create a backup strategy** Finally, you should come up with a backup strategy that makes sense for you, and then you should stick to that strategy no matter what. A typical strategy might go something like this:

Run a Daily backup each day.

Run an Incremental backup once a week. Delete the previous week's Daily and Incremental backups.

Run a Normal backup once a month. When done, delete the previous month's Incremental and Normal backups.

Windows Wisdom

How does the Backup program mark files as backed up? Each file has what's known in the trade as an archive flag, which gets raised when you make changes to a file. When you include a file in a Normal or an Incremental backup, the flag is lowered to indicate that the file has been backed up. Note that a Differential backup does *not* lower the flag.

Windows Wisdom

If you're using Windows XP Home Edition, note that you need to install Backup from the Windows XP Home Edition CD. In the VALUEADD\MSFT\ NTBACKUP folder, launch the Ntbackup.msifile.

Now that we've knocked the whole backup process down to size, let's whip out the brass tacks and get down to business. The Backup program that comes with Windows XP does a fine job of making all-important backup copies of your important files.

To get started, select **Start, All Programs, Accessories, System Tools, Backup.** After a second or two, the Backup or Restore Wizard pulls itself out of a hat. The next two sections take you through the two procedures for backing up: the Backup or Restore Wizard and creating a backup job by hand.

The Backup Wizard's step-by-step approach makes it easy to create and launch a backup job. Here's what happens:

1. In the initial Backup or Restore Wizard dialog box, click **Next.**

2. Activate the **Back up files and settings** option and then click **Next.**

3. The next wizard dialog box gives you four choices (click **Next** when you're done):

- ◆ **My documents and settings** Choose this option to back up your My Documents folder, your Favorites folders, your desktop, and your cookies.

- ◆ **Everyone's documents and settings** Choose this option if you have multiple users on the computer and you want to back up their documents and settings as well as your own.

- ◆ **All information on this computer** Choose this option to be able to completely recover your system in the event of a catastrophe.

- ◆ **Let me choose what to back up** Choose this option to pick out exactly which files to back up.

Windows Wisdom

Windows XP has a collection of files that store what's known as the *system state*. This is the Windows XP configuration, so these are absolutely crucial files, and you'll be able to recover your system much faster if you back them up. To include the system state stuff in your backup job, open the **My Computer** branch and activate the **System State** check box.

4. If you elected to choose what to back up, you'll see the Items to Back Up dialog box shown in Figure 22.4. The idea here is that you use the items in the **Items to back up** list to choose which drives, folders, or files you want to include in the backup. You do this by activating the check box beside each item you want to back up. (Now you see why I suggested you include all your documents in subfolders within My Documents. To back up all your data files, all you have to do is activate the **My Documents** check box. One click and you're done. What could be easier?) Click **Next** when you're ready to proceed.

Figure 22.4

If you decided to select the backup job files yourself, you'll get this dialog box coming at you.

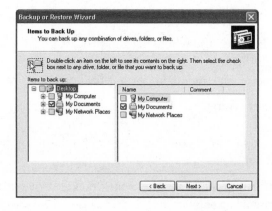

5. Now the wizard wants to know the backup destination. Use the **Select the backup type** list to choose the type of backup medium (such as a file or a tape device) you want to use. Use the **Choose a place to save your backup** list to specify the location of the backup. (You can click **Browse** to choose the location from a dialog box.) You can also enter a name in the **Type a name for this backup** text box. Click **Next** to continue.

6. The wizard displays a summary of the backup job settings. Say "Hold on a minute there, buster!" and click **Advanced.** You'll then run through a series of dialog boxes. Here's a quick summary (click **Next** after each one):

   ◆ **Type of Backup**   Use the **Select the type of backup** list to choose a backup type (Normal, Incremental, and so on).

   ◆ **How to Back Up**   If you have ultra-important data and you don't want anything to go wrong, activate the **Verify data after backup** check box. This ensures that your data was backed up without mishap, but it basically doubles the total backup time.

   ◆ **Backup Options**   You can either append this backup to an existing backup job (this is your best choice in most situations) or have this backup replace an existing backup job.

   ◆ **When to Back Up**   Choose **Now** to start the backup immediately. Alternatively, select **Later** and click **Set Schedule** to run the backup at a future time. (See the "Step 10—Setting Up a Maintenance Schedule" section later in this chapter.)

7. Click **Finish.** Backup gathers the files and then starts backing them up. If the backup medium gets full, you'll be prompted to insert another one. When the backup job is complete, you'll see a report. (If the report tells you that errors occurred during the backup, check to see which files were involved and then back them up again.)

8. Click **Close.**

The Backup or Restore Wizard ensures that you don't forget anything, but it's a bit of a long haul to get from A to Backup. You can usually speed up the entire process by creating a backup job by hand. To give this a whirl, start Backup once again. However, when the Backup or Restore Wizard returns, click the **Advanced Mode** link. (If you find you prefer this method for backing up, you can bypass the wizard in the future by deactivating the **Always start in wizard mode** check box.) Now display the **Backup** tab.

To create the backup job, use the following controls:

- ◆ **Click to select the check box for any drive, folder, or file that you want to back up**   As with the Backup or Restore Wizard, you activate the check boxes beside the items you want to include in the backup.

- ◆ **Backup destination**   Use this list to select the type of backup media you're using.

- ◆ **Backup media or file name**   Use this text box to enter the backup location (or click **Browse**).

Windows Wisdom _____

If you want to include Windows XP configuration data in your backup (which is a darn good idea), be sure to activate the *System State* check box.

To choose the backup type, follow these quick steps:

1. Select **Tools, Options** to ask the Options dialog box to come out and play.

2. Display the **Backup Type** tab.

3. Use the **Default Backup Type** list to choose the backup type.

4. Click **OK.**

To launch the backup, click the **Start Backup** button. Again, Backup gathers the files and then performs the backup. When you see the report, click **Close.**

Step 7—Run the Automated System Recovery Preparation Wizard

If a system goes kaput, one of the most common reasons is a corrupted system file that Windows XP requires to get itself out of bed in the morning. Therefore, you can often resurrect a seemingly dead system by repairing those mucked-up files. This sounds like it would be hard, but the Backup program has a feature that makes it relatively easy. It's called Automated System Recovery, and I'll show you how to use it in this section.

Look Out! _____

Automated System Recovery requires a floppy disk drive. If your computer doesn't come with one, you can't use this feature.

The safety net created by Automated System Recovery is actually composed of two parts:

- ◆ A full backup of your Windows XP installation (not including your data files; you need to back those up separately).

◆ A special floppy disk called the Automated System Recovery Disk. This disk contains information about your system that can be used to repair a broken Windows XP configuration.

Here are the steps to follow to create these things:

1. Launch Backup and, if the Backup or Restore Wizard appears, click the **Advanced Mode** link to get to the Backup window.

2. In the **Welcome** tab, click the **Automated System Recovery Wizard** button. Alternatively, select **Tools, ASR Wizard.** The Automated System Recovery Preparation Wizard (what a mouthful!) slides down the pole.

3. Click **Next.** The Backup Destination dialog box appears.

4. Select your **Backup media type,** choose a **Backup media or file name,** and click **Next.**

5. Click **Finish.** Backup creates a backup of your Windows XP configuration. When it's done, Backup asks for a blank, formatted disk. This will be your ASR disk.

6. Insert the disk in drive A and click **OK.** Backup tosses the repair info onto the disk and then lets you know when it's done.

> **Cross-Reference**
>
> To learn how to recover your system using Automated System Recovery, in Chapter 23, see the section titled "Recovering Using Automated System Recovery."

7. Click **OK** to end up at the Backup Progress dialog box.

8. Click **Close.**

At this point, it would be a good idea to label the disk (use "ASR Disk" or "Emergency Repair Disk" or something equally as dull) and put it in a safe place.

Step 8—Check For Updates and Security Patches

Windows XP is a moving target. Oh, it might look stationary, but while you're busy learning where things are and how things work, the Microsoft programmers are busy fixing bugs, improving existing features, and adding new features. In previous versions, these changes were packaged into massive *service packs* that you could download from the web or get on CD. With Windows XP, however, Microsoft is taking a different tack and is going to have individual fixes and improvements available on a special website called Windows Update. In fact, you no longer even have to go that far because Windows XP comes with a feature called *automatic updates* that will check for new Windows trinkets and then download and install them automatically.

After Windows XP sees that your computer has Internet access, you eventually see yet another icon in your taskbar's notification area, as well as a message titled **Stay current with automatic updates.** This is the Automatic Updates icon, and its job is to let you know when Windows Update has something new to install.

Before you can use this feature, you have to run through a brief setup procedure:

1. Click the **Automatic Updates** icon or the message. The Automatic Updates Setup Wizard comes by.

2. Click **Next.** The wizard asks you how you want to be notified of updates:

Windows Wisdom

If you have Windows XP Service Pack 2 installed, the Automatic Updates icon is replaced by the Security Center icon. I discussed the Security Center in Chapter 19.

Windows Wisdom

If you want to do all the updating by hand, the Windows Update website is located at windowsupdate.microsoft.com.

- **Download the updates automatically...** This is the no-brainer option because Windows XP handles all the dirty work behind the scenes. When an update is available, Windows XP downloads it and then displays the Automatic Updates icon with a message telling you that the update is ready to be installed. All you have to do is click the message to make things happen.

- **Notify me before downloading...** Choose this option to force Windows XP to ask your permission before downloading a component. It's a bit more work, but at least you'll always know what Windows XP is up to.

- **Turn off automatic updating...** Choose this option if you prefer to go to the Windows Update website yourself.

3. Click **Next.**

4. Click **Finish.**

After that's done, the Automatic Updates feature runs in the background and checks for new components for your computer automatically. If you're connected to the Internet and a new component is available, Automatic Updates either downloads it behind the scenes or lets you know if an update is available (if you chose the **Notify me before downloading...** option, earlier).

If the latter is the case, click the **Automatic Updates icon** or the message, and you'll see a list of the updates that are available. Leave the check marks activated beside each update you want downloaded and click **Start Download.** Note that if you need to disconnect from the Internet while downloading the update, click the Update Reminder icon and then click **Pause.** To continue the download, click the icon again and then click **Resume.**

When the download is done like dinner, the Automatic Updates icon displays a message letting you know that you have a new component to install. To install the component, click the message or the icon, which gets you to the Ready to Install dialog box. You have three choices from here:

◆ **Details**   Click this button to see what the heck was downloaded. Note that each item has a check box beside it. If you prefer not to install an item, deactivate its check box.

◆ **Remind Me Later**   Click this button to bypass the installation for now. The Update Reminder icon will pester you about it again later on.

◆ **Install**   Click this button to install the new component.

To change your Automatic Updates settings, click **Start,** right-click **My Computer,** and then click **Properties.** In the System Properties dialog box that appears, use the **Automatic Updates** tab to adjust your settings. Note, too, that this tab also has a **Previous Updates** section that enables you to be notified again of any earlier updates that you turned down for some reason.

Step 9–Check for Security Vulnerabilities

Microsoft regularly finds security vulnerabilities in components such as Microsoft Internet Explorer and Windows Media Player. Fixes for these problems are usually made available via Windows Update. However, to ensure that your computer is safe, you should download and regularly run the Microsoft Baseline Security Analyzer. This tool not only scans your system for missing security patches, but it also looks for things such as weak passwords and other Windows vulnerabilities. Download the tool at www.microsoft.com/technet/security/tools/mbsahome.mspx.

After you install the tool, follow these steps to use it:

1. Select **Start, All Programs, Microsoft Baseline Security Analyzer 1.2.** The program's Welcome screen appears.

2. Click **Scan a computer.**

3. Your computer should be listed in the **Computer name** list. If not, choose it from that list.

4. Use the **Options** check boxes to specify the security components you want to check. For most scans you should leave all the options selected.

5. Click **Start scan.** The program checks your system and displays a report on your system's security (and usually offers remedies for any vulnerabilities it finds).

Step 10—Set Up a Maintenance Schedule

Maintenance is effective only if it's done regularly, but there's a fine line to be navigated here. If maintenance is performed too often, it can become a burden and interfere with more interesting tasks; if it's performed too seldom, it becomes ineffective. So how often should you perform the maintenance steps listed in this chapter? Here are some guidelines:

◆ **Checking your hard disk for errors**   Run a basic scan about once a week. Run the more thorough disk surface scan once a month. (The surface scan takes a long time, so run it when you won't be using your computer for a while.)

◆ **Checking free disk space**   Do this about once a month. If you have a drive in which the free space is getting low, check it about once a week.

◆ **Deleting unnecessary files**   If free disk space isn't a problem, run this chore about once every two or three months.

◆ **Defragmenting your hard disk**   How often you defragment your hard disk depends on how often you use your computer. If you use it every day, you should run Disk Defragmenter about once a week. If your computer doesn't get heavy use, you probably need to run Disk Defragmenter only once a month or so.

◆ **Setting restore points**   Windows XP already sets regular system checkpoints, so you need only create your own restore points when you're installing a program or device or making some other major change to your system.

◆ **Backing up your files**   Perform a full backup of all your documents, as well as a backup of the system state, about once a month. Do a differential backup of modified files once a week. Do an incremental backup of modified files every day. Remember, too, that the Backup program enables you to schedule backup jobs. In the Backup Utility window, display the **Schedule Jobs** tab and click **Add Job.**

◆ **Checking Windows Update**   If you've turned off automatic updating, you should check in with the Windows Update website about once a month.

- **Checking for security vulnerabilities**   Run the Microsoft Baseline Security Analyzer once a month. You should also pay a monthly visit to Microsoft's Security and Privacy site to keep up to date on the latest security news, get security and virus alerts, and more: www.microsoft.com/security.

The Least You Need to Know

- If you highlight a hard disk in My Computer and then select **File, Properties** in the **General** tab of the resulting dialog box, click **Disk Cleanup** to remove unnecessary files; also, on the **Tools** tab, click **Check Now** to run Check Disk, or click **Defragment Now** to run Disk Defragmenter. (On Windows XP Pro systems, you can also click **Backup Now** to run Backup.)

- To run Check Disk and Disk Defragmenter, you need to log on to Windows XP with Administrator-level privileges.

- Bad hard disk sectors can cause all kinds of woes. Therefore, you should activate Check Disk's **Scan for and attempt recovery of bad sectors** check box about once a month or so.

- You should run Disk Cleanup every couple of weeks, Check Disk every week (and the bad-sector check every month), and Disk Defragmenter every week (every month if your machine gets only light use).

- If you want your version of Windows XP to always be up-to-date, be sure to turn on the XP new Automatic Updates feature and let it handle everything for you.

Chapter 23

Troubleshooting and Recovering from Problems

In This Chapter

◆ Determining the source of a problem

◆ Using general troubleshooting strategies to solve common problems

◆ Troubleshooting problems using websites and newsgroups

◆ Using Windows XP recovery tools: Last Known Good Configuration, System Restore, and Automated System Recovery

◆ If worst comes to worst: Reinstalling Windows XP

A long time ago, somebody with way to much time on his or her hands proved mathematically that it's impossible to make any reasonably complex software program problem-free. As the number of variables increase, as the interactions of subroutines and objects become more complex, and as the underlying logic of a program grows beyond the ability of a single person to grasp all at once, errors inevitably creep into the code. Given the status of Microsoft Windows XP as one of the most complex software packages ever created, it's certain that there are problems lurking in the weeds. (Actually, considering the richness, depth, and immense intricacy of Windows XP—its lines of code are numbered in the tens of millions—the fact that to date relatively few problems have been reported is borderline miraculous.) And, the good news is that the great majority of these problems are extremely obscure and will appear only under the rarest of circumstances.

However, this doesn't mean you're guaranteed a glitch-free computing experience. Far from it. The majority of computer woes are caused by third-party programs and devices, either because they have inherent problems themselves or because they don't get along well with Windows XP. Using software, devices, and device drivers designed for Windows XP can help tremendously, as can the maintenance program I outlined in Chapter 22. Nonetheless, you need to know how to troubleshoot and resolve the computer problems that invariably will come your way. In this chapter, I help you do just that by showing you my favorite techniques for determining problem sources, and by taking you through all of the Windows XP recovery tools.

Determining the Source of the Problem

One of the ongoing mysteries that all Windows XP users experience at one time or another is what might be called the now-you-see-it-now-you-don't problem. This is a glitch that plagues you for a while and then mysteriously vanishes without any intervention on your part. (This also tends to occur when you ask a nearby user or someone from the IT department to look at the problem. Like the automotive problem that goes away when you take the car to a mechanic, computer problems will often resolve themselves as soon as a knowledgeable user sits down at the keyboard.) When this happens, most people just shake their heads and resume working, grateful to no longer have to deal with the problem.

Windows Wisdom

Software glitches are traditionally called *bugs*, although many developers shun the term because it comes with too much negative baggage these days. There's a popular and appealing tale of how this sense of the word *bug* came about. As the story goes, in 1947 an early computer pioneer named Grace Hopper was working on a system called the Mark II. While investigating a problem, she found a moth among the machine's vacuum tubes, so from then on glitches were called bugs. A great story, to be sure, but this tale was *not* the source of the "computer glitch" sense of "bug." In fact, engineers had already been referring to mechanical defects as "bugs" for at least 60 years before Ms. Hopper's actual moth came on the scene. As proof, the *Oxford English Dictionary* offers the following quotation from an 1889 edition of the *Pall Mall Gazette:*

"Mr. Edison, I was informed, had been up the two previous nights discovering 'a bug' in his phonograph—an expression for solving a difficulty, and implying that some imaginary insect has secreted itself inside and is causing all the trouble."

Unfortunately, most computer ills don't get resolved so easily. For these more intractable problems, your first order of business is to track down the source of the snag. This is, at best, a black art, but it can be done if you take a systematic approach. Over the years, I've found that the best method is to ask a series of questions designed to gather the required information and/or to narrow down clues to the culprit. Here are the questions:

♦ **Did you get an error message?** Unfortunately, most computer error messages are obscure and do little to help you resolve a problem directly. However, error codes and error text can help you down the road, either by giving you something to search for in an online database (see "Troubleshooting Using Online Resources," later in this chapter) or by providing information to a tech support person. Therefore, you should always write down the full text of any error message that appears.

Windows Wisdom

If the error message is lengthy and you can still use other programs on your computer, don't bother writing down the full message. Instead, while the message is displayed press the **Print Screen** key to place an image of the current screen on the clipboard. Then open Paint or some other graphics program, paste the screen into a new image, and save the image. If you think you'll be sending the image via e-mail to a tech support employee or someone else who can help with the problem, consider saving the image as a monochrome or 16-color bitmap to keep the image size small.

If the error message appears before Windows XP starts, but you don't have time to write it down, press the **Pause/Break** key to pause the startup. After you record the error, press **Ctrl+Pause/Break** to resume the startup.

♦ **Did you recently change any Windows settings?** If the problem started after you changed your Windows configuration, try reversing the change. Even something as seemingly innocent as starting the screen saver can cause problems, so don't rule anything out.

♦ **Did you recently change any application settings?** If so, try reversing the change to see if it solves the problem. If that doesn't help, check to see if an upgrade or patch is available. Also, some applications come with a "Repair" option that can fix corrupted files. Otherwise, try reinstalling the program.

♦ **Did you recently install a new program?** If you suspect a new program is causing system instability, restart Windows XP and try operating the system for a while without using the new program. If the problem doesn't reoccur, then the new program is likely the culprit. Try using the program without any other programs running. You should also examine the program's "readme" file (if it has

Cross-Reference

To learn how to uninstall a program, in Chapter 6, see the section titled "Giving a Program the Heave-Ho."

one) to look for known problems and possible workarounds. It's also a good idea to check for a Windows XP–compatible version of the program. Again, you can also try the program's "repair" option, or you can reinstall the program.

♦ **Did you recently upgrade an existing program?** If so, try uninstalling the upgrade.

♦ **Did you recently install a device driver that is not Windows XP–compatible?** Windows XP allows you to install drivers that aren't Windows XP–certified, but it also warns you that this is a bad idea. Incompatible drivers are one of the most common sources of system instability, so whenever possible you should uninstall the driver and install one that is designed for Windows XP. Windows XP automatically sets a system restore point before it installs the driver, so if you can't uninstall the driver, you should use that to restore the system to its previous state. (See "Recovering Using System Restore," later in this chapter.)

♦ **Did you recently apply an update from Windows update?** Before you install an update from the Windows Update site, Windows XP creates a system restore point (usually called Windows Update V4). If your system becomes unstable after installing the update, use System Restore to revert to the pre-update configuration.

♦ **Did you recently install a Windows XP hotfix?** It's ironic that hotfixes that are designed to increase system stability will occasionally do the opposite and cause more problems than they fix. You can often remove a hotfix using Control Panel's **Add Or Remove Programs** icon. Look for a Windows XP Hotfix entry in the **Change Or Remove Programs** list. If you have multiple hotfixes listed, make sure you remove the correct one. To be sure, check with either the Microsoft Security site or the Microsoft Knowledge Base, both of which I discuss later. Note, however, that many hotfixes cannot be uninstalled. You can try using System Restore to revert to a recent restore point, but there's no guarantee this will work.

♦ **Did you recently install a Windows XP service pack?** If you installed a service pack and you elected to save the old system files, then you can uninstall the service pack using Control Panel's **Add Or Remove Programs** icon. Look for a Windows XP Service Pack entry in the **Change Or Remove Programs** list.

General Troubleshooting Tips

Figuring out the cause of a problem is often the hardest part of troubleshooting, but by itself it doesn't do you much good. Once you know the source, you need to parlay that information into a fix for the problem. I discussed a few solutions in the previous section, but here are a few other general fixes you need to keep in mind:

♦ **Close all programs**   You can often fix flaky behavior by shutting down all your open programs and starting again. This is a particularly useful fix for problems caused by low memory or low system resources.

♦ **Log off Windows XP**   Logging off clears the memory and so gives you a slightly cleaner slate than merely closing all your programs.

♦ **Reboot the computer**   If problems exist with some system files and devices, logging off won't help because these objects remain loaded. By rebooting the system, you reload the entire system, which is often enough to solve many computer problems.

♦ **Turn off the computer and restart**   You can often solve a hardware problem by first shutting your machine off. Wait for 30 seconds to give all devices time to spin down and then restart.

♦ **Check connections, power switches, and so on**   Some of the most common (and some of the most embarrassing) causes of hardware problems are the simple physical things: making sure a device is turned on; checking that cable connections are secure; ensuring that insertable devices are properly inserted.

♦ **Use the Help And Support Center**   Microsoft greatly improved the quality of the Help system in Windows XP. The Help And Support Center (select **Start, Help And Support**) is awash in articles and advice on using Windows XP. However, the real strength of Help And Support is, in my opinion, the "Support" side. In the Help And Support Center home page, click the **Fixing a problem** link to see more links for general troubleshooting and for fixing specific problems related to software, multimedia, e-mail, networking, and more. Note, too, that the Help and Support Center offers a number of troubleshooter guides that take you step-by-step through troubleshooting procedures.

Troubleshooting Using Online Resources

The Internet is home to an astonishingly wide range of information, but its forte has always been computer knowledge. Whatever problem you may have, there's a good chance that someone out there has run into the same thing, knows how to fix it, has posted the solution on a website or newsgroup, or would be willing to share it with you if asked. True, finding what you need is sometimes difficult, and you often can't be sure how accurate some of the solutions are. However, if you stick to the more reputable sites and if you get second opinions on solutions offered by complete strangers, then you'll find the online world an excellent troubleshooting resource. Here's my list of favorite online resources to check out:

- **Microsoft Product Support Services**   This is Microsoft's main online technical support site. Through this site you can access Windows XP frequently asked questions, see a list of known problems, download files, and send questions to Microsoft support personnel. See support.microsoft.com.

- **Microsoft Knowledge Base**   The Microsoft Product Support Services site has links that enable you to search the Microsoft Knowledge Base, which is a database of articles related to all Microsoft products including, of course, Windows XP. These articles provide you with information about Windows XP and instructions on using Windows XP features. But the most useful aspect of the Knowledge Base is for troubleshooting problems. Many of the articles were written by Microsoft support personnel after helping customers overcome problems. By searching for error codes or keywords, you can often get specific solutions to your problems.

- **Microsoft TechNet**   This Microsoft site is designed for IT professionals and power users. It contains a huge number of articles on all Microsoft products. These articles give you technical content, program instructions, tips, scripts, downloads, and troubleshooting ideas. See www.microsoft.com/technet.

- **Windows Update**   Check this site for the latest device drivers, security patches, service packs, and other updates. See windowsupdate.microsoft.com.

- **Microsoft Security and Privacy**   Check this site for the latest information on Microsoft's security and privacy initiatives, particularly security patches. See www.microsoft.com/security.

- **Vendor websites**   All but the tiniest hardware and software vendors maintain websites with customer support sections that you can peruse for upgrades, patches, workarounds, frequently asked questions, and sometimes chat or bulletin board features.

- **Newsgroups**   Computer-related newsgroups exist for hundreds of topics and products. Microsoft maintains its own newsgroups via the msnews.microsoft.com server, and Usenet has a huge list of groups in the alt. and comp. hierarchies.

Before asking a question in a newsgroup, be sure to search Google Groups to see if your question has been answered in the past. See groups.google.com.

Recovering from a Problem

Ideally, solving a problem will require a specific tweak to the system: a setting change, a driver upgrade, a program uninstall. But sometimes you need to take more of a "big picture" approach that reverts your system to some previous state in the hope that you'll leap past the problem and get your system working again. Windows XP offers four tools that enable you to try this approach: Last Known Good Configuration, System Restore, reinstalling Windows XP, and Automated System Recovery, which should be used in that order. The next four sections discuss these tools.

Booting Using the Last Known Good Configuration

Each time Windows XP starts successfully, the system makes a note of the drivers and hardware configuration that were used. If you make driver or hardware changes and then find that the system won't start, you can tell Windows XP to load using the configuration that worked the last time. (That is, the configuration that doesn't include your most recent hardware changes.) This is called the *Last Known Good Configuration*, and the theory is that by using the previous working configuration, your system should start since it's bypassing the changes that caused the problem. Here's how to start Windows XP using the last known good configuration:

1. Restart your computer.

2. When the OS Choices menu appears, press **F8** to display the Windows Advanced Options Menu. (If your system doesn't display the OS Choices menu, press **F8** immediately after your system finishes the Power-On Self Test, which is usually indicated by a single beep.)

3. Select the **Last Known Good Configuration** option.

Recovering Using System Restore

The Last Known Good Configuration is most useful when your computer won't start and you suspect that a hardware change is causing the problem. You might think that you can also use the Last Known Good Configuration if Windows XP starts but is unstable, and you suspect a hardware change is causing the glitch. Unfortunately, that won't work because once you start Windows XP successfully, the hardware change is added to the Last Known Good Configuration. To revert the system to a previous configuration when you can start Windows XP successfully, you need to use the System Restore feature.

I show you how to use System Restore to set restore points in Chapter 22. Remember, too, that Windows XP creates automatic restore points each day and when you perform certain actions (such as installing an uncertified device driver). To revert your system to a restore point, follow these steps:

Windows Wisdom

If restoring your system makes things worse or causes additional problems, you have a couple of choices. To undo the restore, launch System Restore, activate the **Undo my last restoration** option, and click **Next.** Alternatively, you can run System Restore and revert the system to an even earlier restore point.

1. Use either of the following methods to launch System Restore:

   ◆ Select **Start, Control Panel, Performance and Maintenance, System Restore.**

   ◆ Select **Start, All Programs, Accessories, System Tools, System Restore.**

2. Activate the **Restore my computer to an earlier time** option and click **Next.** The Select a Restore Point window appears, as shown in Figure 23.1.

Figure 23.1

Use this window to choose the restore point you want to revert to.

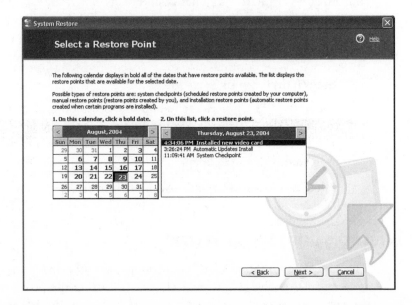

3. Use the calendar to click the date on which the restore point was made. System Restore displays that day's checkpoints in a box to the right of the calendar.

4. Click the restore point you want to restore. (Note that the **System Checkpoint** items are the restore points created automatically by Windows XP every 24 hours.)

5. Click **Next.** System Restore asks you to close all open programs and warns you not to do anything with your computer until the restore is done.

6. Click **Next.** System Restore begins restoring the restore point. When it's done, it restarts your computer and displays the Restoration Complete window.

7. Click **OK.**

> **Windows Wisdom**
>
> System Restore is available in safe mode. So if Windows XP won't start properly, and if using the Last Known Good Configuration doesn't work, perform a safe mode startup and run System Restore from there.

Reinstalling Windows XP

If you can't get Windows XP back on its feet using the previous methods, you may be able to fix things by reinstalling Windows XP over the existing installation. This won't affect your data or any personal settings you've adjusted, but it may cure what's ailing Windows XP either by reverting the system to its default settings or by installing fresh copies of corrupted system files. Here are the steps to follow to reinstall Windows XP:

1. Insert the Windows XP CD-ROM.

2. Restart your computer. If your system prompts you to boot from the CD, press the required key or key combination.

> ### Hacking Windows
>
> If your system won't boot from the Windows XP CD, you need to adjust the system's settings to allow this. Restart the computer and look for a startup message that prompts you to press a key or key combination to modify the settings (which might be called Setup or something similar). Find the boot options and either enable a CD-based boot or make sure the option to boot from the CD comes before the option to boot from the hard disk.

3. When the Welcome To Setup screen appears, press **Enter** to choose the **To Set Up Windows XP Now** option.

4. When the Licensing Agreement appears, press **F8** to accept it. Setup then displays a list of Windows XP installations on your computer.

5. If you have more than one Windows XP installation, select the one you want to fix.

6. Press **R** to choose the **To Repair the Selected Windows XP Installation** option.

Recovering Using Automated System Recovery

If nothing can get Windows XP up and running again, you have no choice but to start with a clean slate. This means either formatting the hard disk or, if hard disk errors are the culprit, replacing your hard disk. This will be less catastrophic if you followed my advice and used the Automated System Recovery Preparation Wizard to make backups of your system files (see Chapter 22). If so, here are the steps to follow to recover your system:

1. Insert your Windows XP CD and reboot your computer. If you're prompted to press a key to boot from the CD, go ahead and press whatever key you like. Watch the bottom of the screen for the following message:

```
Press F2 to run Automated System Recovery (ASR)...
```

2. Press **F2** while the message is displayed. Setup asks for the ASR disk.

3. Insert the disk into drive A and then press whatever key strikes your fancy. Setup starts the recovery process.

4. When the repair is complete, restart your computer.

From here, the Setup program proceeds normally, except that it uses the information on the ASR disk to restore your system files and settings from the backup you made using the ASR Preparation Wizard. If you also backed up your application and data files, use the Backup Utility to restore those now.

The Least You Need to Know

◆ If a problem occurs soon after you changed something on your computer—a Windows setting, a program, a device, and so on—try reversing that change to see if this fixes the error.

◆ You can often recover from problems just by either shutting down all running programs, logging off Windows XP, or rebooting the computer.

◆ Take advantage of online resources such as Microsoft Product Support Services (particularly the Knowledge Base), vendor websites, and newsgroups (particularly the Google Groups search engine).

◆ To recover from a more serious problem, use the following tools and techniques, in this order: Last Known Good Configuration, System Restore, reinstall Windows XP, and Automated System Recovery.

The Complete Idiot's Command Card

General Windows Keyboard Shortcuts

Press	To
Alt+Print Screen	Copy the active window's image to the Clipboard.
Print Screen	Copy the entire screen image to the Clipboard.
Ctrl+Alt+Delete	Display the Windows Task Manager.
Ctrl+Esc	Open the Start menu.
Ctrl+Z	Undo the most recent action.

Keyboard Shortcuts for Programs

Press	To
Working with Program Windows	
Alt+Esc	Cycle through the open program windows.
Alt+Tab	Cycle through the active programs.
Alt+F4	Close the active program window.
F1	Display context-sensitive Help.

continues

Keyboard Shortcuts for Programs (continued)

Press	To
Working with Documents	
Ctrl+N	Create a new document.
Ctrl+O	Display the Open dialog box.
Ctrl+P	Display the Print dialog box.
Ctrl+S	Save the current file. If the file is new, display the Save As dialog box.

Keyboard Shortcuts for Working with Data

Press	To
Backspace	Delete the character to the left of the insertion point.
Delete	Delete the selected data or the character to the right of the insertion point.
Ctrl+A	Select all the data in the current window.
Ctrl+C	Copy the selected data.
Ctrl+X	Cut the selected data.
Ctrl+V	Paste the most recently cut or copied data.

Keyboard Shortcuts for Dialog Boxes

Hold Down	To
Tab	Move forward through the dialog box controls.
Shift+Tab	Move backward through the dialog box controls.
Ctrl+Tab	Move forward through the dialog box tabs.
Alt+Down arrow	Display the list in a drop-down list box.
Spacebar	Toggle a check box on and off; select the active option button or command button.
Enter	Select the default command button or the active command button.
Esc	Close the dialog box without making any changes.

Keys to Hold Down While Dragging and Dropping

Hold Down	To
Ctrl	Copy the dragged object.
Ctrl+Shift	Display a shortcut menu after dropping a dragged object.
Esc	Cancel the current drag.
Shift	Move the dragged object.

Windows Explorer Keyboard Shortcuts

Press	To
+ (numeric keypad)	Display the next level of subfolders for the current folder.
– (numeric keypad)	Hide the current folder's subfolders.
* (numeric keypad)	Display all levels of subfolders for the current folder.
Backspace	Navigate to the parent folder of the current folder.
Delete	Delete the selected object.
Ctrl+A	Select all the objects in the current folder.
Shift+Delete	Delete the currently selected objects without sending them to the Recycle Bin.
F2	Rename the selected object.
F3	Display the Find dialog box with the current folder displayed in the Look In list.
F4	Open the Address toolbar's drop-down list.

Internet Explorer Keyboard Shortcuts

Press	To
Alt+Left arrow	Navigate backward to a previously displayed web page.
Alt+Right arrow	Navigate forward to a previously displayed web page.
Ctrl+A	Select the entire web page.
Ctrl+B	Display the Organize Favorites dialog box.
Ctrl+D	Add the current page to the Favorites list.
Esc	Stop downloading the web page.
F4	Open the Address toolbar's drop-down list.
F5	Refresh the web page.
F11	Toggle between full screen mode and the regular window.

Shortcuts That Use the Windows Logo (⊞) Key

Press	To
⊞	Open the Start menu.
⊞ +E	Open Windows Explorer.
⊞ +F	Find a file or folder.
⊞ +M	Minimize all open windows.
⊞ +Shift+M	Undo minimize all.
⊞ +R	Display the Run dialog box.

Index

T

U

X–Y–Z